PENGUIN BOOKS

NOT THAT YOU ASKED

Today Andy Rooney is perhaps best known for his weekly cantankerous essays on *60 Minutes*. Rooney, who was one of the original writers and producers for the show, which began in 1968, has been on the air since 1978.

Since 1981 he has written four collections of essays: *A Few Minutes with Andy Rooney*; *And More by Andy Rooney*; *Pieces of My Mind*; and *Word for Word*. His syndicated column appears three times a week in 265 newspapers.

Not That You Asked...

ANDREW A. ROONEY

PENGUIN BOOKS

Many thanks to Jane Bradford for all her good help

PENGUIN BOOKS
Published by the Penguin Group
Viking Penguin, a division of Penguin Books USA Inc.,
40 West 23rd Street, New York, New York 10010, U.S.A.
Penguin Books Ltd, 27 Wrights Lane, London W8 5TZ, England
Penguin Books Australia Ltd, Ringwood, Victoria, Australia
Penguin Books Canada Ltd, 2801 John Street,
Markham, Ontario, Canada L3R 1B4
Penguin Books (N.Z.) Ltd, 182–190 Wairau Road,
Auckland 10, New Zealand

Penguin Books Ltd, Registered Offices:
Harmondsworth, Middlesex, England

First published in the United States of America by Random House, Inc., 1989
Reprinted by arrangement with Random House, Inc.
Published in Penguin Books 1990

10 9 8 7 6 5 4 3 2 1

This work is based on a syndicated column from 1986–1988 by Tribune Media Services, Inc.

Grateful acknowledgment is made to Edward B. Marks Music Company for permission to reprint an excerpt from the song "I Wonder Who's Kissing Her Now" by Joseph Howard, Harold Orlob, Frank Adams, and Will Hough. Used by permission of Edward B. Marks Music Company.

LIBRARY OF CONGRESS CATALOGING IN PUBLICATION DATA
Rooney, Andrew A.
Not that you asked—/Andrew A. Rooney.
p. cm.
Reprint. Originally published: New York, N.Y.: Random House, 1989
ISBN 0 14 01.3172 8
1. American wit and humor. I. Title.
[PN6162.R6328 1990]
814'.54—dc20   89-29703

Printed in the United States of America
Designed by Bernard Klein

Preface

A writer doesn't often tell a reader anything the reader doesn't already know or suspect. The best the writer can do is put the idea in words and by doing that make the reader aware that he or she isn't the only one who knows it. This produces the warm bond between reader and writer that they're both after because it feels so good.

The fact is, there really isn't anything new in the world and what I've always hoped to do with my writing is to say, in so many words, some of the ideas that lurk, wordlessly, in the minds of a great many people.

There's no way of knowing how we get to believe what we believe. We're all trapped within ourselves. We have this much and no more. We have our genes and our youth, during which our opinions are formed.

Most of us don't change those opinions once we get them. Instead, we spend a lot of time looking for further proof that we're right.

If we formed our opinions the way we should, we'd get all the facts together and then compare them, using logic and good sense to arrive at the right places. We don't do it that way very often, though, and as a result we acquire a lot of wrong answers that we're stuck with for life. I haven't changed my mind about anything since I was twenty-three. In my head I know I must be wrong about some things but in my heart I don't think so.

As an indication of what you'll find in the body of this book, what follows is a hundred opinions I'm stuck with. There ought to be something here to anger almost everyone:

1. I do not accept the inevitability of my own death. I secretly think there may be some other way out.

2. It's good to be loyal even when what you're loyal to doesn't deserve it.

3. We are selling things better than we're making them in the United States.

4. Capitalism and the free-enterprise system are not working very well. There are too many very rich and too many very poor in the United States. Fortunately, the economic system that doesn't work as well as capitalism is communism. Communists are almost all poor.

5. When I was young I always assumed I'd get to like carrots when I got older but I never did.

6. In spite of all the kind things people are always saying about the poor and homeless, people with jobs and houses are usually more interesting and capable and I prefer to be with them.

7. I am often embarrassed by the people I find agreeing with me.

8. Big Business talks as if it doesn't like Big Government but the fact of the matter is, Big Business is in business with Big Government. Big Business is closer to Big Government than Big Government is to the people, but neither wants anyone to know it.

9. Most poetry is pretentious nonsense.

10. The people of the United States never worked so well or so hard or accomplished so much as they did during the four years of World War II. We need to find some substitute for war as a means of motivating ourselves to do our best. Money isn't the answer, either.

11. I don't favor abortion although I like the people who are for it better than the people who are against it.

12. Good old friends are worth keeping whether you like them or not.

13. Although I went to Sunday school for several years at the Madison Avenue Presbyterian Church, I was not persuaded that Mary never slept with anyone before Jesus was born.

14. I'm suspicious of the academic standards of a college that always has a good basketball team. When a college loses a lot of games, I figure they're letting the students play.

15. A person is more apt to get to be the boss by making decisions quickly than by making them correctly.

16. Until we can all have the medical attention a President gets, there will not be too many doctors.

17. A great many people do not have a right to their own opinion because they don't know what they're talking about.

18. The least able among us are having the most children. Among women, college graduates are having the fewest babies; high school

graduates are having the next fewest and the people who don't get to high school or drop out once they do are having the most babies.

The most capable women are getting the best jobs and are least apt to have big families . . . or sometimes, any family at all.

19. If I were black, I would be a militant, angry black man, railing against the injustices that have been done me. Being white, I think blacks should forget it and go to work.

20. If I were a woman, I would be an angry woman. Men are satisfied having women be something women are not satisfied being. We have a problem here.

21. There are facts too painful to face. I cannot watch a documentary about the slow death facing all elephants and whales.

22. The people who speak up in public for or against something almost always lose my support by being too loud about it.

23. It doesn't interest me to watch a movie or read a novel in which the characters are put in difficult situations by a writer. I'm not interested in being reminded of difficulties. It's already on my mind.

24. It's hard for me to believe that, in the next 150 years, we'll have as many important inventions and discoveries as we've had in the last 150. What is there left comparable in importance to the electric light, the telephone, the gas engine, radio, flight, television, nuclear energy, space exploration, computers and Coca-Cola?

(If anyone were to read that paragraph 150 years from now, I'm sure they'd laugh at my ignorance.)

25. People like to say, "You're only as old as you feel," but it isn't true. It's just something old people say to make themselves feel good about their age. You're as old as you are.

26. I spent fifty years of my life working to become well known as a writer and I've spent the last ten hiding from strangers who recognize me.

27. I dislike loud-mouthed patriots who suggest they like our country more than I do. Some people's idea of patriotism is hating other countries.

28. Politicians deserve better treatment than they've been getting and we should stop using the word "politician" as an epithet. Most of them are honestly trying to accomplish something good for all of us.

29. I spent four years in the army but do not belong to any veterans' organization. As a way of getting together socially with people your own age and background, veterans' groups are fine but I disapprove of them as a pressure group. I'm suspicious of professional veterans who wear overseas caps at conventions. Except for the men who were disabled,

to whom it owes everything it can give, our country owes veterans nothing. We got what was coming to us, a free country.

30. I wish people spent less time praying and more time trying to solve the problems religion was created to help us endure.

31. It seems wrong for the United States to try to protect democracy by undemocratic means like overthrowing the government of a foreign country by undercover action.

32. A lot of people assume that we live in an orderly world where every event has a meaning and every problem has a solution. I suspect, however, that some events are meaningless and some problems insoluble.

33. I believe a lot of things I can't prove. I think homosexuality is wrong but I wouldn't want to have to explain why. I'm more sympathetic to homosexuals who can't help it than I am to those who made the choice.

34. Women have better natural instincts than men and are more apt to do the right thing.

35. I'd make a bad nun. Material possessions give me great pleasure even though all the best advice we're given for happiness advises us to ignore them.

36. When someone says, "You know what I mean?" I don't usually know what they mean and I know they don't know. If someone knows what they mean, they ought to be able to tell you. I mean, you know what I mean?

37. My only war wound is an aversion to German accents.

38. We need chefs more than headwaiters and mechanics more than car salesmen. We need good doctors more than health plans.

39. The evolution of every business enterprise is away from quality. Products always get smaller, worse and more expensive.

40. If someone chooses to live in the United States, they should learn to speak English. I recognize that this is a small, meanspirited, right-wing opinion but I hold it.

41. People will generally accept facts as truth only if the facts agree with what they already believe.

42. The accuracy of political polls is sad evidence of our predictability.

43. Most religions are designed to trick us into doing the things we'd do anyway if we used our heads.

44. It's a lot easier to object to the way things are being done than it is to do them better yourself. Being a revolutionary, even in a modest way, is a lot more fun than having to take over and do it. Castro was

a great revolutionary. It wasn't until he won and started running things himself that he went wrong.

45. A lot of companies spend more to package, advertise and sell their product than they spend on making it. The toothpaste in a tube that costs $1.79 probably doesn't cost 10 cents to manufacture. Something's wrong here.

46. I think women should be paid as much for doing the same job as men . . . although I don't think they can lift as much.

47. I don't believe in flying saucers or the Loch Ness monster and I'm not on drugs or religion. I don't know my astrological sign.

48. If all the truth were known by everyone about everything, it would be a better world.

49. If all the truth were known by everyone about everything, most people wouldn't like it, though. If their future depends on logical decisions based on all the evidence, they're nervous. They don't think they're smart enough to make the right decision. If, on the other hand, success and happiness depends on their astrological sign or on hoping and praying or on winning the lottery, then they feel better. They think their destiny is in better hands than their own.

50. In view of how many of them are regularly found out to be scoundrels, I have an unreasonable faith in and affection for doctors. In this regard, I am very suspicious of anyone who uses the title "doctor" who is not an M.D. There are some very good optometrists but I do not call them "doctors."

51. People are too careful with books. If you like a book, you ought to mark it up with a pencil. Publishers put too much money in the flimsy paper dust jacket on books. The first thing I do with any book that doesn't have my picture on the jacket is throw the jacket away.

52. I don't like to lock anything or take precautions against having it stolen because every time I do, I get the feeling the bastards have beat me a little by making me do it.

53. It doesn't make sense to be against abortion and for the death penalty.

54. I am racist to the extent that I think there's a difference between ethnic groups now after centuries of evolution. I'm otherwise at a loss to know how to explain the consistent behavior of one group and its predictable variation from the behavior of another.

55. It's too bad we seem to need six or seven hours' sleep. Someone's going to invent a way for us to sleep faster.

56. It seems wrong for a state to take money from the poor and

ignorant by selling them lottery tickets to collect money to help the state provide welfare and education to the poor and ignorant.

57. People talk as though they like the country better than the city but they move to the city.

58. Farmers have been quitting the farm and moving to the city for years but you never see any of them there.

59. There's an acute shortage of well-known people in America. The same ones keep appearing on television talk shows. Of course, maybe what we need is not more well-known people but fewer talk shows.

60. Ronald Reagan wasn't as successful reducing the size of government as Franklin Roosevelt was in increasing it.

61. No one wants to read a lot of good writing. There's just so much good writing a reader can take.

62. If the reviews talk about how good the acting is in the movie, I don't go see it. Like writing, there's just so much good acting I can take. Acting and writing shouldn't call attention to themselves.

63. It no longer makes any sense to bother to use an apostrophe between the *n* and *t* in words like *dont* and *isnt.*

64. Most evenings I have two drinks of bourbon before dinner even though I am uneasily aware that the practice is difficult to defend against the charge that drinking is no different from using drugs. Drinking also isn't compatible with my belief that our best hope for happiness is clear thinking, but I try to have my thinking out of the way for the day by the time I have my first drink.

65. Journalists are more honest than other businesspeople because honesty is a hobby with them. They're amused by it. They talk about honesty at lunch. They aren't naturally any more honest, but it's on their minds.

66. There are more beauty parlors than there are beauties.

67. It's harder to avoid listening to something you don't want to hear than it is to avoid seeing something you'd rather not see.

68. We're all proud of admitting little mistakes. It gives us the feeling we don't make any big ones.

69. I'm always surprised when a light bulb burns out.

70. It's amazing that bees keep making honey, cows keep giving milk and hens keep laying eggs all their lives. There certainly isn't much in it for them.

71. It's too bad Jesus didn't have a family.

72. Getting up early in the morning is a good way to gain respect without ever actually having to do anything.

73. It sounds funny in the house without the television set on.

74. I'd get a lot more reading done in bed if I read when I woke up in the morning instead of when I crawled in at night.

75. People who are wrong seem to talk louder than anyone else.

76. I don't like any music I can't hum.

77. Ice cream was just as good when they only had three flavors, vanilla, chocolate and strawberry.

78. The middle of the night seems longer than it used to.

79. I'm satisfied with the money I make until I read how much baseball players are making.

80. No matter how big the umbrella you carry or how good your raincoat is, if it rains you get wet.

81. When the telephone rings in a store, the person behind the counter will spend five minutes explaining something to the caller while all the customers who have bothered to come to the store stand there waiting.

82. They keep talking about how low the rate of inflation is but I notice that when I buy something that cost me only $1.98 last year, it costs $2.42 now.

83. If I'd known how many problems I was going to run into before I finished, I can't remember a single project I would have started.

84. Computers may save time but they sure waste a lot of paper. About 98 percent of everything printed out by a computer is garbage that no one ever reads.

85. Lawyers are more interested in winning than in justice.

86. There aren't many times in your life when your body has absolutely nothing wrong with it.

87. Vacations aren't necessarily better than other times, they're just different.

88. When someone tells you, "It was my fault," they don't expect you to agree with them. When they say, "You're the boss," they don't mean it.

89. No one who goes to prison ever admits he did it.

90. It gives you confidence in America to hear so many people talk who know how to run the country better than the President.

91. Doctors ought to think of some name for their outer office other than "waiting room."

92. It's lucky glass makes a loud noise when it breaks.

93. If dogs could talk, it would take a lot of the fun out of owning one.

94. People aren't called "the working class" much anymore unless they're unemployed.

95. Most people don't care where they're going as long as they're in something that gets them there in a hurry.

96. Blue jeans cost less when they were called dungarees.

97. When I get sleepy driving, the only thing that really wakes me up is starting to fall asleep.

98. People in Florida talk more about the weather than people anywhere else in the world. I think it's because weather is what they're paying for and if it's good they feel it justifies the expense. If it's bad they like to think it isn't as bad as it is some places.

99. Never trust the food in a restaurant on top of the tallest building in town that spends a lot of time folding the napkins.

100. After thinking something through as well and as completely as I am able, to be sure I'm right, it often turns out that I'm wrong.

Contents

PROBLEMS 73

TRUTHS 97

DILEMMAS 121

HABITS AND OCCUPATIONS 135

PEOPLE 167

PLACES 191

ANIMALS AND PETS 205

HOUSES 219

HOLIDAYS AND VACATIONS 237

PLEASURES 251

CHANGES

A Text for Textbook Writers

All I remember about the textbooks I had in school is that most of them weren't very good. We learned more from the teachers than from the books, and the teachers who relied most on textbooks were the weakest.

I have a letter written by Barbara Everett, "editor, Language Arts Department, Elementary-High Division" of the Merrill Publishing Company, one of the biggest in the textbook business.

You can bet that when anyone announces herself as editor of the Language Arts Department of anything, you're in for trouble.

It turns out that Barbara wants my permission to use an essay I wrote for inclusion in one of their seventh-grade textbooks, but she wants to make some changes in it.

"I have marked the changes we would like to make," the letter says. "I have made slight additions to paragraphs one and two so that the readability will be closer to seventh grade. In paragraph five I deleted references to cookies, which are junk food and therefore may not be mentioned in textbooks."

Well, Barbara, in answer to your question of whether Merrill may use my essay in its textbook, no.

I think seventh graders would probably understand the essay the way I wrote it but even if they could not, I have no inclination to try to make it any easier for them. No writer, except maybe Bill Buckley, likes to exclude anyone from understanding what he's written but it is always wrong for a writer, or for that matter a parent or a teacher, to talk down or write down to anyone. If you write simply and directly, children will understand. Even if they are a little confused at first, they'll get the general idea. Then they'll associate the general idea with the words you've used and get to understand them. This is the learning process.

By the time children reach the seventh grade, teachers should be talking to them the way they talk to adults. For one thing, it is almost impossible for an adult to judge what changes should be made in a sentence to make it simpler for a child to understand, so the best course to follow is to say it or write it as well as you are able. Don't give them seventh-grade baby talk.

The trouble with most textbooks is they've turned into characterless pap. So many groups are applying so much pressure to teachers, boards of education and textbook publishers that by the time everything anyone objects to has been deleted there's nothing of any substance left.

Children should be exposed to all the ideas there are so they can choose for themselves. One of the best teachers I ever had would have been thrown out of a lot of schools or colleges because he was left of liberal. As kids we talked and laughed about how favorably he looked on communism, but it didn't make any of us into communists. People underestimate the ability of young students to sort things out.

Now, Barbara, while I have your attention, let me talk to you about cookies. I don't know how to start but let me just say that the cookies Aunt Anna made were not junk food. There are a lot of commercial cookies that aren't junk food, either. Have you tried Pepperidge Farm's crisp molasses cookies recently, or their oatmeal raisin? On behalf of the cookie makers and cookie eaters of the world, amateur and professional, I resent your slurring reference to our product.

Have you never enjoyed an Oreo, a Hydrox, a Social Tea? Are you knocking Fig Newtons? There may not be a lot of wheat germ, fiber or vitamin B in Animal Crackers but are they really bad for kids? Marijuana and cocaine I can understand not mentioning, but chocolate chip and macaroons? Does Merrill really think that by never mentioning the word *cookie* in one of its textbooks, it will improve the health of the nation?

No, Barbara, I don't want anything I've written used in a junk textbook.

"Hey, Romeo, I'm in the Bedroom—Come On Up"

Romance is either dead or seriously ill, having been swept off its feet by sex. Too bad there isn't room for both.

The conventions of a love affair, beginning with an introduction and the gradual process of getting to know someone better, are things of the past. Young women are no longer coy or reserved. They're as aggressive as young men.

The word "courting" has all but disappeared from the language and if a young man asked a girl's father for his daughter's hand in marriage, the father might assume the boy was on drugs.

Engagements are scarce. Every once in a while you read of one but it usually means the couple has been living together for a few years and decided there's some tax advantage in making it official and want to warn their friends in advance.

Women are as capable of opening a car door as men and yet there is something good about a world in which lovers' manners call for the door to be opened by the man on certain occasions. When a man stands behind a woman and pushes the chair forward as she sits down at the dinner table even though she doesn't need the help, it establishes a civilized relationship on a dinner date that can last the whole meal.

The novelists of the nineteenth century wouldn't be published today, because their characters seldom get undressed or go to bed together in the pages of their books. Women in hoop skirts dropped their handkerchiefs as if by accident as a trick for getting the attention of young men. Characters in old novels actually blushed. I haven't read of a woman blushing in a novel for years. You don't blush lying down.

Would Romeo have had to climb up the trellis to reach Juliet on the balcony if he were wooing her today? He would not. She'd stand on the balcony and say, "Hey, Romeo, I'm in the bedroom—come on up." Romeo would go in the front door and walk up the stairs, waving hello to her parents in the living room as he heads for their daughter's bedroom.

I came across a letter Victor Hugo, the great French author, wrote to his true love, Adele Foucher, in 1822. He told her of dreaming that they would go away together before they were married.

"But do not think, my noble Adele, that I would have taken advantage of so much happiness," he wrote. "You would have been the object most worthy of respect, the being most respected by your Victor. You might on the journey have even slept in the same chamber without fearing that he would alarm you by a touch or even have looked at you. Only I should have slept, or watched wakefully in a chair, or lying on the floor by the side of your bed, the protector of your slumbers. The rights to watch over you would have been the only of your husband's rights that your slave would have aspired to, until a priest had given him all the others."

Victor may have been laying it on a little heavy in that letter and was probably hoping he'd be invited to sleep somewhere except on the floor but still it shows you how far in the wrong direction the world has traveled when it comes to romance.

It's hard to believe there will ever be a revival of the light, romantic little songs of not so long ago. "Don't sit under the apple tree with anyone else but me." It just wouldn't make a rock video.

"I wonder who's kissing her now? I wonder who's teaching her how?" The song didn't even have a double meaning when it was popular. "I wonder if she . . . ever tells him of me . . . I wonder who's kissing her now?"

Now the lyrics of most popular songs, as Ed Newman says, seem to be mostly "Ba-buh, Ba-buh, Ba-buh."

Romance, Romance, wherefore art thou, Romance?

The Country We Love to Hate

The worst Russian of all for Americans may be Mikhail Gorbachev.

Gorbachev appears to be making so many good changes in the Soviet Union that it's getting harder and harder for us to complain about our favorite enemy, the Russians. What are we going to do without someone to hate?

"We are going to deprive you of our 'enemy' image," a Soviet official told the CBS correspondent Lesley Stahl.

Given the fact that there are eighteen million bureaucrats in the

Soviet Union, one off-the-record statement by a lone official like that may not mean much but it's a great remark, and if our basic distrust of the Russians begins to be undermined by their doing the right thing, Americans won't know how to behave.

If the Russians ever deprive us of the great pleasure and righteous satisfaction we've derived from hating them all these years, it will be difficult for us to replace it. Every individual, every ethnic group, every country needs another individual, another ethnic group or another country to hate. Hate is what makes the world go round. Some people's idea of patriotism is to hate other countries.

If the Russians start behaving like civilized citizens of the world, we're going to have to look for someone else to be the bad guys in our movies.

When I was growing up in the 1930s, Hollywood was still using World War I German submarine commanders with monocles as their villains. Erich Von Stroheim was the perfect evil enemy as he looked through his periscope and saw an American battleship in the crosshairs.

During and immediately after World War II, Nazis, Gestapo agents and sneaky little Japanese served Hollywood as our enemy prototypes. Peter Lorre played some of those parts.

For at least thirty-five years now, the Russians have served our need for bad guys and they've been perfect for the job. Their evil dictatorship, their closed society, their secretiveness, their building of the Berlin Wall, their ruthless KGB, their refusal to let their own citizens out or to let the rest of the world in all made Russia the perfect target for our hate. In addition, Russians look so much like Americans that casting was easier than when the Japanese were the enemy right after World War II. There was a limited supply of Japanese actors and none of them were very convincing.

If Gorbachev opens the Soviet society, lets us in and Russians out, as it appears he is doing, and then tears down the Berlin Wall, what in the world are we going to do for an enemy?

Who do we have who could play the Ayatollah Khomeini . . . and would he be a proper opponent for Sylvester Stallone? Most of us wouldn't recognize an Iranian if we saw one.

There was a time, years ago, when Americans couldn't distinguish a Japanese from a Chinese. Today, none of us would know an Iranian from an Iraqi, so neither of those would make good Hollywood enemies.

It seems apparent that the Russians are coming our way. Their socialized society isn't working as well as our free-enterprise system—

which isn't working very well, either—and they're trying to change it. Difficult as it may be for some of us to revise our dislike and distrust of everything Russian, it may be time for cautious change.

I've had some terrible times in three visits I've made to Russia as a working journalist. It was frustrating and I was often scared. Our daughter Ellen studied Russian in college and I took her with me on one trip. She went out at night with some Russians she'd made friends with. I gave her $100 and thought she'd change them into rubles at a bank. She came back that night, after having bought dinner for everyone, with $500 worth of rubles. She'd traded on the black market.

I had visions of both of us spending six years in a Russian prison.

Every American who has gone there has had the same emotion when he or she gets out. You have this great feeling of relief and joy at being in the free world again. It doesn't matter whether the first landing in the free world is Finland, France, London or New York—you feel like kissing the ground. If Gorbachev makes Americans feel at home in Moscow, what fun will it be to go there?

As satisfactory as the Russians have been as enemies, we have to hope that time is over. It would be nice to stop assuming we are about to fight a nuclear war with them. It would be nice to stop thinking of Russia as our enemy. I never met a Russian as mean and macho as Rambo.

Baseball Scholarship

A former president of Yale University is now something he says he's always wanted to be, commissioner of baseball.

This is of particular interest to me, because one of the few jobs I've always secretly thought I could do—without knowing anything about the game—is manage a baseball team. I'd just learn to chew tobacco and spit.

It's interesting when someone leaves what he or she is doing to do something completely different. A person has to have a lot of nerve and ability to do it. Dr. A. Bartlett Giamatti, a renowned scholar and the author of several books, among them one called *A Variorum Commentary on the Poems of John Milton,* had been a successful administrator at Yale and there's no reason to think he can't transfer that ability to baseball. I'm not so sure he'll find a place to use his variorum knowledge of Milton or even a place to use the word *variorum* in baseball.

The question that comes to my mind is this: Could someone who has been a manager in baseball make the same job change in reverse that Dr. Giamatti has made? Could Billy Martin, for example, take over as president of Yale?

I don't think we'll ever know, because baseball is more willing to take a chance on Giamatti than Yale would be to try Billy Martin. I personally know several Yale graduates who wouldn't want Martin at Yale but I don't know any ex–baseball players who mind having Giamatti . . . or who'd ever heard of him, for that matter.

The idea of people changing jobs is a good one, though. More of us should do it. Too many people get stuck doing the same dull thing all their lives without ever finding out whether they have the ability to do something else.

Most of us don't dare change jobs. We're chicken. If we're making an OK living so we're able to pay the mortgage or the rent, the car loan, the insurance premiums and the grocery bills and have good enough credit to borrow for a vacation, we don't want to rock the boat.

Most of us are trapped by the pension system, too. People stick at a job for no other reason than that they've already been at it for eighteen years.

"Three more years, Andy," a friend said to me the other day. "Just three more years and I'm getting out of here. I can't wait."

Someone ought to do him a favor and fire him so he won't waste three years of his life working at a job he doesn't like.

Dr. Giamatti says that he's dreamed of being in big-league baseball all his life. It's nice that he's realized his dream. I've known half a dozen people who have dreamed of being concert pianists, famous actors or best-selling authors but never made it. I have one good friend who is clever with his voice and writes funny material but he sticks at a nine-to-five job because he doesn't quite dare quit and try to make it as a comedian.

I'm not certain he could make it, either. The trouble is there aren't many openings for comedians, concert pianists or acting stars. If you are the 27,000th best insurance salesman, you can make a very good living but there isn't much market for your talent if you're the 27,000th best violinist in the world. And no television network is going to pay a lot of money to even the 270th funniest comedian. My friend may be funnier than 229 million Americans but that isn't good enough.

Other people stick at dull jobs because that's what they do. Work is a nervous habit. They never think of trying to do anything else. They get up in the morning and their routine is so established they never give changing it a thought.

I say, "Hurray for A. Bartlett Giamatti," but his friends at Yale may be quoting his hero John Milton:

> But oh the heavy change, now thou art gone,
> Now thou art gone and never must return!

Tod Wing's Hardware Store

On vacation, when it's too early to have a drink and I'm tired of doing everything else, I drive the thirty miles into town and stop by Tod Wing's hardware store.

If you think hardware stores aren't what they used to be, you haven't been to R. B. Wing's in Albany, New York. R. B. Wing's is just like it used to be. It's a hardware museum, except most of the stock is where you can't see it.

There are no pots, no pans and no fancy displays. There are three wooden floors and most of what they have is hidden away in bins or on upstairs shelves. Tod's got things in stock that his grandfather put in. They'll sell someday. Tod doesn't worry about it.

If I were rich, I'd like to buy the whole store and just go there and play every day, like a little girl plays with her dollhouse. It might be a good way for me to lose weight because I like a good hardware store better than I like to eat. It could never happen, of course. It's Tod's dollhouse and it's not for sale at any price.

You know that anyone who's stuck at one thing for as long as Tod has must have some stubborn qualities. Tod's got them. I like his store but I'm glad I don't work for him. He's one of those bosses who comes in early, eats a quick lunch across the street, stays late and is always watching.

It's hot in the store these days. After I've talked to Tod in his little office, I wander out into the store and always have the same joke with the rest of the guys who are digging into the dark corners to make up the orders.

"Tod says he's going to air-condition the place next week," I tell them.

They nod and smile as if to say, "Oh, sure he is."

He never will, of course. Tod's attitude is that if the place needed air-conditioning, his great-grandfather would have had it done when he opened the store down by the Hudson River in 1845. Tod's father had another chance when they moved into the new store in 1915. The guys are lucky to have electricity. The lights aren't very bright but it must have been a big day for the store when Tod's father decided to put electric lights in at all.

As much as I admire Tod for holding his ship to the wind, when I buy a tool, I often buy it somewhere else because he doesn't have what I want.

You can't get a Makita drill or a Bosch sander in his place. He won't have anything in his store that isn't made in America. The Japanese, the Germans and the English all make better tools than we make in America but Tod doesn't carry any of them.

"Our business is here," Tod says, speaking of America. "We buy here."

Some of the heavier woodworking tools made in America are still good. I bought a big Powermatic table saw made in Tennessee from Tod two years ago, and it's a beauty, but I had to go somewhere else to buy the Freud carbide-tipped blades made in Spain. They're the best but he won't give them shelf space.

The store does so much business with heavy hardware users like contractors and schools that they aren't looking for the Saturday-morning crowd like me anyway.

"They come in looking for a pound of nails," Tod says. "What are you gonna do? We accommodate 'em."

The store sells a lot of tools to local schools too, and many of them are compelled by law to Buy American. Tod wouldn't do it any differently if they weren't. He wouldn't stock a Japanese chisel or a Swedish handsaw if it meant staying in business.

It doesn't look as though R. B. Wing will be going out of business any time soon, either.

The future looks good for R. B. Wing. Tod's son Charles and his grandson Steven are both there now.

Mail Call

The bad news is, it's going to cost you a quarter to mail a letter from now on.

The good news is, you won't be getting as much junk mail.

I called a spokesman for the U.S. Postal Service and he said businesses that use junk mail to sell us stuff will be using it less because of the rate increase. The third-class mail rate was raised 25 percent. It still costs a lot less than first class, though, and I may try sending out some of my letters third class and see what happens. I think you have to leave them unsealed.

I've always wanted to make a deal with some of the businesses that send me their catalogs and advertising material year after year even though I never buy anything from them. If they simply sent me the cash for half what they spend on mailing stuff to me that I throw out, we'd both come out ahead.

The best mail is the letter from a friend or relative. It arrives with good little tidbits of information and a few words in conclusion that reconfirm a relationship with an expression of warmth, respect or love. Sad to say, only 6 percent of all the mail is that kind. The Postal Service people think the old "Dear Mom" letter has been replaced by the weekly "Hi, Mom" phone call. Too bad. A phone call is not nearly so satisfactory as a letter. Who ever heard of putting a phone call in a box and keeping it in the attic for forty years?

The Postal Service is a government agency but it's supposed to operate like a business. It doesn't get tax money so it has to pay for itself. Last year it lost $223 million, but in the last ten years it has made more than it has lost by $560 million.

It seems to most of us that the Postal Service has had more than its share of raises in the past ten years. Every so often I buy a few hundred prestamped penny postcards, thinking I'll answer a lot of mail, but the rate always goes up and makes the postcards obsolete before I use them. I still call them "penny" postcards because that's how much they cost until 1952.

In 1978 they cost 10 cents each. In 1981 they went up twice, first to 12 cents and then to 13 cents. In 1985 they went to 14 cents and now a postcard or a Christmas card you don't put in an envelope will cost 15 cents. Hallmark hates it.

Big-city post offices are places you don't go unless you have to. The people who work there are often rude, no one knows anything and you have to stand in line to find out that what you want isn't available.

Small-town post offices are great. Everyone is pleasant and helpful.

One clear reason for the national decline in affection for the post office is that in 1900 there were seventy-seven thousand of them. Today, with three times as many Americans, there are only forty thousand post offices. You can bet the thirty-seven thousand they closed were all good, small ones.

It might be a better country if we didn't have mail delivery at all. One of the healthiest things for any community is a post office where everyone comes to pick up the mail. When people have to go get their mail every day, it's not only good for people, it's good for the community.

We still pick up our mail in the little community where we live in the summer. Even the fact of having to do it is good for you: "I gotta go get the mail," you say, and no one contests that. It takes precedence over any dirty job you're doing. If you gotta get the mail, you can get out of anything.

If you didn't have to go get the mail in our community, you might never know why the fire siren rang at 3:45 A.M. You might not know that the old Peabody house has been sold to two men from New York who are going to live there. You wouldn't know why Ed Wright isn't speaking to Paul Webberly. Going to the post office is a good thing to do even when you don't get anything but a boxful of junk.

Do Only Women "Wed"?

Pamela Bankert, a third-year law student at Rutgers University, and Rupert Brandt, a carpenter, were married the other day, according to *The New York Times.* The little headline read PAMELA BANKERT WEDS.

No men ever get wed in the *Times,* just women. It doesn't say a thing in the headline about Rupert getting hitched too. Most society pages in newspapers put more emphasis on women than men. You don't see pictures of the men all dressed up in wedding clothes. It's always the picture of the woman in her wedding dress. I resent this. Men get married just as often as women and, when they do, it's just

as important. I don't know why society editors think it's more important to tell people a woman got married.

The short story of Pamela Bankert's wedding leaves a lot of unan-
swered questions. How does a third-year law student get to know a
carpenter? Can a lawyer find happiness with a carpenter and, if so, can
a carpenter find happiness with a lawyer?

One thing Pamela is sure to find when the phone begins ringing off
the hook in their house is that lawyers are a dime a dozen, but everyone
is trying to find a carpenter.

The most interesting part of this wedding story is the last line. "The
couple," the story ends, "will use the surname Bankert."

Why, do you suppose? Is Rupert just an easygoing guy who went
along with the suggestion they use her family name instead of his? Are
there class overtones in this? Is Pam's family reluctant to have her take
the name of a carpenter? I don't envy Rupert the rest of his life. From
now on people will ask him, "What was your name before you were
married?" Is there an equivalent to the phrase *maiden name* for a man?

Mr. Brandt's parents apparently are divorced, because the story says
he's the son of "Harvey Brandt of Somerville, N.J., and Pauline Perkins
of Brockton, Mass."

We don't know from the item whether his mother, Pauline, reas-
sumed her maiden name or got remarried to someone named Perkins.
I think the *Times* owed us quite a bit more or quite a bit less on this
story.

The idea of a man taking a woman's name is new to me. I'd probably
be a male chauvinist pig in Gloria Steinem's pretty blue eyes to oppose
the idea, but if the practice becomes popular it's going to cause a lot
of confusion. Having the woman assume the man's name may be unfair
to women, but it is the established way of doing things, and to change
is going to play havoc with public records.

When Pam and Rupert's children grow up and apply for a passport
years from now, what are officials going to think when they come to
the question MOTHER'S MAIDEN NAME? and see BANKERT written in the
little box? They're going to think the Bankert children made a careless
mistake.

A great many progressive women continue to use their maiden
names in business. This is understandable. Most of them officially
adopt their husband's name for the purpose of signing legal documents
and Christmas cards. This makes good sense.

Still other couples decide to join their two names with a hyphen to
create a third name. If Pamela and Rupert had chosen this course, they

now would be Pamela and Rupert Bankert-Brandt. This may seem like a solution, but it's a shortsighted one. It causes trouble down the line. Say, for example, that Pamela and Rupert Bankert-Brandt have a child named Darcy Bankert-Brandt. Darcy grows up and falls in love with a young man whose parents also had hyphenated their names. The young man's name is Peter Palmer-Williams. If Darcy insists she and her husband share their two names, their names become Mr. and Mrs. Bankert-Brandt-Palmer-Williams.

If, God forbid, Pam and Rupert's marriage doesn't work out, I wonder if Rupert will retain his married name.

Educated—to a Degree

My college education ended after my junior year because I was drafted into the army. After World War II I never returned to school so I never had a graduation of my own. I got an education in four years in the army that no college could match in a hundred years but, nonetheless, I've always felt cheated and just a little bit uneducated without a diploma.

Now I've been to quite a few commencements. I've seen my own children graduate and I've served as a speaker. I enjoy the events even though I'm envious of the young people getting diplomas.

It's the air about a college campus on commencement day that's so good. You don't go to a graduation ceremony for the oratory. The speeches, including my own, range from not very good to terrible. There's something about the event that attracts clichés. Speeches are invariably too long and often boring. They have a certain form and language expected of them that seem to limit how good they can be. Speakers feel obliged to give a lot of fatuous and unrealistic advice.

The valedictorian makes his or her speech and it's a duplicate copy of every valedictory ever given, filled with platitudes that give no indication that this is the smartest kid in the class speaking.

The only really good commencement speech I ever heard was given by a judge whose speech blew away in a strong wind before he could read it. I have no idea what he had on those fifteen or twenty pieces of paper but he shrugged and took off without any notes and was brief and excellent.

Getting their diplomas gives the graduates a feeling of success at having achieved their goal of four years as well as a sense of relief. They're wildly excited with anticipation of a future free of the artificial deadlines and work loads that school has imposed on them all their lives. It's fun to be with them on that day because their enthusiasm is infectious.

I've been to two graduations where the students should have been spanked instead of graduated. They turned what should have been a joyous, civilized event into a near-riot, yelling and screaming at inappropriate times, intruding on tradition and being generally badly behaved. They drank from whiskey bottles hidden beneath their black robes, sprayed champagne on everyone, threw bottles, seat cushions and parts of their clothing. I don't know why they wanted to ruin so important a day in their lives for themselves and for everyone else and I don't think the college administration should have stood for it.

One year I sat for two hours in cap and gown in a steady rain on the raised platform behind President James English as he handed out 516 diplomas and shook 516 wet hands at Trinity College in Hartford, Connecticut.

You might think it was a dreary experience but it was a wonderful one. Every face that came forward was a life about to be lived. I found myself guessing who'd be successful, who not, who happily married, who un. Why did this sweet young girl choose to come forward barefoot, this one in high-heeled black pumps?

Each graduate bounded forward with delight and enthusiasm to reach for the symbolic piece of paper. Yells and cheers came from the crowd as some of their classmates crossed the little stage. One big, awkward blond boy waved his diploma triumphantly and his classmates hooted. You just knew he was the one who almost didn't make it.

It wasn't always clear what evoked the shouts. The person onstage had been involved in some incident memorable only to the shouters. In their minds, the person made their class special—even though every class that ever graduated had one just like him.

Graduation ceremonies aren't what's wrong with the world.

How to Turn Inventions Off

The administration is asking Congress for $6 billion to build a fifty-two-mile tunnel in which to shoot atoms at each other. Two atoms (this is how I understand it) would be started from opposite ends of the tunnel. When they collided somewhere in the middle, the atoms would break apart and scientists would be able to find out what's inside. It seems like a lot of money to spend to break something.

The secretary of energy said the invention and construction of the world's largest research machine would be as scientifically significant as the manned landing on the moon in 1969. This would be damning a project with faint praise to a lot of Americans who can't remember exactly what practical results came from man's walk on the moon.

I'm reluctant to say this $6 billion project is a mistake because I don't understand its implications, but you always have to be suspicious of the people who are coming up with new things. The fact of the matter is, scientists and inventors invent a lot of things the world would be just as well off without and a better machine with which to break atoms might be one of them. For my own amusement, I've been making a list of unnecessary inventions that I've seen in my lifetime:

—Designer telephones in bright colors and strange shapes. Telephones don't seem to work noticeably better since they stopped making them all black and white and one style.

—Elevator music. It suggests all of us have to be entertained, amused or diverted from our own thoughts every minute of the day no matter what we're doing.

—Push-button controls on car radios. Turning two dials, one to find the station and a second to control the volume, was all we ever needed.

—Newspapers printed in color. A headline is a way of getting us to read a story by telling us, briefly, what it's about in an interesting way. It shouldn't be necessary to add color to the pictures or the type. "There it is, in black and white."

—Froot Loops, bubble gum, cranapple juice, frozen waffles, Diet 7 Up.

—Spray paint in pressurized cans represents very little advance over a can of paint you pry the lid off and spread with a brush.

—Digital watches that can only tell us that it's 8:50, not ten of nine.

—The buzzers in cars that inform you that you haven't fastened your seatbelt. What we need in a car is a buzzer that tells you where you put the keys.

—Designer jeans. Designers have added very little but price to blue jeans.

—Homogenized milk. There is a whole generation of people who don't know that, left alone, cream rises to the top.

—Cute sayings on license plates put there by state governments for promotional purposes. Maine is VACATIONLAND. Maine is also very cold in the winter, but the license plates don't say so.

—Remote-control television. The necessity for having to get up out of your chair and walk across the room to the television set made it more likely that you'd turn the thing off instead of switching from station to station all night, looking for something good that doesn't exist.

—Instant tea. All you do to make instant tea is put a spoonful in a cup and add hot water. All you do to make tea of tea that isn't instant is put a tea bag in a cup and add hot water.

All we can do is hope that this new $6 billion atom breaker-upper is more help to mankind than these items have been. If it's successful, maybe they could develop a machine that would hurl two Twinkies at each other at a billion miles an hour.

Any Day Now . . .
Any Day Now . . .

"I think we're going to see fantastic breakthroughs in aircraft technology in the next ten years or so," says Jerry N. Hefner of the National Aeronautics and Space Administration's Advanced Vehicle Division.

A newspaper story I read recently says that, among other things, new designs could reduce the drag on airplanes by enough to save the airlines $10 billion in gas bills every year.

Sounds good, but don't wait until the airlines pass that savings on to you. I've learned not to get excited about stories that promise "breakthroughs."

After reading that story my mind ran back to a newspaper article I'd read a long time ago so I went searching for it. The search took me almost all of Thursday but I found what I was looking for in an Associated Press story printed February 23, 1951.

"New strides toward the development of the first atom-powered airplane—a craft that might fly 80 times around the world on one pound of fuel—were disclosed today," the story began.

"As the climax of four years of intensive research, the Air Force and the Atomic Energy Commission announced jointly that the first phase in the program to produce an atomic plane had now been completed."

The next phase, the story said, was to be conducted by the General Electric Company at its Lockland, Ohio, plant.

Nineteen fifty-one? I thought to myself. That was thirty-eight years ago. I don't think I've ever ridden on a nuclear airplane and I know darn well they haven't developed an airplane that can fly eighty times around the world without stopping because they made that big deal about the *Voyager,* the plane that flew around it once without stopping. Maybe they're keeping it secret.

So I called General Electric to ask about the atom-powered airplane. When I mentioned the atom-powered airplane to a pleasant woman I talked to in the public relations office, she broke into gales of laughter.

She said she thought there was a model of the engine they worked on in their little museum upstairs but confessed she didn't really know much about it.

Next I called the air force. A Colonel Greer in public relations said he couldn't remember anything about it but he said he'd go to their historical section and see what he could find. That's where I stand on my report on atomic-powered airplanes . . . nowhere.

There must be a great breakthrough graveyard in the sky for new developments that sound good but never get beyond their one announcement. I remember one invention I looked forward to with great anticipation. On the cover of the last issue of *Collier's* magazine, there was a picture of a man standing on a small, round platform that could lift him off the ground and take him up and over anything for short distances.

Have you seen one of those in your hometown recently? They don't seem to be selling them in mine even though, back in 1956, *Collier's* promised we'd all have one pretty soon.

World's Fairs are a great place to see wonderful inventions you never see again in real life. When I was in high school I saw the "World of Tomorrow" at the 1939 World's Fair in New York. GE had a walking, talking robot that was going to take over a lot of dirty jobs for all of us in the future. In 1982 I saw another robot that was going to do all those jobs, at the World's Fair in Knoxville, Tennessee, but I don't notice a robot doing the dishes in our kitchen.

Maybe the most promised, least delivered technological improvement around is the video telephone with which you could see the person you were talking with and be seen too. The first time I saw a demonstration of something called Phone-A-Vision was at another World's Fair, in 1964. It was right around the corner . . . and it's still around the same corner twenty-five years later.

The moral to the story is, when you read about a new invention, don't hold your breath until it's available.

You Can't Go Back to School Again

To return or not to return, that is the question when it comes to class reunions.

This was a reunion year for both my college and high school classes and I attended both.

It was alternately great, terrible, exhilarating, depressing, fun and boring. If, as Thomas Wolfe wrote, "You can't go home again," it is equally true that "You can't go back to school again." At a reunion, we're all looking for something that is as gone as yesterday.

I was surprised, though, at how quickly old relationships, both good and bad, were reestablished. The classmates I hadn't liked much in school almost instantly irritated me again and I could see they felt the same hostility toward me. The years hadn't dissipated whatever it was in each of our personalities that rubbed the other the wrong way.

The good part was that when I met the people who had been friends in school, the warmth of our friendship was instantly renewed. It was sweet pleasure to be reminded of why I liked them so much.

You don't talk to anyone for long at a reunion. You envision spending hours reliving old times, but you don't. There is almost no time to listen to anyone else's life story or tell your own.

I saw Carl across the room and headed through the crowd to say hello. We laughed about the Latin class we both failed and then our conversation was interrupted by a classmate. We never talked again, and when I got into bed that night, I remembered that the last time I'd seen Carl was at an Eighth Air Force base in England in 1942, where he'd been a B-17 pilot. Two days later he'd been shot down and spent two years in a German prisoner camp. Such is the condensation of reunion conversations that it never came up.

There were students around, and they had a proprietary air that amused me. It was as though it were their school and we were intruders for the day. Those young students had no way of understanding that we knew the school as well as they did. I looked at the blackboards, the familiar cracks in the marble floors, the locker room, the stairways and a desk I'd sat at for three years and I smiled at the students. It was their turn to be young.

I talked to Walt. We sat next to each other in chapel because his last name began with *R* too. We had been friends but not close friends. He wasn't in my group, I guess you'd say.

"I never did much here," he said. "I certainly didn't distinguish myself."

It had never occurred to me before that he had thought that about himself when he was in school.

"What are you doing now?" I asked.

"I'm a heart surgeon practicing in Los Angeles," he said.

It was one of the depressing moments. I realized how cruel and exclusive a small group of us had been. We thought of ourselves as the leaders and the doers, and as much as half the class was shut out simply because of some quirk of personality that made them less acceptable to other kids when they were young.

What business did we have shutting out of our group a fifteen-year-old boy with the ability inside him to become a heart surgeon?

I don't know whether I'll go to another reunion. Today I wouldn't but in five years I may. I like the continuity lifelong friendships provide but there is something artificial about the reunion setting.

Schools encourage graduates to return to their reunions because reunions generate the kind of enthusiasm for the school that induces alumni to give money. I was thinking that there are some other groups of people I've spent important parts of my life with who I'll never see again simply because there's nothing in it for the organizations to which we belonged. They have no interest in bringing us together and we wouldn't bother on our own.

Maybe just as well.

The Race Against Time

Well, it looks now as though it's going to be a race against time for those of us past forty years old to see whether we live forever. They keep chipping away at the things that are killing people and it looks as though there's a good chance they'll have everything licked in our lifetime.

The Food and Drug Administration announced that it has approved a new drug, lovastatin, that will lower our cholesterol level. Cholesterol is the one that clogs up your veins and arteries like rust in a pipe and produces heart attacks when the blood can't get through.

I read the headline on that story and went to the kitchen to get a bowl of ice cream, but when I came back to the living room to finish the story and eat the ice cream, I found that the medical experts were saying you should still keep your cholesterol level down for the drug to work effectively.

"The drug works best," Nobel Prize–winning Dr. Michael S. Brown said, "when taken in conjunction with a low-fat, low-cholesterol diet."

Nothing is ever perfect—that's the trouble with all these new discoveries.

The scientific and medical communities are going to have to step up the speed of their inventions, preventions and discoveries if they hope to have all the illnesses known to the human mind and body either cured or preventable before one of them catches up with us. Some of us don't have all the time in the world left.

What I want, if any of you medical scientists are reading this, is a small pill that can be taken once a day before dinner, with a martini, that will cure anything I already have and prevent anything I might catch in the future. In addition to inhibiting cancer, heart disease, cirrhosis of the liver, kidney failure and shingles, I'd expect this little pill to keep me from getting Alzheimer's and palsy and at the same time restore any names to my memory that I can't think of. Neither do I want to read a lot of warnings on the label telling me that if I take too much of the stuff it could produce bad side effects. This all-purpose, live-forever pill should be 100 percent side-effects-less.

I know you medical scientists can do it if you put your minds to it. If some of you were a little older, you might have more incentive to work harder on the problem.

Lovastatin will be sold by the Merck drug company by prescription under the name Mevacor. Don't ask me how they arrived at these names or why they're changing it from "lovastatin" to "Mevacor" when they sell it.

You can't knock the drug companies that are developing all these miracle medicines, though. It's capitalism at its best. The drug companies want to get rich and they spend a lot of money developing new medicine to that end. That's the way capitalism is supposed to work. Merck and Company developed lovastatin and it deserves to make a lot of money.

Just as soon as science has licked old age and all the diseases we humans die of, we're going to have to face the problem of where all of us are going to live. If no one ever dies, there's going to be a honey of a housing shortage. Between our new liberal attitude toward promiscuous sex, the outlawing of abortion and the elimination of death, this is going to be one crowded planet in another hundred years.

I just wanted to make sure you heard the good news about this new drug. Lovastatin will sell for about $1.25 a dose and doctors estimate a person with a high cholesterol level will need four doses a day, so it isn't going to be cheap.

I figure that if lovastatin costs $5 a day for the next hundred years, that'll run me $182,500. Listen, the way I enjoy life, it'll be worth it, even if I have to borrow.

The Hollow Breadbasket

It's always surprising, considering how slowly things seem to progress from day to day, how quickly great changes take place in the world.

Remember the Egypt of your history books? Remember what happened to Rome and Greece? In recent times Great Britain has gone from one of the dominant world powers to a quaint country with waning influence in world affairs. Japan has developed from an inconsequential maker of cheap trinkets for our five-and-ten-cent stores to the biggest producer of quality goods in the world.

Is it possible some major and terrible change is taking place in our great country? Are we seeing it happen without knowing it's that big?

We can console ourselves with the thought that there was probably never a time in the two hundred years since the Constitution was written when it didn't seem as though things were getting worse. If that's true, these must be typical times because things sure seem to be getting worse.

What do I mean? I mean American industry isn't making most things very well. I mean our scientific work is being done more and more by foreign visitors and less and less by native Americans. The brightest kids in many of our schools weren't born here. Our money isn't worth much in foreign countries. Our manufactured goods don't sell well abroad.

A typically discouraging "these days" story appeared in the paper the other day. General Electric and General Motors are fighting a battle with the government, trying to get permission to use Soviet rockets for lifting their communication satellites into space. They want to use the Russian rockets because our space program doesn't have any.

Can you believe it? GE and GM going to the Russians for help? Here are two of the biggest corporations in the United States admitting that if they want to put their satellites in space, they have to use Russian rockets because the Russians are making them better than we are. Here are two companies that ought to be spending more time making their products, like rockets maybe, and less time making money, pleading to their government to let them use Soviet products. It's a sad day. First thing you know, the Russians will be selling us light bulbs, toaster ovens and tanks, which George Bush says they make so well.

In spite of its rockets, the Soviet Union doesn't yet seem about to bury the United States economically, but then who would have thought the Japanese would be doing it twenty-five years ago? I recall we used to laugh at the large parties of visiting Japanese engineers who always were being shown through the technical areas at CBS. There are no longer any Japanese visitors. Obviously, they got what they wanted and now they're selling CBS much of the equipment it uses in those technical areas. I'm waiting for the Japanese to take over Dan Rather and the evening news.

In a typical month recently the United States paid Japan $4 billion more for goods than Japan paid us. Our biggest export to Japan in terms of cash is food. That's cold comfort because the biggest reason we have more food than we can eat and Japan doesn't is that the United States is twenty-five times as big as Japan and has the land to grow it on. Japan isn't even as big as our state of Montana and has half the population of the United States.

What should we do? How do we get back to where we were when

we were making so many things better than anyone else in the world?

Columbia University in New York has hired a Wall Street wheeler-dealer to teach a course in corporate takeovers. It's called "Corporate Raiding: The Art of War." Bright young Americans are being taught not how to make something but how to make money by taking over established companies built on hard work.

Did you ever have one of those days when nothing seems funny?

Under Underwear Ads

For many years, before people had clothes dryers in their basements, every young boy's knowledge of what women wore under their dresses was formed by what he saw hanging from clotheslines in backyards.

It was a more realistic picture of the truth than what a young boy sees today. When underwear was hung out to dry, Sears, Roebuck was advertising women's underwear in its catalog to show how warm and practical underwear was. The women modeling the undergarments were not all built like Marilyn Monroe, and there was nothing about the ads that would cause readers to linger over them if they weren't in the market for the product.

Somewhere along the line, something went wrong. If the ads carried in the slick women's magazines today were printed in *Playboy*, someone would be trying to ban them from the newsstands. Perfectly respectable people who wouldn't dream of having pictures of mostly naked women around the house have these magazines right on the living-room coffee table where everyone can see them.

I'm not complaining, mind you, just commenting. The underwear ads are sexier and more provocative because the women in the ads look like intelligent, likable women. They don't look like the tough, been-around broads who appear naked for *Penthouse*. Even though the women in the underwear ads look prim and proper, it is apparently difficult to get nice women to do this kind of posing. As an inducement to get them to do it, the ones who stand there having their pictures taken in underwear are paid more than the ones who are pictured fully clothed.

My question is this, though: Does the average woman really imagine that she'll look like the women in the ads if she buys the underwear they're selling? Under the underwear, the women in the ads have one-in-a-million, near-perfect bodies. I should think the average woman would feel terrible every time she looked at an underwear ad. How is she ever going to live up to that image? You could say the average man might feel the same inadequacy when he looks at the unnaturally handsome dog in the shirt ad but at least the man in the shirt ad has his clothes on.

It's hard to believe many women are fooled into buying the underwear being advertised because they think they'd look like the women in the ads if they wear it. I even find the ads make a strange assumption. They seem to assume that a lot of people are going to see women in their underwear.

There are lots of fur-coat ads in the magazines and, looking at the underwear ads, you realize why it is women need fur coats.

To do some research, I went to the library to leaf through the magazines that carry ads for women's underwear. A trendy magazine called *Working Woman* has pictures of young women so scantily dressed you'd think NOW, the National Organization for Women, would object to the models being associated with working women. You wonder what their work is. I couldn't help noting, too, that the less women's underwear covers, the more it costs.

Magazines like *Cosmopolitan, Glamour, Mademoiselle* and *Vogue* have underwear and outerwear ads on adjacent pages, and I notice a new phenomenon here. While the women in the underwear ads are wearing elaborate and lacy undergarments that obviously cost a lot of money, the women in the pictures who are considered to be fully dressed seem to be wearing little or no underwear at all. If the women wearing dresses had on the undergarments pictured in the ads, the underwear would be showing, and it isn't.

Of course, some of the underwear is so elaborate and some of the outerwear so skimpy that it's hard for a man looking at these pictures to know which is which. What often appears to be a nightgown turns out to be an evening dress.

The Fake Fat of the Land

Many of you will probably be getting thinner pretty soon now because several companies have announced that they've made a new low-calorie, cholesterol-free substitute for fat that they'll have in food in the grocery stores next year.

I'm sorry I won't be joining you in losing weight by eating this stuff. If I lose any weight, it's going to be by cutting down on food, not by eating imitation fat. I have never tasted any imitation food that was close to the real thing. When the label says "with a real buttery flavor," it means there's no butter in it, and if it tastes like butter to you simply because they call it "buttery," you're a poor judge of both butter and good food.

The NutraSweet Company, part of Monsanto, one of the country's largest makers of chemical products, announced something called Simplesse. The company says Simplesse has been made to taste, feel and look like fat but will have 80 percent fewer calories. It would be used in things like ice cream, mayonnaise, yogurt, salad dressing and cheese spreads. One of the shortcomings this new product has as a substitute for butter or shortening of any kind is that you can't cook with it. You can't heat it.

I have some observations about all this:

—The ingredients in commercial cheese spreads are already as suspect as the ingredients in a cheap hot dog. If I want a cheese spread, I buy good cheese and spread it.

—If we're going to have salad, I make a salad dressing. I don't understand anyone who buys bottled salad dressing that's half as good and costs four times as much.

—I like yogurt but most commercial yogurt is so chemically concocted anyway that if they want to play around with a food, yogurt would be a good one for them to concentrate on.

—NutraSweet already makes the artificial sweetener aspartame. I have no objection to aspartame and occasionally buy a Diet Coke that's made with it. Just don't try to tell me it tastes like sugar.

I don't care what they put in cheese spreads or salad dressings or soft drinks but I object to anyone tampering with ice cream. Laws governing the ingredients in ice cream have been effective and have kept the quality of commercial ice creams at a high level compared to many products. It would be a shame if they started fooling around with ice cream by making it with fake anything. If you don't want the calories in ice cream, don't eat ice cream.

I'd prefer that Monsanto left our ice cream alone and stuck to the things that made the company big in the first place . . . things like fertilizers and herbicides.

Just as I hate to see dog food in the same aisle with the cans of tuna fish in the supermarket, I don't like a fertilizer company making food.

Anyway, we already have enough companies trying to improve their profits by trading on the great American dream of looking beautiful by dieting.

Procter & Gamble, the soap company, has a new product too. It is called Olestra. I don't know where it got the name. Maybe it was the name of the original Mr. Procter's wife.

Olestra is different from Simplesse. Olestra is purely synthetic and goes right through your body without changing itself or your body. Simplesse, on the other hand, is a protein that your digestive system has to work on.

Monsanto's NutraSweet Company takes protein particles from egg whites and milk, grinds them up and heats them and makes them into the same shape as fat particles. I don't know how they do that.

"This creates the smoothness and richness our tongue knows as fat," says Robert Shapiro, head of NutraSweet. "It's really an illusion of the taste buds."

Maybe, Mr. Shapiro, but my taste buds are very experienced and hard to kid. I don't want any of your fake food. I don't want to be fooled. If I'm going to overeat, I want the real thing.

As my father used to say, "Even if it was good, I wouldn't like it."

Handpicked Genes

The scientific loser of the century, as far as anything of practical importance to mankind goes, was the landing on the moon. It was a great $25 billion television show but not much else.

Nothing fascinates us more than considering what changes will take place on Earth after every one of us alive today is dead and gone.

Most of the science fiction written about the future centers on space exploration and life on other planets. There are always rocket ships on the book jackets. Maybe, though, the greatest changes will take place right here on Earth.

The National Research Council is spending $200 million a year on a fifteen-year effort to find out all about the genes that make people the way they are. In fifteen years, spending at that rate would cost us $3 billion. It sounds like a better place to put our money than on the moon.

You may recall from high school biology that every human being has forty-six chromosomes. When a man and a woman have sex that results in the fertilization of the egg in the female by a sperm from the male, the chromosomes divide evenly. The new life gets twenty-three of them from the man and twenty-three from the woman but no one can predict in advance which ones the baby will get. The chromosomes contain the genes, and it's the mixture of all these little rascals from two human beings that produces a totally different third human being.

"She looks just like you" means the baby got your blue-eyed gene or your snub-nose or blond-hair gene, but chances are the kid has more traits from ancestors of yours that you never knew than she does of yours.

If she's lucky, she didn't get your bad-temper gene or the gene that makes one of your toes go in the wrong direction.

In talking about their proposal, the scientists emphasize how much the study of our genes would mean in the elimination of some forms of cancer, cystic fibrosis, Alzheimer's and manic depression. You can bet, though, that this isn't where the study of genes is going to get into trouble. The trouble will come when they start fooling around with what we're really like.

What's the Supreme Court going to rule when a hospital starts advertising that, for $1,500, it can get you the baby you want, boy or girl. If we end up with twice as many boys as girls, would the government pass a law forcing people to have girl babies until the numbers were equal?

What will the whole human race look like in a thousand years if everyone's father and mother can choose how their child will look and act? If blacks decide they're discriminated against because they're black and wish, therefore, to be a different color, will black parents take on different color genes? Everyone will want to be taller. Will we fit into our cars or our houses? Will they have to raise the hoop on the basketball court? And if our cars and our houses get bigger to fit us, will there be room on Earth?

If scientists can locate the genes that control intelligence, the whole world should end up smarter. Will smarter make people happier?

The danger, of course, is that we'd all end up too much alike. It is the stray, freak, longshot gene or combination of genes that produces the unpredicted genius and makes the human race so interesting. It's those aberrant genes that no scientist could plan that gave us Albert Einstein.

If anyone could lay down the law and make fooling around with genes illegal everywhere in the world forever, it would be a good idea, but whenever there is knowledge about anything, someone uses that knowledge and you can bet that if gene-changing doesn't take place in the United States, it'll take place somewhere else in the world.

Americans will be six-footers in an eight-foot world.

Bigger Isn't Better

The easy stores to go to are the big ones that have a lot of everything. You can go to a department store in a mall that has dresses, pants, paint, books, golf clubs, underwear, watches and wastebaskets. Upstairs they have furniture and rugs. Downstairs they have refrigerators and television sets. These stores are owned by a company whose name is listed on the stock exchange. There is a store just like it in the next city and the refrigerators and television sets are downstairs there, too.

As an addicted recreational shopper, I go to these big stores and I like them, but I mourn the gradual decline in the number of small stores that have just one thing and are owned by one person, not a corporation.

The Small Business Administration in Washington says 600,000 new small businesses have started up every year in the 1980s. During the 1970s there was an average of only 365,000 new small businesses a year. I hope that in the year 2089, a few hundred of the small family businesses that start up this year will be celebrating their hundredth year and will have a little footnote in gold letters on the sign out front saying EST. 1989. I hope the great-grandchildren of the founder will still be in the business, but in spite of this optimistic announcement by the SBA, you can't tell me there aren't fewer little businesses than there used to be.

The trouble is that according to an old rule of thumb in the business world, four out of five new businesses go belly up within five years. We lose something every time a small store or a small company that makes something goes out of business. It's more like a death in the family than a business failure. When the little bakery is bought by the big bakery, the bread is never so good again. No big corporation taking over a smaller company has ever improved the product. I could name a thousand products whose quality declined under the new management of a corporate takeover. To tell you the truth, it's hard to think of a big brand product whose quality has not declined in the past ten years.

One of the reasons it's becoming more difficult for a small store to stay in business is that the small manufacturer, which once supplied the store with good quality products that were distinctive and different from those mass-produced for the chain stores, has been absorbed by the giant competitor or driven out of business. The small retail store, without a small manufacturer, ends up buying many of the same products the chain stores sell and the chain stores sell them for less. No one, not even a small-store customer as myself, can stand to pay $2.68 for an item he knows he can get for $1.98 someplace else.

I am not ungrateful to the big chain bookstores that sell millions of books. My heart, though, is with the small bookstore in your own town or in your neighborhood. It is likely that the proprietor—more often than not a woman—has read most of the books in the store and, while she's in business to make a living, she loves books better than money. In the big chain bookstore, a book may sell for 10 percent off but the salesperson has not read it or, very likely, any other book in the store, either.

The big stores have had a bad effect on the little stores in another way too. The little guys often have to band together and buy from some kind of cooperative so they can buy in volume. They get all their merchandise from one supplier, which puts them in a better competitive position with the giants. The bad part is, the quality of the merchandise in the small stores then isn't any better than the quality in the big ones. Furthermore, one small store is just like another.

I think you fellows in the sales department at newspapers that depend a lot on big chain stores for advertising revenues know this is all in good fun. Just kidding, fellas.

Graduation: End or Beginning?

May seems early for graduation ceremonies but a lot of colleges have them then. The more a college charges, the earlier it has its graduation.

Graduation day is one of the most abrupt endings we come to in our whole lives. Most things dwindle away or, little by little, we change what we're doing. Not graduation. That's it. The end. Period.

Because of the abrupt interruption in life's activities for the graduate, there are very few times in anyone's life so bittersweet as that final day at high school or college. Graduates are glad it's over but they're sad it's over, too, and they're scared about their future.

Considering how much hostility and suspicion there is toward any really educated person by almost everyone with less than a high school education, we're lucky so many young people recognize what a good thing a higher education is.

Some people consider it almost a badge of honor not to have gone to high school. If they've been successful at all or even if they haven't, they brag about how little education they've had, just as if their ignorance had helped. They don't consider anything a college graduate does for a living as real work.

Last weekend I was joking with a friend of mine who never went to high school.

"I been working all day," he said. "You probably ain't done a decent day's work in your life. Real work, I mean."

He was kidding but only sort of. The fact that I get up at 5:37 every morning and don't come home until 6:30 in the evening doesn't impress him at all. He doesn't know how I spend my time but he's not willing to concede it's work because I wear a necktie and don't lift anything.

I suppose the resentment the uneducated have toward others is natural enough. One of the simple pleasures of life is to feel superior to someone. It doesn't have to be a mean feeling. Everyone needs to feel superior about something and there are lots of people who manage to feel superior about some pretty funny things. If I know how to change the oil in my car and you don't, I feel superior to you in this one regard even though you may be a nuclear physicist. All I have to do to feel pleasantly superior is to think about what I know, and ignore what you know that I don't.

The argument that will never be resolved in education is how much the process should be directed toward teaching practical subjects that will help students make a living and how much education should be pure academic work, the only practical end to which is the pleasure of knowing.

There isn't much money in just knowing things, as any out-of-work college professor can tell you, but I hope we never give up on education for its own sake. Even though there isn't any great commercial demand for philosophers, Shakespearean scholars or experts on the works of Byron, Keats and Shelley, I hope we continue to have students who devote their education to these matters.

Kingman Brewster, once president of Yale, said, "Perhaps the most fundamental value of a liberal education is that it makes life more interesting.

"It allows you to think things which do not occur to the less learned and it makes it less likely that you will be bored with life."

I like my proud know-nothing friend but the world would be a sad place without young people who go to the trouble of suspending their lives for four years while they go to college.

A Death in the Family

I've listened to a hundred dutiful clergymen try, without success, to mitigate the sorrow of death for weeping survivors by quoting the Twenty-third Psalm or by soothingly suggesting death is something other than a tragedy. No one, though, uses words so well as to make friends and relatives of the deceased feel good at a funeral.

The death of an institution can never be so sad, but the end of a newspaper has many of the elements of the death of a friend. *The Knickerbocker News* in Albany, New York, was laid to rest at 2:30 P.M. on April 15, 1988, and nothing I can say about its demise can mitigate the sorrow for those who knew it. I knew it.

The Knick, as it was familiarly known, was part of my life because I grew up with it. When I was eight I waited for it to come. My friend Bud Duffie and I would spread it on the front porch to read the latest comic-strip episodes of Buck Rogers, Ben Webster and Little Orphan Annie.

When I was ten, I made the first money I ever had that wasn't given to me by my father. I delivered the paper to thirty-seven homes, or in the bushes near those homes, over a ten-block area in Albany.

One summer during my college years, I worked briefly in the newsroom of *The Knick* as a copyboy. While the job itself wasn't much, it was on the strength of an overstated line in a résumé regarding the importance of my work there that I was whisked out of the Seventeenth Field Artillery Battalion on maneuvers in Land's End, England, and assigned to the army newspaper, *The Stars and Stripes,* in London.

I have yellowing clippings from *The Knick* containing my name that Margie and my mother cut from it during World War II: ALBANY BOY FLIES BOMBERS OVER GERMANY.

And for the past eight years my column has appeared in *The Knickerbocker News* three days a week. How could I be anything but sad on the day of the death of an institution that has been so much a part of my life?

On reading of the demise of any newspaper, newspapermen and -women everywhere hear the faint, faraway toll of Hemingway's bell. There's a newspaper disease that's killing a lot of afternoon papers. No one is certain what causes it, what to do for the patients that have it or how to keep the healthy afternoon papers from getting it. In 1970 there were 1,429 daily afternoon newspapers published in the United States. By 1986 there were only 1,188. In 1987 23 more afternoon papers ceased publication and the number was down to 1,165. *The Knickerbocker News* is part of the statistic for 1988.

If *The Knick* were human someone would certainly say now, on the occasion of its demise, "It's a blessing." The poor *Knick* was old and desperately ill. It had suffered terribly. It had the best care there is in the business, but there wasn't much the newspaper doctors could do. Even though it had no chance for survival, no one wanted to unplug the support systems that kept it alive. Everyone kept doing what they could for it even though they'd known for several years it was hopeless.

Those who knew *The Knick* when it was younger and healthy, would hardly have recognized it in its last, dying days. There's something sad and wrong about being left with the memory of someone you've loved as he or she looked and acted toward the very end of a good, long life. We should all be remembered, by those who survive us, for how we were at our very best. It seldom happens that way, and a dying newspaper is hardly at its best in its waning months. Giving reporters time to dig for information is expensive and not always productive. Editors on a tight budget have to go for the sure things.

If you believe that information, knowledge and decisions made by people who have all the facts is the best chance the human race has for prosperous survival, you have to mourn the closing of any source of those things. That's what *The Knickerbocker News* was.

Going Feet First

You look at your body for signs of deterioration. Most men notice a change when they get out of competitive contact sports at the age of about twenty-three. They have the sad feeling they've peaked already and will never be in such good shape again. A general deterioration becomes noticeable at thirty.

When I make a casual checklist of body parts, I start at the top and work down. Right now I think my feet are going first. When I was thirty-five I noticed a slight thinning of my hair, but there hasn't been much change. I'm still a long way from being bald. My hair turned gray, but I don't mind gray.

I just spent two sessions with my dentist. He says my teeth are generally in good shape. I like an optimistic doctor of any kind, even if he lies a little. I don't like a dentist who looks in my mouth, shakes his head and says, "Oh, oh."

My dentist finds good things to say. Last time he was drilling away and he said, "Boy, you really have hard teeth."

I stand pain better when he flatters me.

My face looks a little weather-beaten but it's got a lot of good years left in it. My eyes are fine. I wear glasses for reading and writing, but I can still read without glasses if I have to. My ears are as good as new. I guess your ears don't deteriorate the way your eyes do. Almost everyone over forty needs glasses, but only 3 million Americans wear hearing aids. To tell the truth, most of us hear better than is absolutely necessary. Most of the sounds we're exposed to every day are so loud that we could hear them just as well with half our hearing ability. If my ears were adjustable, I'd have the sound turned down most of the time.

You never know about your heart. My doctor says my heart is OK, but, of course, a lot of people who die of heart attacks have just been reassured by their doctors that they're in great shape.

After that recent announcement about aspirin being good for potential heart-attack victims, I've been taking an aspirin a lot of nights before I go to bed. I don't know what it's doing for my heart, but my feet hurt less when I get into bed.

My lungs must be in good shape because I can run on the tennis court without being winded. With the exception of one year when I got hooked on how much fun a pipe was, I've never smoked. I worried about my tongue with a pipe, not my lungs.

My legs are clearly in better shape than my feet, which seems unfair. My hands and arms are actually stronger than they were when I was younger because of all the woodworking I've been doing. Sometimes I think I'd be better off standing on my hands half the time and on my feet the other half.

There have been so many reports about people who start getting Alzheimer's disease when they reach the age of sixty that I worry about my brain. Every time there's a name I can't remember, I think I may have it. The only thing that saves me from real worry is that I can remember I never remembered anyone's name when I was twenty, either. As far as I can tell, my brain works as well as it ever did. I realize, of course, that statement makes me vulnerable to some smart remarks.

If it weren't for my feet, I'd be in great shape. Feet are poorly designed to stand up for a lifetime. I don't have any complaints with the basic construction of any other part of my body, but feet are not well made. They're fragile and funny-looking. What in the world are all those toes for? Does anyone use his or her toes separately, as we would use our fingers? Toes are leftovers from the time we hung from trees.

Day after day, week after week, month after month, year after year I've been walking, running and banging my two hundred pounds down on these poor little old size 8½ EEEs of mine. They're sick and tired of it and they're not going to take it anymore.

A Nun's Tale

Sister Mary Rose came to see me the other day. She understands my position in regard to nuns but she won't be discouraged and I admire her for that.

I first met Sister Mary Rose Christy in Arizona when I was making a film there in 1968. At that time she was trying to save the Indians. Sister Mary Rose is always trying to save someone, whether they need it or not. On the occasions she's written to me, she never fails to end the letter by asking God's blessing for me. She wants to save me.

The results of these blessings are not all in, but naturally I have high expectations. A request from a nun would carry more weight than if I'd asked for God's blessing myself.

At the present time Sister Mary Rose is busy saving the homeless in San Francisco and they're lucky to have her on their side. She rejects my contention that she could use a little saving herself. For one thing, she's eating better than is absolutely necessary. She's a wonderfully good-hearted person, though, and I suspect she thinks of herself last.

Anyway, as you can tell, I like Sister Mary Rose a lot, and that's why I'm so upset with a recent trend in her life-style. In the past few years she's started doing something I can't excuse her for. She's stopped wearing her nun's habit. When she comes to my office now she's dressed like anyone else looking for work. That means she doesn't look like a nun. It would be fair to say she's gotten out of the habit.

If you're going to be a nun, you ought to look like a nun and act like a nun. I've told Sister Mary Rose this. I've told her that if she doesn't wear that black costume, I'm not going to call her "Sister" anymore. I'm just going to call her Mary Rose . . . or possibly even just Mary. Pope John Paul II has laid down the law to Catholics in so many ways that I wish he'd come up with a pronunciamento on dress for priests and nuns. I'm sure it's an area in which the Pope and I agree. You certainly aren't going to find Pope John Paul II wearing blue jeans or a sports coat and I'll bet he expects proper dress among his workers in the vineyard where the grapes of wrath are stored.

I like to see a nun or a priest here and there. They are black and white dots in a colorful but otherwise anonymous crowd. You can identify them for what they are. If a salesman, a doctor or a Russian spy goes by, you never know because they look like everyone else. When a properly attired nun goes by, you know who she is. You can divert yourself with whatever thought you usually have about nuns. I called the Catholic archdiocese in town and the man in their communications office just laughed when I asked if priests and nuns were wearing their official clothes less frequently.

"Oh, my, yes . . . ever since the Second Vatican Council," he said. I recognized, by the tone of his voice, that "the Second Vatican Council" was a phrase that held great meaning for him, so I didn't display my ignorance by asking how it bore on nuns' habits. He said "Second Vatican Council" the same way a Secretary of State might say "Ever since Geneva," or "Ever since FDR, Churchill and Stalin met at Yalta."

Why have nuns dropped their habits? Aren't they as proud of being nuns as they once were? Do they think they can be more effective wearing civilian clothes? Why, for that matter, do so many priests go out wearing regular shirts and ties when we expect something more of them? Men of the cloth ought to wear their regular cloth. Priests, ministers and nuns ought to be as identifiable as policemen in case we need one in an emergency.

Don't come back, except in black, Sister Mary Rose.

Let the Salesman Beware

Recently I got that urge most men try so unsuccessfully to resist every few years. I went in to look at a new car. I know buying a new car is silly when the old one is running perfectly well, but we all know how to overcome good sense when it comes to thinking about a new car. We say, for instance, "I don't want to have to start spending a lot of money on an old car. It'll be cheaper in the long run to turn it in now."

It won't be cheaper but that's what we say when we're talking ourselves into buying a new car.

I like dealing with car salesmen. (I have never dealt with a car saleswoman.) For one thing, I don't feel the usual compulsion to be absolutely honest. There is an unwritten understanding between car buyers and car salesmen, who are otherwise perfectly decent people, that anything goes. It's a poker game. Buyers don't know what the dealer is holding. We know there's a profit margin he can cut into to give us a better deal but we aren't sure how much he has to play with or how deep he's willing to cut into it to make a sale.

Years ago I went to a Ford showroom looking for a station wagon. I saw one I liked and started dickering over the price. Finally, in a desperate attempt to push me over the brink, the salesman said, "It's the last car like this on the whole East Coast. If you want it, you better grab it because it'll be gone tomorrow."

This was a challenge to me. I don't like to be browbeaten by a car salesman.

"Oh, gosh," I said. "That's really too bad. I have a good friend and we always buy identical cars. I was looking for two of these, one for him and one for me. If you only have one, it's no deal."

"Listen," the car salesman said, "that's what someone told me. Just let me go in the office and check to make sure."

Sure enough, of course, he found one at another Ford dealer in the next town. Just lucky, he said.

I didn't buy the two wagons.

The big news I got from car dealers I spoke to last week was that the hot color is red. They can't get enough red cars.

Next to black, red is the last color I'd want. The pigment in red paint doesn't seem to hold up as well as other colors, and while a red car might look attractive and catchy when it's new, there is nothing so old and tired-looking as a two-year-old red car.

The car I drive most is white, and if I get a new one, it'll be white too. A white car doesn't seem to get as dirty as other colors and in the summer it reflects the heat of the sun's rays. I hope everyone doesn't decide to buy a white car some year, though. I enjoy the variety of colors of cars on the road. No color dominates, and that's the way it should be.

The best cars I've ever owned smelled good. We all know a new car smells good, but the best cars have a way of smelling good all their lives. My 1977 wagon still smells good.

I fight cars with a lot of gadgets on them but it's a losing battle. My other car has a panel with little buttons that are supposed to light up when there's trouble. If the brake is left on or the engine oil is low, a red light goes on indicating "brake" or "oil," for instance.

Last week the little light indicating trouble in the "cooling system" came on. I brought the car in and there was nothing wrong with the cooling system but with the wiring in the indicator panel. In four years, the only time the trouble-indicating lights have gone on has been when there was some trouble in the indicator board itself. So much for gadgets.

The one thing I'm happy you can still get in most cars as an option is manual shift. Automatic shift burns more gas and doesn't give a driver the same control over a car as the driver has with stick shift. Shifting the gears of a car is one of life's satisfying little jobs. I like to shift for myself.

NUISANCES

Getting Rid of Leftovers

Has there been a study done at Harvard or Stanford on leftovers? Congress is working on the tax bill and the President is concerned over what to do about South Africa, but is anyone giving any attention to a major element in all our lives . . . what to do with what's left that we can't use but is too good to throw away?

The storage shelves in our house are filled with all sorts of good leftovers that aren't good for anything.

I can spot useless junk everywhere in someone else's house. It's difficult to find any in my own. Maybe what we need in this country is some kind of neighborly mutual-help program. It's a lot easier to throw away someone else's leftovers than it is your own. We might work out some exchange program whereby a friend or neighbor comes to our house while we go to theirs. Each would set aside sentimentality and clean the other's house of leftovers.

The most conspicuous and persistent leftovers, of course, go in the refrigerator in little plastic boxes. At any given time, there are eight to ten lumps of leftovers aging on the shelves of our refrigerator. Just last night I put what amounted to about half a serving of squash in a container that was big enough to hold ten times that much. I know perfectly well what the future holds for this pitiful little morsel. It will sit there for a week, gradually finding its way to the back of the refrigerator, where a jar of pickles sits. The pickles were opened six weeks ago. I hope the jar of pickles and the summer squash can find something in common because they're going to spend a lot of time together. Then, some day down the road, I'll be rooting around back there looking for the mayonnaise, and wonder what's in the plastic box.

I'll open it up and detect a strange odor emanating from the lump of yellow in the bottom.

"Yuck," I'll say to myself and scrape it into the garbage.

When something you've cooked is fresh and your palate is reminding your memory of how good it was, it's difficult to discard it. When that same dish is tired and stale and nothing more than a space-taker in the refrigerator, it becomes a pleasure to cast out.

The trick to getting rid of leftovers is to anticipate how you're going to feel about those items in two weeks.

And it isn't just the refrigerator. There are leftovers in life no matter what we're doing. Every time I buy an electrical appliance, there are parts in the box it comes in that I don't use and can't throw away. As soon as a month later, when I come across them in a drawer, I can't figure out what they're for.

I bought a small antenna for the television set upstairs. It helps the reception, but in the little plastic bag of parts that came with it there are three bolts, a bracket and some kind of insulator left over. These things are all brand new and it would be a crime to throw them away, but the kitchen drawer set aside for miscellaneous items is filled with leftover hardware.

Paint makes a miserable leftover. It's almost impossible to plan a job in such a way that you buy just the right amount of paint and finish with none left over. A quart of paint is so expensive that there aren't many of us who can throw out what remains in the can even though we rarely use it. There's a gallon can in the basement representing what was left over after I painted the twins' bedroom blue fourteen years ago. So much paint dripped down the sides of the can that I am no longer able to read the label. I don't even know for sure whether it's oil- or water-based paint. I doubt if it would make a noise if I shook it. There it is, though. If I ever need it, I know just where to find it.

It's a good thing you don't have to keep paint in the refrigerator.

A Plug for New Electrical Outlets

They're building dams and nuclear power plants and scientists are talking about harnessing the sun's energy to produce electrical power but they aren't doing a thing about the rat's nest of electric cords, outlets and homemade lash-ups around our television sets, behind our living-room couches and under our beds.

Every time I want to plug something in, I have to crawl under a table, move a chair or go down in the basement to find an extension cord or some kind of converter. Something's wrong with electrical outlets in America.

I'd vote for the presidential candidate who stood on a platform that demanded "enough electrical outlets for all!" It's time for each of us to demand enough outlets in our homes. Not only should there be enough but they should be put where we need them and where we can get at them. Why are they always installed along the baseboard, on the longest section of wall, where any fool should know the couch is going to go? How do they expect us to plug anything into the wall behind the couch? And why did they put two outlets there instead of six?

Is there anyone who doesn't have an electric clock in the bedroom? A radio? Some lamps? Possibly even a television set, a hair dryer or an air conditioner? Then why in the world did the people who built the house only install two electrical outlets? Are they in business with the companies that make those gadgets that convert one outlet into three? Do they get a percentage from the makers of extension cords?

The kitchen in this house is lined with a tangle of power-carrying cords. There's a clock over the stove, a blender, a Cuisinart, a toaster oven, an orange juicer, a small black-and-white television set, a radio and on occasions I bring in an electric griddle for pancakes, a popcorn popper, a deep-fat fryer or a small Waring ice cream maker.

A moratorium ought to be declared on the invention and manufacture of new electrical appliances until they work out a better system for plugging them in. Half the time when you start to connect an appliance, you find the maker was so concerned about the possibility you'd be electrocuted, that he put a three-pronged plug on the end of the cord.

There are few experiences in life more frustrating than having a three-pronged plug and a two-hole outlet. In my lifetime I've bought a hundred three-pronged adapters, but where are they when I need one?

I have no objection to grounded plugs if the experts tell us we should use them but then why do they ever put in a wall plug that isn't equipped to take a three-pronged plug? It should be illegal. I could probably go to jail for it but I confess that in moments of frustration I have gone to the kitchen drawer with the pliers in it and used them to bend off the offending ground pin so that the plug will fit into the wall socket.

With so many fools in the world, it's impossible to make the world foolproof. The people trying to make the world safe for everyone are fighting a losing battle and one that makes life difficult for the average person.

Fifteen or twenty years ago some electrical genius decided to make plugs whose prongs were a different size. The larger of the two prongs doesn't fit into the old standard wall plug. I have never understood what this latest development in the field of power cords does for me but I managed to stay alive without being electrocuted for many years before we had plugs in which one of the prongs was bigger than the other.

It seems inconceivable to me that the minds that came up with the fantastic array of electrical appliances available to all of us couldn't come up with some new idea for wall sockets that would be convenient, safe and good-looking. It should not be necessary to hide them under the bed, behind the couch or in the next room, where you can't get at them.

The Privacy of a Public Person

A year ago I was walking along a street in Greenwich Village having a good time doing not much of anything when a man wearing a sweater and blue jeans and carrying a violin case grabbed me by the arm.

"Hey," he said, "aren't you Andy Rooney?"

It seems presumptuous of anyone to grab me under any circumstances but even more so when the person doesn't even know for sure who he's grabbing.

"A lot of people ask me that," I said, and walked on.

"Hey, no kidding," he said, grabbing my arm again, "are you Andy Rooney?"

"Look," I said, "I'm minding my own business. Why don't you mind yours . . . go play your violin."

The young man looked shocked.

"You ought to be in some other business," he said, and walked away.

Should I be in some other business? Does a stranger have a right to grab me by the arm, stop me in the middle of a pleasant, private walk because I appear on television and write a newspaper column?

I have been with close friends, far better known than I am, who are unfailingly gracious in these situations. Walter Cronkite will charm a stranger with his smile, sign his name on a sheet of paper and listen as though he were interested to silly small talk from anyone who stops him. If I could be like Walter, I would be, but I can't.

This all comes to mind because I've been reading about a lawsuit brought by the author of *The Catcher in the Rye*, J. D. Salinger. Salinger, a notorious recluse, won't give interviews to newspeople or appear on television. He certainly won't talk to strangers. He wants to be known for what he writes, not for what he looks like or sounds like. I admire him for it.

The story was about an unauthorized biography of him, publication of which he tried to stop. Most of us would be flattered by even an unflattering biography, but Salinger wants no part of it.

I'm on J. D. Salinger's side and yet the question from the man with the violin often comes to mind after I've been rude to a stranger. Have I sold my right to privacy by appearing in public for money?

A couple named Lipovsky wrote from Vancouver, British Columbia, after I'd laughed at some letters I'd received, to say how pompous and arrogant I was for not appreciating the people who had taken the time to write.

Well, I appreciate about half the letters I get and I get some that I actually treasure but I get a lot of mail from idiots, too, and I see no reason why I should pretend I'm grateful to the people who wrote them.

Considering how desperately hard people work to get themselves a reputation and to become widely known, it's interesting how empty a thing well-knownness seems to be once you have acquired it. I'm nervous every time I sit down to write or do something on television. At that very moment I am nothing until I've produced something. If what I produce is poor it makes my semi-well-knownness seem all the more hollow to me.

There seem to be thousands of people in the United States whose only job in life is to get people with familiar names to loan them out for some good cause. Anyone with any kind of public name at all gets hundreds of requests a year from well-meaning organizations that wish to use the person's name in a long list of names that goes down the left-hand side of their stationery.

It embarrasses me to turn down charitable organizations that ask if they may use my name as a sponsor or honorary committee member on their fund-raising letters, but it doesn't embarrass me nearly as much as seeing my name used that way, endorsing something I know nothing about and in whose work I have taken no part. It's a minor fraud.

It seems to me anyone who becomes well known through what he or she has written owes the people who have liked it nothing but to continue to write as well as possible.

The Keys to Our Kingdoms

We've gone crazy with keys. If we want to get in, we're all forced to carry eight or ten keys around with us. We carry keys all day, every day, that we don't use once every six months. I don't notice the number of thefts going down because of our keys, either.

If keys and locks were the answer to dishonesty, we'd have a theft-free country.

The drawers in which everyone keeps life's bric-a-brac and memorabilia have keys in them we haven't used in years. In many cases we no longer know what it is the keys unlock but we're afraid to throw them away.

Between the dresser drawers, the kitchen drawers and the small, thin drawers in hall and living-room tables, there must be thirty dead keys in our house. I still keep the keys to a couple of cars that were probably turned into scrap and melted down ten years ago. Is there a market for the key to the trunk of a 1957 Ford Fairlane?

People have a terrible time throwing a key away. A key seems like such an important item even though it no longer fits anything we own. If I saved money the way I save keys, I'd have enough to make a takeover bid for IBM.

Most of us have at least seven basic keys. We have two house keys, one for the front door and one for the back door. We have one for the garage, whether we lock the garage or not. We have two car keys, one for the ignition and one for the trunk. (This isn't counting the backup set that comes with the owner's manual.) Many Americans have at least one key that opens a door or a locker at work, and usually we have a small key that opens some kind of padlock we own.

Those are the basic keys, although there may be many more. If you own two cars, you have a total of eight car keys. Often there are two locks on the door of a house, and an office in a city building can mean you'll have to carry three keys. You'll need one to get into your office area, another to get into your office door and a third to unlock your desk.

We pretend keys are more important than they are. How serious an impediment to entry is a lock and key when the only thing that stands between a burglar and the possessions in your house is a pane of glass?

I often ride a train to work, and I'm amused to see businessmen carrying little briefcases with tiny, expensive brass locks on them. It's ridiculous for the same reason a lock on a suitcase doesn't make any sense. If someone wants to steal something in a briefcase or a suitcase, the thief isn't going to stop to unlock it. He's going to take the whole lot in the handy little carrying case you've provided for him. He can open it later, at his leisure, with an ax.

There must be ten tiny keys in my dresser that came with suitcases I've bought. I've never locked anything with them and I've never thrown them out. I always ask a luggage salesman for a suitcase without a lock on it and suggest to him that it should be cheaper. Most suitcases, of course, have locks.

Some of my battered and abandoned suitcases in the upstairs hall closet are themselves repositories for keys. I often find two or three hotel keys for rooms I checked out of seven years ago floating around the bottom of a suitcase along with the other flotsam and jetsam of long trips. All the keys say on them DROP IN ANY MAILBOX, NO POSTAGE NECESSARY. I feel terribly guilty but I never get around to returning those keys.

People make a big deal out of locking their cars with keys. More than a million cars a year are stolen in the United States and I bet all but about four of those are locked tight with the ignition key in the owner's pocket when the car thief comes along. The lack of a key doesn't seem to deter the car thieves.

I have a feeling that if we all threw away the keys, our kingdoms would still be there in the morning.

A Dose of Double-talk

"Delicious," I heard the flight attendant say to the passenger behind me. "It's really delicious," she said.

"OK," I thought to myself, "I'll take that as her opinion even though I can't see what she's talking about."

"I tasted it," the flight attendant continued, "and it's really delicious. I never had anything so delicious. Delicious."

This was five "deliciouses" I'd heard in the space of twenty seconds and it was irritating. I'm easily irritated in flight.

"I'll try some," I heard the passenger say.

"You'll love it," the flight attendant said.

"It's really delicious," I said quickly to myself, mocking what I anticipated the flight attendant would say next. She didn't disappoint me.

"It's really delicious," she bubbled for the sixth time.

I reached in the pocket for the bag provided for passengers who think they're going to be sick. If I wasn't a sweet, mild-tempered person I'd have stood up and whacked this young woman over her pretty head with my seat cushion and yelled, "All right already . . . so it's good."

Is it my imagination or are people repeating themselves more than they once did? I'm continually hearing people say the same thing not twice but four or five times.

It's hard to know what brought this on. It seems as though people either enjoy hearing themselves say these things or they don't trust people to hear what they've said the first time. They want to make sure.

This morning I happened to be outside my office door when the man who delivers the newspapers showed up. He also delivers to Charles Kuralt just down the hall and the personnel office next door.

"I'm going to leave their papers with you too," he said. "I can't get in so I'll leave them with you. The door is locked there and I can't leave them so I'll leave them here."

There's a subject for someone's doctoral thesis here somewhere: "The Theory and Practice of Repetition in Everyday Conversation."

There are phrases people use that have repetition built into them. I have a friend who often says something like "I just had a small little breakfast this morning."

He always uses the words *small* and *little* together as if one improved on the other.

I don't know whether he invented it himself or whether it was written for him, but for a reason I can't figure out, back in 1984, President Reagan started using the phrase "a new beginning."

Are there any old beginnings? It's repeating the same thing over again, twice, repeatedly.

There seems to be a proliferation of unnecessary talk everywhere. I can think of several possible reasons for it.

The first reason may be that there's so much unnecessary noise in the world that in order to carry on a conversation, people have to shout and constantly reiterate. The chances of anyone hearing everything they say the first time they say it is minimal. There's either a radio or a television set blaring away or someone's running a lawn mower or power saw or the street-maintenance people are working with a pneumatic jack hammer nearby.

I often take a cab in New York. Invariably the driver has his radio on too loud and, in addition, he has a two-way radio with someone on it competing with the other sounds, trying to give him the name and address of a customer. When I tell him where I want to go, I notice I often repeat the address to make sure he heard it.

And then there's another reason for all the verbal repetition. I don't want to get over my head in psychology, but I think people are uncertain about so many things in their lives that they get some sort of primal satisfaction from saying something that doesn't call for any thought.

If we expressed an idea just once, telephone calls, interviews and everyday conversations could be cut in half.

Gift Shop Gifts

If it came from a gift shop, please don't give it to me. There is a whole category of things that I don't want for Christmas and most of them come from gift shops. Don't get me a tie rack, for instance.

There's something wrong about a place that specializes in things to be given away. It can't be as down to earth as the everyday store that you'd go into to buy something you need for yourself. Most of the items in gift shops are things no one has any use for. I am uncertain about why they have been categorized as "gifts." Why would anyone decide to give a friend something that the store owner, by designating it "gift," has declared to be something the person wouldn't want for himself?

The only kind of gift to give is something you'd like to own yourself. You aren't dying to have a set of hand-embroidered pot holders, a bag of fragrances for your underwear drawer or a copper-plated watering can.

There are some nice gift shops just as there are nice cups of tea. The people who run them tend to be struggling entrepreneurs who aren't making much of a living. I like the people and I feel sorry for them but they're in the wrong business. We don't need any more gift shops. No one really likes anything that has the look of a gift about it.

The worst gift shops in the world are those terrible places at airports. If you fly into St. Louis, the gift shops at the airport feature caps and T-shirts saying ST. LOUIS CARDINALS on them and coffee cups bearing the likeness of Charles Lindbergh's plane, the *Spirit of St. Louis.*

The names on the caps and T-shirts are about the only distinguishing feature in airport shops across the country.

The shops usually make a failing effort to have some local products. In an airport in Burlington, Vermont, you'll be able to buy maple syrup. The airport in Orlando will send a crate of oranges home for you, and one in Chicago will have ashtrays, highball glasses and key chains featuring the Chicago Bears football team. In San Francisco there are redwood-tree plaques saying HOME SWEET HOME. Everywhere you can find seashells, pictures of movie stars in cheap frames, fancy candles and expensive little calendar books.

It's hard to put your finger on what's wrong with gift shops. They often try too hard to be clever but, worse than that, nothing in the shop is of much use in the real world. The only purpose served by a bread-board with flowers painted on it is as a gift. It's a gift and nothing more because the chances are it never will be used to cut bread on.

What does anyone do with a gift shop gift? No one wants an apron with a crossword puzzle on it or a glass paperweight that gives the impression it's snowing when you turn it upside down.

Our houses are filled with this useless kind of stuff and we don't dare throw anything away because we don't know when the person who gave it to us is going to show up again.

If you've got to bring home a gift from your trip, make sure you buy it in town before you hit the gift shop at the airport. I actually had a friend years ago whose marriage ended in divorce over something he brought his wife from Kennedy Airport in New York.

My friend was about to board the plane when he realized he hadn't bought anything for his wife. Feeling guilty, he rushed back into the terminal and went to the gift shop. From there he brought her a bronzed thermometer in the shape of the Empire State Building.

She was apparently already in sort of a bad mood when he arrived home late, and when he gave her the gift shop gift she took one look at it, threw it at him and left home forever.

I didn't say so to my friend at the time but I thought she had a good point.

Let's Hear It for Silence

They've finally gone too far. The American Civil Liberties Union, one of my favorite organizations in spite of President Bush, is defending the right of people to play musical instruments in New York City subway stations as a means of begging for money.

Some of these young musicians are pretty good. You see them on street corners as well as in subway stations all over town. A friend has a son who walks up and down the lines of people waiting to get into popular movies on weekends, playing his violin. He has a basket attached to his chest for people to drop money in.

Begging like this is the young man's only source of income and his father and mother say he does quite well. Their attitude is strange. I don't think they're proud of him but they don't try to hide it and they seem somewhat amused by it. It's my personal opinion that their son ought to be spanked and put to bed without his supper—or his violin—even though he's thirty years old. I don't say that to them.

Most of these street musicians are inoffensive but I don't believe they have the law on their side and I can't understand why the ACLU has come to their defense. What about the rest of us who like silence, ACLU? Where do our rights start? Why does my friend's son have the right to dominate the sound and atmosphere of a movie line? What if I'm standing with someone I enjoy talking to? If he has the right to play on the street or in the subway, do I have the right to stand next to him with a siren and drown out his noise with a noise of my own?

When one person's freedom to do something infringes on another's, the question of freedom gets into deep water.

Another friend of mine had the best time of his life on a New York subway the other day. He was sitting there reading his paper, when three young punks got on the train with a radio blaring loud rock music. My friend was thinking about moving to another car because, in addition to not liking the noise, he didn't like the looks of the three young men. At this point another passenger, wearing blue jeans and a cap pulled down over his eyes, asked the young men to turn off their radio.

My friend didn't want to be in on any confrontation about something as small as a loud radio, so he kept his nose buried in his paper, but his ears were tuned to the scene down the car. He half expected to be witness to a bloody incident.

"Hey, man," one of the young radio-players said, "why don't you . . ." He uttered a comment that can't be repeated.

"I said, turn off the radio," the man in blue jeans said firmly. The three youths started toward him. At this point the man whipped out his New York City police badge, revealing his pistol holster as he did so. At the next stop the undercover cop handcuffed the three together and took them off the train.

Where would the ACLU stand on that?

Several weeks ago I was lying in bed ready to go to sleep when I heard music wafting in the open window. It was loud, incessant and unusual for the neighborhood. I lay there getting angrier by the minute until I couldn't stand it any longer. I got up, pulled pants on over my pajamas, put on a shirt and sneakers with no socks and headed for the sounds.

As I approached the source of the commotion, a woman, dressed as hastily as I was, came walking toward me.

"What's going on?" I asked.

"Oh, it's a high school graduation party," she sighed. "They have notices posted on the trees saying they'll move inside at midnight."

I turned and headed for home. I wasn't going to be a graduation party pooper. In a case like this, the only thing to do is surrender your freedom to have silence to a group of young people who, for one night, want to be free to have noise with their fun.

Low Marks for High Flight

I've had more comfortable flights in a B-17 bomber over Germany during World War II when we were getting shot at than I've had on some commercial airline trips recently. Deregulation is about as successful for the airlines as a kindergarten class would be for kids without a teacher. It's a dismal failure. The airlines are going the way of our railroads.

Anyone planning a vacation trip for pleasure is going to get off to a bad start because there is no longer anything pleasant about a commercial airline flight. You hold your breath until it's over. People ought to stay home if they don't have to go somewhere. Businessmen and -women should do their long-distance business by computer. Flight is torture.

The same thing has happened to U.S. airlines that has happened to most American industry. The money-changers are in charge. The professionals, who used to get their satisfaction out of trying to make theirs the best airline in the business, are gone. Pilots who used to be proud to work for Pan Am, Eastern, Delta, TWA, American, United, are now bad-mouthing their own airlines, and for good reason.

Ticket agents, flight attendants and pilots seem not only good but exceptionally good by any standard you use to judge employees. They aren't the problem. Service has deteriorated because there aren't enough of them.

The women who do the dirty work on board the aircraft, the flight attendants, formerly "stewardesses," are a remarkably capable, interesting, intelligent and attractive group of all-American women. They perform the service of waitress, nurse, bartender, psychiatrist, hat-check girl and cocktail-party conversationalist and still maintain their pleasant manner in the face of rude, dissatisfied, unruly passengers like me.

There have been numerous instances of violence by passengers on board airlines and there are going to be more. You often read of a passenger who is arrested when the plane lands.

Rage comes easily to people under the circumstances found on commercial airlines. Plane interiors have been redesigned so the cabins are incredibly crowded and uncomfortable. There are too many people jammed into too little space, often on a hot aircraft. The claustrophobia factor is high. You're trapped in a confined space, bumper-to-bumper with several hundred strangers. Baggage service is so bad that too many people have brought too many bags on board and there's no room left to store a necktie. If an airline cabin were a prison, it would be illegal.

The food in flight is no longer fair. The thought of asking the attendants for anything beyond their routine is out of the question. They simply don't have the time to do it. You're lucky if they have the plate off your lap before you land.

On a Delta "dinner flight" I took, cocktails weren't served until after dinner . . . which is as appealing as having dessert for breakfast.

First-class flight is prohibitively expensive for most people and I'm one of them. I have flown what they call "business" class several times. That's expensive too and not nearly as good as the so-called tourist or economy class of ten years ago.

The pilot always politely suggests you stay in your seat with your belt fastened, ostensibly "for your own safety," but practically because they've jammed too many seats in the plane and the aisles are so narrow there's no room to move around in the cabin. You're lucky if you can get to the bathroom.

If the mechanics are being pushed as hard as the ticket agents and the flight crews, there is no way mechanics can maintain those airplanes in good condition. Maintenance must be on the same level of quality as everything else. If that's true, we're in for trouble . . . by which I mean there are going to be lots more crashes in the next few years.

Airlines, chronically behind schedule, ought to be ordered to list travel time instead of flight time. Their schedules should read from the time they tell you to be there, not from the time the flight is supposed to take off. What difference does it make that the flight is scheduled for five hours if it leaves an hour late and you have to be there two hours in advance of the scheduled departure? For practical purposes, your travel time is eight hours.

On a recent American Airlines flight of about 110 miles that takes thirty-five minutes in the air, I paid $99 for a one-way ticket and was told to show up half an hour before flight time. I got there nine minutes before flight time and the gate to the plane was closed.

I complained to the people at the desk. They rapped on the window, and got the ground personnel to bring the stairs to the small commuter-type airplane back down.

"What time do you have?" I asked the man who had closed the door.

"I don't know," he said. "I don't have a watch."

I suggest that American Airlines make the ownership of a watch mandatory for people in charge of closing doors on time.

Don't fly if you're looking for a good time.

On Becoming a Credit Risk

It finally happened. I dreaded the day but I knew it would happen sooner or later. My credit card didn't pass.

The item I was buying was a tent costing $64.95. We're replacing the old garage that used to be an icehouse, up in the country, and I had to empty it out. I was buying a tent as a temporary storage place. I didn't have $64.95 cash with me so I took out my Chemical Bank

Visa card. There were several people behind me in the cashier's line. I hated to hold them up with a credit card, but I had no choice.

The young woman at the cash register did the thing where they put your card in the little printing press and pull the handle to get a duplicate of it. She typed some number off my card into a device that looked like an adding machine and waited. Finally she looked up at me and said, "I'm sorry, sir. Your credit has been stopped."

I looked at the next person in line behind me and laughed nervously.

"Boy, these banks," I said, suggesting that it was just a bookkeeping mistake by the bank. A wonderful person like me would never have failed to pay a bill.

An assistant manager came along.

"Here, give me the card, I'll call," he said.

He called some Visa main office, waited a minute, then turned and said, "I'm sorry, Mr. Rooney. You have an unpaid outstanding balance. You can't charge anything."

By this time the people in line behind me were impatient.

"There must be some mistake," I said as I walked sheepishly out to my car without the tent. I could feel all the eyes in the store following me. They might as well have had my name up in neon lights with bells and sirens going off: ATTENTION, ATTENTION. ANDREW A. ROONEY DOESN'T PAY HIS BILLS!

Driving home, I remembered a letter I'd recently received from the bank. I pay bills to individuals the day I get them, but I'm apt to leave institutional bills in a pile of undone things. Apparently I'd done that with my Visa bill.

The late notice, which I found the next morning, said, "The amount overdue on your account is $5.00. Please see that payment is made within the next five days. Sincerely, Collection Department." I doubted a collection department's sincerity but I remembered getting the notice now.

I realized I had to do something about this cloud hanging over my financial reputation so I set out to pay it quickly.

For a year I've been paying my Visa bill by phone but I'd lost the number. I finally got the phone to ring at the Collection Department and was greeted by a recorded message.

"Thank you for calling Chemical Bank," it said. "All our agents are busy. Please stay on the line and your call will be answered by the first available agent."

Nine minutes of terrible music later, Mrs. Piro answered. Mrs. Piro had never heard of being able to pay by phone.

"Let me give you my supervisor," Mrs. Piro said.

This time it was only six minutes of recorded music later before Mrs. Hobbs came on the line.

Mrs. Hobbs did not think it was possible to pay my Visa bill by phone either, but because I'd been paying them that way for a year by transferring money out of my Chemical checking account into my Chemical Visa account, I knew she was wrong.

"I'll give you the number for Customer Service," Mrs. Hobbs said. All agents were busy again but the music was livelier and, when Mrs. Manza finally answered, she agreed that it could be done by phone.

I exonerated myself forthwith, but those people who stood in line behind me yesterday will never think of me as an honorable man again.

And, if it rains, all the good junk in the garage will get wet because I don't have it under a tent.

Figuring Out Insurance-Company Figures

One of the most frustrating jobs known to man is trying to get information out of an insurance company. Insurance companies are faced with so many people trying to cheat them that you have to be a little sympathetic to their efforts to protect themselves. But boy do they protect themselves! And let's face it—insurance companies have us where they want us.

Six weeks ago I had surgery to correct a hernia. Before undergoing surgery, I went to an internist, who gave me a very thorough examination.

You don't shop around trying to find the cheapest doctors when you're having work done on a body you can't turn in for a new one. Both the internist and the surgeon I used are the very best kind of representatives of the medical profession. They are not only medically expert but socially aware. It gives me a lot of confidence in both of them that they are each other's doctors.

The charge for the medical examination, including all the tests that went with it, was $314.

I paid the doctor by check and sent in the Prudential Insurance

Company forms for reimbursement. In two weeks Prudential sent me a check . . . for $11.20.

"Your family deductible," the form said, "is now satisfied."

Well, OK, but obviously Prudential was more satisfied than I was.

The surgeon's charge for the operation, a hernia with minor complications, was $1,550. It did not seem out of line for an outstanding surgeon in an expensive part of the country.

I paid the surgeon, and this time the Prudential check came with a semi–form letter. It said:

"Your group plan provides only for reimbursement of usual and prevailing fees.

"In determining a usual and prevailing fee, we refer to statistical profiles of physicians' charges for the same or similar services in the area."

The check from Prudential for the surgeon's fee was for $840. They pay 80 percent of the figure they assign to the operation . . . $1,050.

I decided to try to find out more about the billing. I talked to three people at Prudential, then to an administrator at the hospital, a Blue Shield executive, two people at the State Commission on Hospitals and Health Care and four doctors, not including either of mine.

The doctors said $1,550 was a normal charge.

The Prudential people were polite but evasive.

In answer to my question "How do you determine 'usual and prevailing,' " they hedged.

"It depends; we have different ways."

"We divide the country into two hundred and fifty-two areas and do it that way."

The nice young man whose name was at the bottom of the letter finally said, "Gosh, I probably shouldn't be talking to you about this at all." He must have thought he'd given me some information, and that's the last thing an insurance company wants one of its employees to do.

When I complained to another about getting only $840 back on the $1,550 bill I paid, he said, "We update our 'usual and prevailing' rates every quarter. You probably just missed an update."

My employer provides the insurance coverage, so I spoke to the company expert and got the biggest surprise of all.

Prudential, he said, doesn't really insure me. My company pays the medical bills. All Prudential does is the book work for a fee. My employer "pays" Prudential about $58 a month for each employee, but it's only a bookkeeping figure. Actually, he said, my employer deposits that amount in a bank account out of which medical costs are paid. It must be a common practice but I'd never heard of it and was surprised to find my company in business with an insurance company. Obviously my company doesn't mind when Prudential keeps the costs down.

The whole episode wasn't a total loss. I got my hernia fixed and I feel a lot better. Even though I never found out how the insurance company decided I'd only get back half what I'd paid out, I learned something.

That's about as good as you can expect to do.

Driving Still Drives Me Crazy

Last weekend I was making my 150-mile drive north from New York City when a nut in an old red Camaro came careening through the traffic behind me. He must have been doing ninety.

As he came nearer, I pulled closer to the truck in front of me, thinking it would keep the Camaro from cutting in. It didn't and the driver made a dangerous move as he veered into the narrow gap between me and the truck, forcing me to hit my brakes. He immediately cut to the inside of the truck, passed that and flew on.

I was still simmering mad four miles down the road when I saw the flashing red lights of a cop car pulled over to the side of the road. He'd caught the smart alec in the red Camaro! It is the kind of event that makes it impossible not to take pleasure from someone else's misfortune. I was delighted.

There was time enough for me to slow down and room enough for me to pull up next to the police car, where the officer was sitting, writing a ticket. I rolled down my window and, as the surprised officer looked up, I yelled, "I hope he loses his license!"

I pulled back on the highway and drove off, hoping I never meet the driver of the red Camaro in a dark alley.

There has been a recent rash of shootings on California highways and several times a year you read the story of an argument between drivers in a minor accident that leads to a fight or a shooting.

If you're a driver, you can understand how it happens. My angry reaction to the driver of the Camaro was a symptom of the same disease that leads to shootings. In the course of any trip you take, long or short, some other driver does something you think is wrong. If you're an aggressive driver, you're angry. Go get 'em, cowboy! You have this weapon in your hands, your car, and your tendency is to use it.

"I'll go get him and cut him off at the next light . . . give him a taste of his own medicine."

Some drivers are saints. They plug along slowly but surely and nothing bothers them. They're not competitive with everyone else on the road. They don't anger easily.

These safe and sane drivers are, unfortunately, often responsible for the accidents other drivers have and they are not always good at handling their cars. The slow, cautious driver arouses unreasonable resentment from me when I'm behind the wheel and I'm convinced they cause many of the accidents. I hate to say so but the nut in the red Camaro knows more about how to handle his car than the very slow driver does.

There are a handful of driving maneuvers that bring out the worst in me. Traveling at five or ten miles an hour above the legal speed limit, which is average in America, I keep a respectful distance from the car or truck ahead of me. I hate it when another car passes me on the right or left and pulls into that space, forcing me back.

When someone who has just passed me slows down at an intersection and waits until he has started to make a turn before putting on his turn signal, I lay on my horn in protest. By the time he starts turning, he no longer has to put on his flasher to let me know about it. He's too late.

"You dumb SOB," I mutter under my breath to nobody. I'm not a nice person in a car.

The best truck drivers are better than the average passenger-car driver but there are some terrible ones. Some enjoy coming up a mere eight or ten feet from your rear bumper. If you hit the brake, you're going to have a truck in the backseat. Truck drivers do this to let you know you're in their way and that they own the road.

On the highway, there's always the driver who passes you at eighty and then slows down in front of you to fifty-four. My blood boils.

The next new gadget they might consider building into our cars is a hypnotic windshield wiper that talks: *"Don't fight. Don't fight. Don't fight."*

Stamp Out Fake Tag and Garage Sales!

There ought to be some legal standard for what can be called a tag sale. A real tag sale is a great American tradition that also may be called a garage sale or a yard or lawn sale, but now there are imposters who are ruining tag sales for the rest of us.

The original idea was that, since once in about every ten years the average American household accumulates a lot of things the owners no longer use but they can't bring themselves to throw away, they have a friendly little sale on their front lawn, in their backyard or in their garage. The spoilers are making a business of tag sales. Some neighborly-appearing con artists have a tag-sale sign they bring out every year to trap unsuspecting passersby.

The unwritten rule about these sales always has been that they offer no newly acquired items specially bought to be resold. No tag sale was ever intended to be a bargain basement. Just as soon as someone starts having a tag sale every summer, you know these people are not playing the game fair and square. They are in the tag-sale business and can't be trusted. Chances are, they travel around to other tag sales, buy junk, mark it up and sell it on their own front yards as genuine homemade junk when, in fact, it's imported.

Naturally, exceptions will be allowed to the resale rule. If something is acquired at a tag sale that seems like a good idea to buy at the time but which turns out to be a terrible idea, this is a legitimate item for resale.

Any longtime tag-sale devotee knows the genuine tag-sale items when he sees them. The following are examples of genuine tag- or garage-sale items:

—An old bicycle, slightly rusty, usually junior-size.

—A souvenir plate with a picture of Richard and Pat Nixon on it.

—A bundle of *National Geographic* magazines for the years 1951 through 1953, tied with string.

—Two used jigsaw puzzles with some missing pieces.

—A hand-push lawn mower that hasn't been used since the power mower was invented.

—A Christmas-present scarf, unused and still in its original wrapping
with the see-through plastic cover.
—A set of six cute little pronged forks with tiny handles shaped to look
like ears of corn, designed to hold ears of corn while they're being eaten.
—An old iron with a frayed cord.
—A wooden box of rusty old tools.
—Bad wood carvings or porcelain figurines.
—Several unopened copies of *Reader's Digest Condensed Books*.

Almost anything goes in a tag sale, but it must be an average American household's attempt to unload junk it doesn't want. Money should
not be the first consideration in a genuine tag sale.

In all my years of tag-sale buying, my favorite purchases, aside from
seventeen Underwood No. 5 typewriters I've lugged home, have been
a six-foot wooden toboggan, a brass coal scuttle, an old, small wooden
plane, a set of four heavy wheels eight inches in diameter with rubber
tires, and a souvenir mug with Spiro Agnew's picture on it.

It's possible to get lucky at a tag sale. People look for that painting
worth $10,000 that they buy for $12 because it has been hidden in
someone's attic for forty years, but that doesn't happen at tag sales in
real life. Those are just newspaper stories. In real life, the old painting
you buy for $12 is actually worth only $3.

The luckiest you can be at a tag sale is to see a big, homely old chair
you want to buy and discover it's too big to fit into your car. Anything
you can't buy at a tag sale, for whatever reason, is usually a blessing.

I call on Congress to pass tag-sale legislation that will protect this
great American institution from ending up as just another chain store
on the stock exchange.

Everything's Coming Up Rosiest

There is so much competition for our attention that everyone is
using up all our good superlatives to get it. I say "using up" because
there's just so often you can use a superlative before it loses its compara-
tive effectiveness.

Advertisers and salesmen of all kinds are describing things in ultimate terms in order to get us to buy. Even friends talking together
about everyday things describe them in superlatives.

Here are some conversations you're apt to hear:

"How was your weekend?"

"Terrific."

A weekend experience is never described with any of our middle-ground adjectives like "good." If a weekend wasn't either "great" or "terrific," it was "a real disaster" or "the pits."

If you go out for dinner and you're asked the next day how it was, you say: "Absolutely delicious. The best I ever tasted."

"How was the dessert?"

"Fabulous. Absolutely fabulous."

In foreign affairs, nothing is merely a "problem." Everything is described as "a crisis in foreign affairs." Or, "The United States faces its worst crisis in this decade."

When local police find cocaine in someone's apartment, it is usually described as "one of the biggest drug busts in history."

Movie actors and good athletes are no longer mere stars. They're all superstars. Never mind that you never heard of them before. Someone who is only a "star" is practically an unknown. Superstars play football in the Super Bowl. They're "world class" athletes.

On television and in the newspapers, games are hardly ever simply "won." Michigan "crushes" Ohio State or Ohio State "destroys" Michigan. A good play by an athlete is always described as "unbelievable." The word "awesome" is beginning to get quite a bit of play too.

Book reviewers and movie critics don't ever seem to read or see anything that's average. Books are "brilliant" or "trash." A movie may be either "provocative," "superb drama" or "spectacular."

Every movie I see advertised these days is called "One of the year's ten best."

No movie is ever "funny" anymore. The movie is at least "hilarious." The comedy also may be "a sheer delight." You wouldn't want to see a movie that was just a plain "delight," without being a "sheer" one. One movie being advertised now is called "a raucous rib-tickler . . . Steve Martin is savagely funny . . . one of the year's ten best films."

Some serious movies are "haunting."

A movie with dancers in it may be "dazzling" or "mind-boggling." The fact that most of us don't understand exactly what it would mean to have our mind "boggled" doesn't stop people from using the word.

Movies also may be "stupendous" or "monumental in scope." The photography is "gorgeous" and chances are the movie has been "brilliantly directed" by someone.

When a store has a sale, it doesn't simply "reduce" prices. Its prices are DRASTICALLY REDUCED!!! Often its reductions are described as ONCE IN A LIFETIME BARGAINS!!!

For some reason, it seems more acceptable for a commercial enterprise, like a store or a movie theater, to use nothing but superlatives in describing the things they're trying to sell. We all know you have to take advertising with a grain of salt. It seems too bad that our ordinary, everyday conversation between friends has degenerated to the point where the frequent and thoughtless use of the superlative as a trick to attract our attention has lessened the importance of language generally.

Thank you very, very much for listening, Readers. You're the greatest.

May I Help You?

When you go through the office door into the waiting room, there's usually a receptionist behind the desk. Sometimes she's behind a glass partition because she also answers the phones. (I have never seen a male receptionist, and as a male, I resent it.)

"May I help you?" the receptionist says, nice as pie, just as if she really wants to help you. You know darn well she hates you but she tries to act as if she's helping. You can tell she hates you, because if she didn't hate you she wouldn't make you feel as though you didn't have any business there.

After taking your name she says, "Please sit down."

She doesn't say it in a nice way as though she wants you to be comfortable. She doesn't mean it when she says "Please." It's more of an order she's giving. "SIT DOWN!" is what she's really saying.

Very often I don't want to sit down. I don't feel like sitting down. I'm not tired. Whether it's the office of a dentist, a lawyer or a tax accountant, I'm more apt to be nervous than tired.

I don't want to give receptionists the idea I'm relaxed, either. I don't want them to think time doesn't matter to me and they can keep me waiting as long as they feel like it once they have my weight off my feet. That's why I always remain standing.

Gradually, a clearly visible tension mounts between me and the receptionist until she reluctantly admits that the person I've come to see will see me. You can tell that, if she had her way, I wouldn't get in until I'd darn well sat down the way she told me to.

I don't know why receptionists, whose job ought to be to make people feel at home, are so unfriendly. They have a way of making you feel unwanted every time.

At home at night receptionists must practice making people feel unwanted. They have phrases they use.

"What is this in reference to?" they ask.

If you wanted to talk to a receptionist about something, you'd have made the appointment with her in the first place. It's none of her business what you want to talk to her boss about. Maybe you're someone who wants the job she has. How would that sound if you told her that?

"Yes. I'd like to talk to your boss about getting your job. You're such a sourpuss that he's trying to find someone nice."

That's what I always feel like saying.

Receptionists have a hundred unfriendly ways of greeting people who come through the door.

"Do you have an appointment?"

"May I say who's calling?"

What does she mean "May I say . . ."? Why is she being so condescending? Why doesn't she come right out and ask, "What's your name?"?

I'd rather find an armed guard at the door than the average receptionist. At least I know where I stand with an armed guard. He doesn't give me a lot of artificial charm. He just says, "You can't go in there, buddy."

The receptionist says, "I'll see if Mr. Jones is in." That's what she says even though she knows darn well Mr. Jones is in because she was sitting at the desk when he showed up for work and she has seen him go to the coffee machine twice and the bathroom once, since then.

Just once, I'd like to be confronted with an honest receptionist in an office.

"Hi," I'd say as I came in. "Ed Jones around?"

"Yeah," my ideal receptionist would say. "He's goofing off somewhere back there."

"Can I talk to him?"

"Let me see if he's off the phone with his wife yet. He spent the last hour talking to the school principal about one of his kids and he's having an awful time collecting from an insurance company on a car he cracked up last week. I'll see what he's doing now."

You never find a receptionist like that, though. They're all the same. They ought to be called "rejectionists."

Silence the Blowhards

The same government that passed the idiotic law that limited automobile speed to fifty-five, whether the car is traveling on an eight-lane highway without a curve for the next hundred miles in the middle of Wyoming or on a bumpy, two-lane macadam trail in a mountainous area of Colorado, might have done everyone a bigger favor if it had banned horns on cars.

On at least 98 percent of the occasions when a horn is blown by a driver, it is a sign of impatience, not imminent danger to anyone. If there's danger, it's best for the driver to keep both hands on the wheel and hit the brakes. If the driver has time to blow the horn, chances are nothing serious is about to happen.

Most frequently the driver who blows the horn is mad at the driver of the car in front. Horns have no practical influence on the average driver whatsoever. We blow at the drivers in front of us with full expectations that they'll get out of our way. We are angered when they do not but it doesn't occur to us to move over when the drivers behind us lean on their horns.

Last night at about quarter to ten, I was taking one last look at the newspaper when I heard a car horn up the street from our house. It blew once and then there was a pause. Then there were two short honks and finally a series of longer blasts.

Who is so rude, in a street with a row of houses on both sides of it, to sit outside one of them and blow a car horn for attention? Doesn't this idiot understand that it will inconvenience several dozen people attracted to the sound and forced, against their will, to wonder what or who it's for?

Whenever a street is blocked by a garbage truck, a person parking a car, an accident or a sticky traffic light, someone in the rear of the line of cars always starts to blow. Does that driver think all the cars in front are sitting there from choice? Is the sound of the horn really the thing that's needed to get traffic moving? Would it, if the driver didn't blow, stay where it is all day?

When I take the train home from work to the commuter station, there are always fifteen or twenty wives waiting in cars for their husbands. One of them invariably blows the horn to get her husband's attention. Of all the cars in the station, what makes this woman think she is justified in being the only one blowing her horn? Has she considered what it would sound like if all the wives of all the husbands getting off the train blew their horns? (I recognize that I have assumed it is always a wife waiting for a working husband doing the blowing. That just happens to be the way it is at the station I use. If I ever see a husband waiting for his wife to come home from work and hear him blow his horn to attract her attention, I'll report to you.)

In most noisy cities, car horns are part of the orchestra. The fire engines clang past, little noted. The sirens of the ambulances wail notice of their approach, pass and diminish in the distance. A car horn attracts no attention whatsoever except from the driver who gets some kind of perverse satisfaction from blowing it.

If it would be dangerous to eliminate the horns on cars altogether, and probably it would, then at the very least horns ought to have meters attached to them. A meter could be tied into the odometer. Every driver would be given two free horn honks for every hundred miles of driving. Any horn blowing in excess of that would cost a driver a use tax of $25 per honk.

The most annoying horn blowers are the repeaters. They are the drivers who hit the horn three or four times every time they hit it at all. No quick beep for them. A horn-use tax would hit these drivers hardest.

Automobile horn blowing is one of the principal causes of noise pollution in America. A horn-blowing tax might not help solve the national debt but it would have a great quieting effect.

Some Days Everything Seems Wrong

Is it just a mood you get in once in a while or are a lot of things not as good as they used to be?

—The streets in our cities and the roads around them have certainly deteriorated. No major highway twenty years old is in good condition and there's so much traffic on them that they can't be closed and rebuilt the way they should be. As a result, the original concrete gets a little cosmetic dab of asphalt once in a while.

—Most brands of paper handkerchiefs (I'm avoiding saying the name we all call them) are smaller and less substantial. You need two where one used to do the job.

—"Wash and wear" shirts look good when you buy them, and you can wash them but you can't wear them. All the synthetic fabrics itch in hot weather and are not nearly as comfortable as shirts were when they were made of cotton. Today, you have to search for "all cotton." Synthetic fabrics are progress at its worst.

—Our lakes, our rivers and our beaches are no longer any fun to go to for a vacation. If they're any good and have clean water, they're too crowded. Most of them aren't any good, don't have clean water and are too crowded anyway. We have ruined most of our great water, and why it isn't more of a concern of government I don't know.

—And don't think you can climb a mountain and enjoy the pristine beauty of nature, either. Climb the highest mountain and you'll find an orange peel and three empty beer cans.

—Breakfast in a good hotel used to be one of the great luxuries. Forget breakfast. The chef doesn't come in until 11 A.M. and then he starts to prepare lunch.

Most breakfast menus advertise "fresh orange juice," but it almost never is fresh, especially in Florida.

Ellen stayed in the Hilton in Boston last week. The menu said "fresh-squeezed orange juice." Ellen has knowing taste buds. She challenged the waiter, then the head waiter. (Like father, like daughter.) The head waiter insisted it was fresh orange juice.

"If you don't believe me," he said, "I'll show you the bottle." Fresh orange juice, as John McPhee once wrote, "is juice that's still in the orange when you order it."

—Tomatoes are a joke except for about three weeks a year. Tomatoes used to be dark red, juicy and full of flavor. Now they're used like food coloring or parsley. They're merely decoration. They're pink, hard, dry and tasteless.

—House paint is not as good as it once was. It peels. One reason is that manufacturers are no longer allowed to use lead in their paint because small children, who ate loose paint in deteriorating houses, became ill.

It's probably a necessary law that prohibits the use of lead, but it sure makes poor paint and it's too bad we couldn't stop kids from eating paint instead.

—Postal service is a joke compared to what it was twenty-five or thirty years ago when everyone got two deliveries a day. Can you imagine that? Two deliveries a day? You're lucky to get one some days.

I hope it's just things, not people, that are deteriorating.

A Room at the Inn

Hotels are on my mind because I slept in one for a week recently in Atlanta.

Atlanta is a good hotel city. Architect John Portman started the trend toward those huge atrium lobbies. He thinks a hotel should be an experience, not just a place to sleep. Portman has changed the look of big, expensive downtown hotels in America and made them more interesting. They're no longer big boxes with a lot of little boxes inside.

I stayed in one of Portman's hotels, the Westin. It was a very nice hotel and although I'm impressed with his work, I'm not as interested in an experience as I am in a night's sleep. In his successful effort to be interesting, Mr. Portman sacrifices some convenience for the guests. Many hotels have little scorecards they leave for guests to fill out. They ask a guest to rank the hotel's various services. I never fill them out, but here are several comments I have that would apply to most hotels in America:

—I wish the bellman carrying my bags to the room would stop asking those same questions: "Did you have a nice flight?" "Have you stayed with us before?" and "How long are you going to be with us?"

—There is too much knocking at your door in most hotels. I'm not doing anything sneaky, but I don't like hotel employees knocking at the door to check on something all the time.

—They can turn down the bed if they want to while I'm out for dinner, but please stop leaving me those two little chocolates on the pillow.

—Hotels have got to wake up to the fact that seven o'clock is too late to begin serving breakfast. Because they start so late, it is often difficult to get into the dining room for breakfast by eight o'clock and room service is all jammed up between seven and eight. It isn't unusual to wait forty-five minutes for toast and coffee to be brought to your room . . . for $11.95, "SERVICE NOT INCLUDED."

—Hotels ought to get together on a shower-control mechanism. Most of them work OK if you know how they work but if you've never seen the type before, they can be difficult. You can either freeze or scald yourself. One problem they don't consider is that about half of all Americans need glasses and you can't wear your glasses in the shower, so you can't read the directions on the shower control.

—The new thing is for American hotels to pretend they have a concierge. The concierge is one of the best things about staying at a hotel in Europe. This man is available in the lobby at all times of day and night. He knows everything and can do anything. If you want reservations at a good restaurant or tickets to the opera, he knows how to get them.

American hotels don't have the vaguest idea what a concierge is and they should be prohibited from giving the word a bad name by using it.

—The price for a good hotel room has gone out of sight. Prices have risen higher and faster than any other single item I can think of. The rooms at the Westin are $130 for one person and $190 for two. Wow!

—Hotels ought to stop putting so much of their own advertising literature around the room. I'm renting the room and they ought to leave the space on top of the dresser and the television cabinet for me, not for their own commercials. And if you put all their literature in a drawer, the maid takes it out and puts it back where they want it the next day.

—The lights near or over the bed are almost always impossible to read by and very often the on/off switch is hard to find or inaccessible from a prone position.

—Hangers are too often cleverly designed so they're hard for a guest to take home, but they're hard to use, too.

Please come back and see us again real soon.

PROBLEMS

Withering Away with the Weather

Sometimes I get the feeling the Earth doesn't really want us. It sure makes it difficult to live here.

Last night when I got home just before dinner, I stopped and looked at the thermometer outside the kitchen door. The sun hits it in late afternoon so it isn't really an accurate indicator, but it read 94 degrees. On the radio they were calling it an official 90.

I went upstairs to change into my old sitting-around clothes, but I didn't stay up there long because it must have been 100 in the bedroom. We have an air conditioner but it hadn't been turned on because no one was going to be in the room. I hate to spend money cooling an empty room.

This morning I left the house at 6:10 and the same thermometer that had read 94 degrees last evening was at an even 40 degrees. Do you think some force is using weather to drive us crazy or make us move somewhere else, off Earth?

Driving to work, I got to thinking about how near the Earth is to being uninhabitable. I've never read what temperatures the human body can take for high and low extremes but it seems likely that parts of this planet are close to being outside the range of human tolerance at times. The temperature gets into the high 120's in Death Valley, California, and it has been as high as 134 degrees. That's in the shade and there isn't any shade out there. The Earth's temperature has peaked at 136 in Libya. Muammar al-Qaddafi aside, this is reason enough for me not to book a two-week vacation there.

In Vostok, Antarctica, temperatures have been recorded as low as 126 degrees below zero. Can the same body that would stay alive in

136-degree heat also keep going 262 degrees below that? I remember reading about a place in Montana where the temperature fell from 44 degrees above zero around noon to 56 degrees below zero late that night. That's putting heating systems and the human body to the test.

Somehow we seem to live through extreme temperature changes. Air-conditioning and central heating make it easier, but the human race survived before it had either. I don't see how.

Nature is always making things tough for us. If it isn't temperature, it's another kind of terrible weather or natural phenomenon that makes life difficult. Sunday there was a picture in my newspaper of a row of expensive beach houses that are in imminent danger of being washed away because the ocean has eroded the sand out from under them, leaving the houses precariously perched on top of their telephone pole–like stilt pilings.

At another time of year, that same page of the same paper might have a picture of snow drifts burying a row of cars on a highway near Buffalo or of a house being washed downstream by the overflowing Mississippi in the delta. Just when you think you're lucky to be in the one safe part of the country, something strikes you. I look with some sense of sad superiority at the stories of raging fires coming down the canyons in California or of twisters sweeping the Kansas plains.

While I was worrying about all the bad luck the rest of the country was having last fall, a hurricane struck the East Coast while we were in Maine. We drove home to Connecticut the following day, following detours where the road had been blocked off by fallen telephone poles, and found the lawn in front of our house with enough major branches down so that I had to call a tree surgeon to clear them away.

I am always worried that the Earth will become too warm, too cold, too wet or too dry for humans. We are, after all, fragile creatures. It wouldn't take much of a change to make life on Earth impossible.

Fortunately for me, I have something more important to worry about today. I think my checking account is overdrawn.

More Is Not Merrier

I don't mean to be selfish. I don't want to keep the world to myself and a few friends, but there does come a point when a crowd ruins everything. We have all the people this country needs now. I associate overpopulation with poverty and unhappiness, not with joy and plenty.

If the Bible were rewritten this year with some quotations from God, I think he'd probably want to change that line in Genesis where he's quoted as saying, "Be fruitful, and multiply, and replenish the earth . . ."

For all we know, God may have been misquoted in the first place. You know how inaccurate reporters are. A second Bible I have quotes God as saying, "Be fruitful, and multiply, and *fill* the earth."

The present occupants of the planet earth have more than fulfilled that biblical command. We've filled the earth and ought to stop multiplying before it overflows and we spill out into space.

We ought to have a grand plan for the planet's future that would include arrangements for maintaining some relationship between the number of people trying to live on earth and earth's ability to sustain that many.

We've already ruined all the rivers from the Yangtze to the Mississippi. Do you know of a lake you can drink from? Lake water was all drinkable before we started dumping our garbage, our sewage and our commercial waste in it. Now we've started ruining our oceans and, big as they are, they'll be seas of slop before long.

We often find ourselves breathing air we'd prefer not to have in our lungs, but we have no choice. That's all the air there is. Breathing Los Angeles air must be the equivalent of three packs a day.

The increase in the number of people is greatest in the countries least able to take care of them. On television, you see emaciated women in Ethiopia with emaciated babies, both dying of starvation. Nine months later you see dying women with week-old babies. The women must have been dying when they conceived the children.

Does it never occur to these people that it would have been better for her, better for the child and better for the world if she had said no to the guy? If the pope had been there and she could have asked his advice, what would he have said? Would he have advised her to go ahead and be fruitful and replenish the earth?

He's a good pope. He probably would have said, "In your case, I'm going to make an exception. The earth doesn't need any more people in Ethiopia this year, thank you."

It's a pain to those who feel strongly about the tragedy of the black condition in America to see so many blacks assuring themselves and their children a dismal ghetto future by reproducing beyond their ability to take care of their children.

If birth control of one kind is wrong, you'd think birth control of any kind would be wrong. The most effective method of birth control is the widely—but reluctantly practiced—inhibition of desire. It's why all women are not constantly being attacked. Men curb their desire or rape would be rampant. It's birth control at the beginning. Do opponents of birth control oppose it?

It's difficult to understand how any society, government, philosophy or religion could encourage its constituents to do any more than reproduce its own numbers.

We could do great things in the world if we could stabilize the population and then gradually reduce it.

I'd like to see the world return to the way it was in the 1930s, when I was growing up.

Maybe they'd tear down some of the buildings they've put up on the vacant lots we used to play in.

They could tear up some of the wide concrete strips that cross the country and give us back some of those lovely little dirt roads that wound their way among the farms.

The line at the motor vehicle bureau might get shorter.

In summer, there might be a place at the shore big enough to spread a blanket again for a picnic.

The people who like to fish might find a quiet pond far from the noise of a radio.

There'd be seats on the bus, no traffic jams with the shopping carts at the supermarket.

Who knows, we might get a little of our privacy back if the world stopped having more babies than it can happily hold.

Doctors, Doctors Everywhere

There are too many doctors, according to a report issued by the American Medical Association.

For me to believe that, the report would have had to be issued by patients instead of doctors. I'd like to get together a panel of patients who had just spent the morning sitting in a waiting room before being admitted for an eight-minute session with the doctor.

It also would be interesting to find out what someone thinks who became desperately ill in say, Kumquat, Iowa, and almost died before he got to the nearest doctor sixty miles away in Fort Dodge.

There are hundreds of communities in the United States that have no doctor. In some of them, a doctor would have a hard time making the doctors' average $108,000 a year, but if a doctor in a small town could make, say $60,000, or about three times as much as the high school principal makes, would that be a bad deal?

The idea that there are too many doctors comes up every year. It's as wrong this year as it was last year. There are not too many doctors. There are not enough doctors, and until each of us is assured immortality, there will never be enough doctors. Let me know when all pain and suffering is over. Call me when cancer is a thing of the past and when AIDS is a memory like diphtheria, and then I'll agree there are enough doctors.

Most of us hold the medical profession in high esteem. I do. We seem to have a higher regard for doctors than doctors have for themselves. I hope they aren't right.

Dr. James Sammons, the executive vice president of the AMA, says there's an overproduction of physicians, and he wants to cut down on the number of people admitted to medical schools and on the number of foreign doctors admitted to practice in the United States.

Dr. Sammons denies it but he's talking about doctors' income, not patients' health, when he says there are too many doctors. The AMA spends too much time on everything but medicine.

The report says too many doctors could mean that a doctor's skill might deteriorate because the physician "may not perform certain procedures frequently enough to maintain a high level of skill." You mean, they need the practice?

The report also says that, because there are too many specialists, some doctors might be driven into general practice. I don't know enough to argue that point but, if true, is it terrible? If enough doctors are driven out of plastic surgery, Kumquat, Iowa, may get a doctor of its own someday. Maybe doctors will even start making house calls again.

The AMA sounds like a bricklayers' union. The bricklayers want to limit membership in the union so there will always be more bricks that need to be laid than there are bricklayers to lay them. Doctors don't want a lot of young doctors offering their services for less so they can pay back the money they borrowed to get through medical school.

Everyone in any business wishes there weren't so many people in it.

Established lawyers complain that law schools are turning out young lawyers faster than the legal profession can absorb them. Newspaper reporters wish there weren't so many bright young people coming out of college who want to be reporters.

In many hospitals across the country, doctors trained in medical schools in India, the Philippines and Mexico are doing the dirty work. They're working the long night shifts, doing the instant surgery on no-pay patients in the emergency rooms and generally providing medical services that would otherwise be neglected.

If foreign doctors are trained in approved teaching hospitals, the only thing wrong with their working here is that they are cheating the country they left. Dr. Sammons objects to their presence for the same reason Lee Iacocca would like to keep Japanese cars out of the United States.

Paper, Paper Everywhere

I wallow in paper.

When the mail comes, it's a plethora of paper, most of which I don't need or want.

At the office, I get originals and duplicates of everything and then Jane makes copies of the copies. Jane and I work together, and she is better organized than I am but she's obsessed with making copies. One year when I got my eight tickets for the Giants' home football games, she Xeroxed my tickets so she'd have a record of them. (I still use the word "Xerox" even though I know it's a patented trade name. The proper word for what I mean is "photocopy" but it's not nearly so good a word as "Xerox." Sorry about that, Xerox. I also call all paper handkerchiefs "Kleenex," all plastic cups "Styrofoam," and sometimes I even call the record player the "Victrola.")

America has gone mad with paper since the invention of photocopy machines, and now the computer printers are spewing forth more printouts of everything than anyone possibly could have a use for.

Once upon a time, every office had a secretary who spent most of the day typing things that didn't need to be typed. Now it no longer takes a secretary to make a duplicate of anything. A walk to the copying machine is as much a part of office routine for the average executive as a walk to the water cooler used to be. The executive often makes copies of things that don't need to be copied while the secretary is at the water cooler.

If you doubt we're using too much paper, walk through the business area of any large city before 6 A.M. and see what the trash people are picking up the most. They're packing huge bundles of paper with printing on it and little holes along its edges into the maw of their compacting trucks.

Making duplicate copies or computer printouts of things no one wanted even one of in the first place is giving Americans a new sense of purpose. Duplicating things makes people feel they're doing something important and, while they're doing that, they don't have to do any real work.

If I were in the paper business, I'd be nervous. Business was never better for these companies than it is right now but certainly there has to be a reaction. At some point the average American is going to revolt. "Enough, already!" they're going to cry. "Stop snowing us under with paper."

A company called Accountemps in New York just completed a study concluding that U.S. businesses waste $2.6 billion annually on unnecessary photocopies. It estimates 350 billion photocopies are made every year and that, of those, one third will end up in the wastebasket.

This is a conservative estimate. I have no way of guessing how many photocopies will be made but I do have a way of guessing what proportion of them will go into the wastebasket. All I have to do is look at my own wastebasket. I throw out 50 percent of all the printed material that comes into my office, without ever opening the envelopes it comes in. I discard another 40 percent of it after giving it a quick glance and determining it's only someone trying to sell me something I don't want. Of the 10 percent I actually read, I save 2 percent.

There aren't enough filing cabinets in the whole United States in which to put all the copies of all the documents being duplicated. If there were enough filing cabinets, there wouldn't be anyplace to put them. If there were filing cabinets enough and storage space enough, there's no one with time enough to read them.

A piece of paper that's been duplicated on a photocopy machine reeks of the same sense of unimportance that a carbon copy used to have. When you were the person who got the carbon copy of something instead of the original, you knew you weren't very important. That's the way most of us feel now when we get something that's been, you'll pardon the expression, Xeroxed.

For Whom Is Bad News Good?

Whenever I hear of people praying for rain in a drought, I think how little faith they have in God.

God has so far ignored the prayers for rain, and his supplicants should concede that, for reasons unknown to them, God knows what's best. Don't they believe there's some grand plan? Don't they have faith that there's something good about drought?

I confess to not knowing whether there's a grand plan in which everything happens for the best or not, but it certainly seems as though something good for someone comes out of everything.

One recent October evening, there began a great storm in the Northeast. By morning there were fourteen inches of heavy snow on the ground and on everything else. The leaves were still on the trees and the weight of the snow caught on them broke their branches, uprooted whole trees and generally caused the kind of damage in the cities and in the forests that would bring tears to the eyes of a tree lover.

Who could possibly benefit from a storm like this? When I started to clean up a small wood lot behind our house in the country, someone who knows more about this sort of thing than I do pointed out that I should leave things the way they were because fallen and rotting trees in the woods provide a great home to all kinds of animals in nature. The bees, the birds, the bugs, the chipmunks, the raccoons, the deer all prefer a casual and messy wood lot to a manicured one.

It's not so clear what good drought in the Midwest does. It's the sort of weather pattern that makes you wonder if the world will end not in ice but in fire. Scientists are suggesting it may be partly due to our having burned away some of the ozone layer that protects the earth from the sun, like dark glasses protect the eyes.

Even so, I have the feeling a drought is part of some rhythm of life on earth. We can't even ignore the possibility that we ourselves are part of that rhythm. Maybe our having burned away the ozone layer is as much part of nature as a snowstorm.

Letters à la Landers

Recently I went to a party in Washington and met Ann Landers. She's small, pretty, carefully dressed and easy to talk to. These are not the things I envy Ann Landers for, though. I envy her all those short, well-written letters she gets asking direct questions that she can make a column out of answering. All the letters I get are three pages long and they never ask me anything. They're always telling me.

Here's a sample of the kind of letters I'd like to get:

Dear Andy,

My husband and I have been married for twenty-seven years and we're always looking for how to be happy. What is the secret to happiness?

Signed
Unhappy

Dear Unhappy,

The secret to being happy is in learning to take pleasure from all the dull, routine and terrible things that keep happening to you in life. Once you have mastered the art of liking drudgery, bad luck and disappointment, you'll be a happy person.

Dear Andy,

My husband told me he's in love with another woman who is seventeen years younger than he is. I'm in love with another man seventeen years older than I am. What advice can you give us?

Signed
Ageless

Dear Ageless,

I'd suggest both of you start acting your ages.

Dear Andy,

If a President was divorced and remarried while still in office, would his second wife still be called the "First Lady"?

Signed
History Scholar

Dear Scholar,

If a President divorced his wife and married another woman while still in the White House, "The First Lady" is not what the other woman would be called most often, especially by the First Wife.

Dear Andy,

Do you like the name "Andrew"? We are about to have a baby and if it's a boy, we're thinking of naming him Andrew.

Signed
Pregnant

Dear Pregnant,

Yes, I like the name Andrew, but if your name is Andrew you get called "Andy," and I don't like to be called "Andy." Unfortunately, I don't like people going out of their way to call me "Andrew" either, so a lot of people just call me "Hey." My advice to you is, have a girl.

Dear Andy,

Do you read Ann Landers' column? If so, do you really think she gets all those letters, or does she write them herself?

Signed
Suspicious

Dear Suspicious,

You are suspicious, aren't you? When I talked with Ann in Washington, the subject never came up so I don't know who writes the letters she answers.

Dear Andy,

This is the first time I've ever written to a columnist. What is your opinion of people who write to columnists and ask for advice? How many people do you think have lived happily ever after because of the advice they got from columnists?

Signed
Truth Seeker

Dear Seeker,

The same number of people have lived happily ever after because of the advice they got from columnists as have made the right decisions in life by paying attention to the astrology columns.

Dear Andy,
   Ever since we were married, my wife has insisted that I make the bed every morning. Do you think a man should make the bed?
                                                       Signed
                                                       Unmade

Dear Unmade,
   Very often the solution to any problem is compromise. Why don't you agree to make your side of the bed?

Frankly, I don't know how Ann Landers does it day after day. The answers are easy but the questions are hard to think of.

Where Am I, Anyway?

I waste too much time getting lost and I'm tired of it! Road maps have got to improve. I thought they'd get better after gas stations stopped giving them away and started charging $1.50 for them, but they haven't.

Some people are better at reading maps than others but maps should be easier, especially for map illiterates like me.

Maps in countries like France, Germany and England are better than ours, but that's probably because those countries are smaller and people have had more centuries to find their way around them. I'd like to see a Chinese road map. I don't suppose they have them at all in Russia because no one is allowed to go anywhere.

You have to be sympathetic to U.S. mapmakers, I suppose. They have to get a long, narrow state like California on the same-shaped piece of paper as they put thin, wide Tennessee on. And what do you do with crazy-shaped states like Florida, New York and Texas? Ideally, for a mapmaker, states would all look like Colorado so they'd fit nicely on a page.

Mapmakers have plenty of problems. There isn't room to write the names of all the places that should be on the map and there isn't room for the road numbers. Roads cross each other and change names and most maps can't handle it. Say you're in the town of Crawfordsville, Indiana. The map you have is twenty miles to the inch. They start the name of the town with *C* at a dot that represents it but by the time you drive to the end of all fourteen letters in C-R-A-W-F-O-R-D-S-V-I-L-L-E, you're halfway to I-N-D-I-A-N-A-P-O-L-I-S. It isn't the map-maker's fault. We need a totally new system for making maps.

But these are all mapmakers' problems. We want answers so we can find our way around. For instance, I don't want one map where an inch represents ten miles and another map on which an inch represents one hundred miles. I want a standard reference so I can look and guess quickly how far it is from one city to another. Modern science has left road maps behind.

They've talked for years about some finding device for cars but can't seem to come up with it. I think it's science fiction.

What we need is a screen that can be mounted in some good place, like the back side of the sunshade, so the driver can see it easily. A small, bright light should indicate the present position of the vehicle . . . and the position of police speed-patrol cars in the area. With the press of a button that would be as simple as changing the station on the radio, you'd be able to select a map of the whole country, the state, the town or the block you're on.

The screen would show you the whole United States if you wished to plan a trip from San Diego to Baltimore by way of Madison, Wisconsin, or it would show you the name of the street three blocks down the road from where you are.

It also should be possible to press a button to get a list of hotels, motels and restaurants in any area. Asking for a list of restaurants to avoid would probably be asking for too much.

This electronic map might even include the phone book and the Yellow Pages. Why not? Is this the computer age or isn't it? What are we waiting for?

I'm tired of getting lost when I'm driving someplace. My car doesn't have any problem moving along faster than the speed limit but if I'm not going in the right direction, why do I want to go that fast?

Half the time on a map you can't tell a river from a superhighway. The mapmaker has the name of the Mississippi once up near Duluth, Minnesota, and doesn't have it again until way down near Baton Rouge, Louisiana. The names of the cities go across the map but often the river names are printed up and down, the way the rivers run, and are hard to read.

It wouldn't do any harm to put a staff of smart people to work on nothing but figuring out a new way to fold a road map so you could put it back the way it was when you unfolded it without hiring a Japanese gadget packer to do it for you.

America the Not-so-Beautiful

Next to saving stuff I don't need, the thing I like to do best is throw it away. My idea of a good time is to load up the back of the car with junk on a Saturday morning and take it to the dump. There's something satisfying about discarding almost anything.

Throwing things out is the American way. We don't know how to fix anything and anyone who does know how is too busy to come so we throw it away and buy a new one. Our economy depends on us doing that. The trouble with throwing things away is, there is no "away" left.

Sometime around the year 500 B.C., the Greeks in Athens passed a law prohibiting people from throwing their garbage in the street. This Greek law was the first recognition by civilized people that throwing things away was a problem. Now, as the population explodes and people take up more room on earth, there's less room for everything else.

The more civilized a country is, the worse the trash problem is. Poor countries don't have the same problem because they don't have much to discard. Prosperity in the United States is based on using things up as fast as we can, throwing away what's left and buying new ones.

We've been doing that for so many years that 1) we've run out of places to throw things because houses have been built where the dump was, and 2) some of the things we're throwing away are poisoning the earth and will eventually poison all of us and all living things.

Ten years ago most people thought nothing of dumping an old bottle of weed or insect killer in a pile of dirt in the backyard or down the drain in the street, just to get rid of it. The big companies in America had the same feeling, on a bigger scale. For years the chemical companies dumped their poisonous wastes in the rivers behind the mills or they put it in fifty-gallon drums in the vacant lots, with all the old, rusting machinery in it, up behind the plants. The drums rusted out in ten years and dumped their poison into the ground. It rained, the poisons seeped into the underground streams and poisoned everything for miles around. Some of the manufacturers who did this weren't even evil. They were dumb and irresponsible. Others were evil because they knew how dangerous it was but didn't want to spend the money to do it right.

The problem is staggering. I often think of it when I go in a hardware store or a Sears, Roebuck and see shelves full of poison. You know that, one way or another, it's all going to end up in the earth or in our rivers and lakes.

I have two pint bottles of insecticide with 5 percent DDT in them in my own garage that I don't know what to do with. I bought them years ago when I didn't realize how bad they were. Now I'm stuck with them.

The people of the City of New York throw away nine times their weight in garbage and junk every year. Assuming other cities come close to that, how long will it be before we trash the whole earth?

Of all household waste, 30 percent of the weight and 50 percent of the volume is the packaging that stuff comes in.

Not only that but Americans spend more for the packaging of food than all our farmers together make in income growing it. That's some statistic.

Trash collectors are a lot more independent than they used to be because we've got more trash than they've got places to put it. They have their own schedules and their own holidays. Some cities try to get in good with their trash collectors or garbagemen by calling them "sanitation engineers." Anything just so long as they pick it up and take it away.

We often call the dump "the landfill" now, too. I never understood why land has to be filled, but that's what it's called. If you're a little valley just outside town, you have to be careful or first thing you know you'll be getting "filled."

If five billion people had been living on earth for the past thousand years as they have been in the past year, the planet would be nothing but one giant landfill and we'd have turned America the beautiful into one huge landfill.

The best solution may be for all of us to pack up, board a spaceship and move out. If Mars is habitable, everyone on Earth can abandon this planet we've trashed, move to Mars and start trashing that. It'll buy us some time.

Where There's Smoke

When the federal jury held the company that made Chesterfield and L&M cigarettes before 1966 partly to blame for the death of Rose Cipollone, it was striking at the very heart of our American way of life.

Rose died of lung cancer at age fifty-eight after smoking a pack and a half a day for more than forty years. The jury ruled that the Liggett Group, which must have been Liggett & Myers tobacco company once upon a time, knew cigarettes were bad for people and should have said so in their advertising. The company was ordered to pay Rose's husband, Antonio Cipollone, $400,000. The award was relatively low because the jury found that the tobacco company wasn't all to blame. It said Rose was 80 percent to blame herself for continuing to smoke after she knew the risk.

That seemed like a pretty reasonable conclusion for a jury to come to. I'm tired of everyone blaming someone else for everything that happens and I was ready to be indignant if the jury laid all the blame on the tobacco company. Anyone would have to be an idiot not to know smoking a pack and a half of cigarettes was bad.

The big news, though, was not who was guilty in this case. The big news was the jury's decision that advertising ought to be honest. Are they crazy?

The lawyer who won the case said the jury concluded the tobacco company was lying in its advertising. He pointed out that one ad for L&M cigarettes claimed they were JUST WHAT THE DOCTOR ORDERED and another for Chesterfields said PLAY SAFE—SMOKE CHESTERFIELDS.

The tobacco industry was pleased that it got only 20 percent of the blame but was nervous because the verdict in this jury case might bring on a flood of lawsuits from people dying of lung cancer.

This isn't what worries me. I'm worried not about the possible decline and fall of the cigarette industry, but about the effect the case will have on the advertising industry itself. Does this mean that in the future ads will have to be honest? Are they kidding? One of the things that makes America great is the unwritten understanding between advertisers and consumers that it's a lot of baloney.

Women know in their hearts that beauty products won't make them beautiful.

Men understand they'll never look like Jim Palmer in Jockey shorts.

We all know foreign countries don't look as exotic as the travel ads picture them.

If advertising has to be absolutely honest, does this mean that GRANDMA'S ORIGINAL HOMEMADE MOLASSES COOKIES would have to be made by Grandma at home?

Can you imagine how ads would read in newspapers or sound on television if they had to tell all? The classifieds would be hard hit:

JOB WANTED: INEXPERIENCED AND UNWILLING TO LEARN, LAZY HIGH SCHOOL DROPOUT LOOKING FOR HIGH PAY FOR LITTLE WORK.

The real estate ads would change:

HOUSE FOR SALE: TWO DRAFTY BEDROOMS AND ONE YOU COULD PUT A COT IN. TWO HALF BATHROOMS. BASEMENT LEAKS, FURNACE ABOUT SHOT. ON WOODED LOT IF YOU CALL TWO TREES A WOODED LOT.

The secondhand-car ads would say something like:

FOR SALE: RUSTY 1981 PONTIAC. SEEN BETTER DAYS. $4,300 OR BEST OFFER OVER $2,000. LOADED WITH GADGETS YOU DON'T NEED. GETS 14 MPG DOWNHILL. FRONT SEAT UNCOMFORTABLE ON LONG DRIVES. MISSING CIGARETTE LIGHTER.

Insurance-company ads wouldn't emphasize how quickly they pay claims. They'd be more like this:

DON'T LOOK FOR YOUR MONEY TOMORROW IF YOU'RE INSURED WITH US. IF WE PAID EVERY CLAIM EVER MADE, WE'D BE OUT OF BUSINESS.

I don't know how many cigarettes the tobacco companies would have sold if they'd had to tell all they knew all these years:

IRRITATE YOUR FRIENDS AND YOUR THROAT, SHORTEN YOUR LIFE, ACQUIRE A FILTHY HABIT. SMOKE UNLUCKY STRIKE CIGARETTES. THEY'RE WORST FOR YOU!

No Thief to Catch

We're afraid of thieves. We're wary of the con artist trying to swindle us. We don't dare put down a suitcase in an airport while we go to the bathroom. We lock our houses, our cars, our bicycles, our windows. We put our treasures in safe-deposit boxes instead of leaving them out in the open where we can enjoy them. If someone approaches us on the street at night, we're nervous. It's gotten so we take dishonesty for granted. We assume people are dishonest until they prove otherwise. That's a sad state of affairs.

There are 547,000 people in prisons and jails in the United States. That's 1 person in every 500. You have to figure that for every criminal who's caught, there are 5 who are not. Still, it leaves us with a nation of honest people. The average American would never consider stealing anything. Even better, the average American who found a purse or a wallet with cash and the owner's name in it would seek out and return both with no thought of a reward.

Think how nice life would be if everyone was honest:

—We wouldn't need locks on our doors.

—If we didn't have locks on our doors, we wouldn't need to carry keys so we wouldn't ever lose our keys or misplace them.

—Windows wouldn't have those little butterfly things on top to prevent them from being opened from outside. Ground-floor apartments in big cities wouldn't need bars on their windows.

—It wouldn't be necessary to stand in line waiting while the clerk writes your driver's license number and a credit-card number on the back of your check so they'll know where to get you if the check bounces. People would never bounce checks and, if they did by mistake, they'd rush back to make them good.

—Late-night walks on dark streets would become popular.

—We'd only need a few lawyers, and I can't think why we'd even need them. Our courtrooms would be empty because there'd be hardly any lawsuits.

—When there was a trial, a jury could come to a decision quickly because they'd know they were getting the truth, the whole truth and nothing but the truth.

—Women could leave their pocketbooks anywhere.

—No one would break a contract because a contract would just be a spoken agreement between two parties that neither would ever break because they'd given their word.

—Arrangements for a house sale would be done with a handshake agreement.

—We wouldn't need police except to direct traffic and tell strangers in town how to get somewhere.

—There wouldn't be any guns. Why would anyone need a gun if there were no criminals?

—We wouldn't have to spend a lot of money inspecting Soviet missile sites because, if everyone in the whole world was honest, we could trust them when they told us how many they had. All our spies could come home and all their spies could go home.

—If there were things we wanted to know about a foreign country, we'd ask them and they'd tell us.

—We'd save money on the Federal Bureau of Investigation because they could go out of business for lack of any wrongdoing to investigate.

The dishonest handful among us make life difficult and less happy for everyone. We ought to be angrier at them than we are.

Making a Killing Killing

When you read that we're going to spend $9 billion on a wonderful new weapon capable of killing everyone but us, don't worry. It probably won't work.

There's no reason to have a lot of confidence in the people who design and make weapons. They've been wrong too often. They mean well. They want their weapons to kill people but usually the weapons don't work. If all the weapons ever made worked perfectly, everyone on earth would have been dead years ago. Weapons makers are more successful making money than war.

Every new weapon seems like the ultimate one but usually turns out to have something wrong with it. Our newest Star Wars weapon idea is some kind of laser beam to be aimed at an enemy from a satellite. The trouble with a lot of these highly technical weapons is, wars end up being fought in the mud and the weapons don't work in the mud. It's impossible for someone sitting at a desk in an office to know what a soldier will need in the mud. The writer has been in the mud.

One of the problems with a new weapon is that you can't really test it until there's a war. Then, if it doesn't work, it's too late. In training sessions, our army and navy practice with new weapons but it isn't the same. "Maneuvers," as they call these practice wars, are only some officer's guess what might happen. The officers doing the teaching have usually not been at war themselves. They're teaching what they've been taught. Most maneuvers are expensive jokes. If we'd fought our wars the way we maneuvered, we'd have lost. The writer has been on maneuvers, too.

The Defense Department says that Iranian airliner with 290 people on board was shot down in 1988 because of human error by navy men, not because there was anything wrong with the complicated tracking systems being used. Well, if the people charged with operating the equipment can't work it, there's something wrong with the equipment.

During World War II, half the weapons given American soldiers to fight with were poorly designed or wrong for the job. Things haven't changed just because weapons are more complicated.

The Norden bombsight was going to revolutionize the air war over Germany by making "pinpoint" bombing possible. They always used the word "pinpoint." The bombsight must have worked perfectly in theory but bombardiers either couldn't master it or were too busy being shot at to fool with it. They got near the target, pressed the bombs-away button and hoped for the best.

Everyone thought the B-24 bomber was going to be an improvement over the B-17. It was faster, carried more bombs and was more maneuverable. For a variety of reasons that wouldn't show up in peacetime testing, it never matched the B-17. No B-24 pilot agrees.

When the army came up with a nifty little rifle called the carbine, it looked like the answer to a soldier's prayer. It was a small handy weapon that was infinitely easier to carry and store than the seven-pound M1. For a short time, every infantryman tried to get his hands on a carbine. The carbines were cute, they felt good and they were light.

It didn't take soldiers long to find out that the difference between the carbine and the M1 was the difference between a water pistol and a real weapon. They abandoned the carbine and went back to their M1's.

We developed a new tank for the invasion of France and it was hopelessly wrong for the job. Tanks usually are. The Jeep was more successful helping to win World War II than the M1 tank.

We've spent billions developing the new stealth bomber that's supposed to be able to fly into enemy airspace undetected. We'll see. The British built a two-engine bomber made of wood called the Mosquito forty-five years ago for a lot less money. It went undetected by German radar.

What the Pentagon needs from weapons makers is a money-back guarantee. Too many companies have made too much money over the years producing weapons that don't work.

Learning to Weed

Considering how poorly so many things are made and how sloppily so much work is done, it's surprising how many people still recognize excellence when they see it. The fact that there are still people who prize excellence is a good sign. Maybe there's still hope.

Excellence is rare. It calls attention to itself wherever it exists. Last weekend we stopped by the best little vegetable stand I know of. The woman who runs it said they would be closing next weekend. It's always a sad day but it's an inevitable one because she sells only the things they grow, and their growing season is over. She doesn't bring in avocados from California, oranges from Florida or melons from Colorado to stay in business.

In June, she begins to get raspberries and asparagus. By July she has beans, peas, green and yellow squash, potatoes and cauliflower. In August the corn, tomatoes and melons come. Hers are the best. The little parking area in front of her stand is jammed with randomly parked cars. People drive ten or twelve miles, passing six or eight supermarkets on the way, just to get her fresh vegetables.

The thing that worries me most is that while she may have a hundred or more customers a day, the supermarkets, with vegetables picked a week before and shipped in from faraway places, have thousands.

Excellence attracts a crowd but there's so little of it that it's always a sellout.

The best doctors can't take any more patients. You can't afford the best lawyers and, even if you could they're too busy to take your case.

There are always one or two builders in town who do excellent work. They're booked.

This summer we got hold of a fine builder and he put a nice little addition on our house out behind the kitchen. When he finished, he got the best painter to do the inside and outside of the addition. Painting is one of those jobs that seems easy enough for anyone to do. All I have to do to see the difference between a do-it-yourself job and a good professional one is to compare a job I've done with his.

We were so pleased with the paint job that we talked with the painter about doing one of the upstairs bedrooms.

"You better make up your mind quick if you want me," he said. "I'm already booked through April."

That's the way it is with excellence. You'd think there'd be more of it if so many people want it.

The things I've owned that were made according to high standards of excellence stand out in my mind. Just offhand I can think of a watch, two kitchen knives, a car, several tools, a camera and an overcoat, all of which have been a great pleasure to own because of their excellence.

You can spot excellence a mile away. If you go into a strange restaurant, you can tell within ten seconds whether the food's going to be any good. You can tell almost everything about a restaurant before you even sit down. There are hundreds of signs that suggest excellence or, more often, mediocrity.

Too many Americans are settling for mediocrity. Too many are buying the cheapest of everything without regard to its quality. If they can buy it for less, they take it. At the supermarket it's the lowest-quality merchandise that sells the fastest. Junk-building-material stores that sell the poorest-grade paint, plywood and tools are proliferating. "Outlet" stores with cheap goods are pushing the quality department stores out of business.

All of us ought to be putting the pressure on manufacturers to make things better, not encouraging them to continue making them cheaper. We ought to be letting them know they can't pass off their junk on us.

Maybe our schools should teach courses in the appreciation of excellence. Too many people today aren't bothering to drive the ten miles to the vegetable stand.

TRUTHS

Spring in the City

All the poems and the songs about spring make it sound as if it only happens in the country. Spring may be a happier occasion some places than others but it happens everywhere equally. Spring is just as spring in the city as in the country.

It is considered normal for all of us to speak positively about the country and negatively about the city. It doesn't matter what city. Country life is known to be innocent, serene and wholesome; city life is artificial, evil and filled with misery and corruption.

While I have no intention of breaking with this tradition, I would like to point out that spring is just as noticeable to a city person in the city as it is to a farmer in the country. Furthermore, I suspect that while spring is as noticeable to a city person in the country as it is to the farmer, spring in the city might go unnoticed by the farmer.

It's interesting that even though all the talk is about how wonderful the country is, most people choose to live in the cities. This could be attributed to better chances of making a living in a crowd, but something happened this morning that made me wonder about that.

I was sitting at my desk, staring idly out a window in my office, when a bird of undetermined species came and sat on the sill. All I can say for sure is it was neither a robin nor a pigeon. I don't know whether the bird had been south for the winter or not but he must have come from somewhere because it's the first I've seen him . . . or perhaps her.

I looked at the bird for a while and then watched it soar away. "This bird," I thought to myself, "is free as a bird. He could go anywhere he wants but he chooses to be here in the city with all the evil, corruption and misery. Why?"

Why does any bird choose to land on my cement windowsill when he could just as easily go to the country and live under the eaves of a barn?

The bird suggests to me that living in the country is not always all it's cracked up to be. Farmers may be leaving the farm in droves because they borrowed a million dollars from the bank and can't pay back the loans, but birds don't come to New York because they're head over tails in debt. They come because they want to live here. It gives me some hope that I'm not crazy for wanting to live here myself.

Spring has sprung in New York City. Signs of it are everywhere. It is light now at 6 A.M. and the rumble of the garbage trucks begins earlier. The loud sounds of honking horns being blown by irritated drivers of cars trapped behind the garbage trucks on narrow streets can be heard all across the city an hour earlier too.

The sirens and flashing lights of the police cars going for coffee are just a little brighter, just a little louder and moving just a little faster because it's spring.

And don't tell me about the little shoots from the spring plantings that are beginning to push their little heads up through the soil on the farms of America. What do you think that green stuff is emerging from the dirt that has become trapped between the divisions of the cement sidewalks? We may call them weeds in the city but they are clearly related to the growing things the farmers are borrowing millions to encourage in their fields.

The homeless emerge from the city shelters at this time of year and sleep, once again, on the sidewalks, warmed only by the hot air coming up through the grates covering the basement power centers of the tall buildings.

The street peddlers emerge and spread their wares in everyone's way on the sidewalks; tens of thousands of city buses that crisscross Manhattan, which for months have been too cold, suddenly become too hot.

Don't tell a city person that spring is a country phenomenon.

The Right Stuff on College Campuses

College students are protesting the fact that their college administrators have invested some of their money in companies that do business with South Africa. College students are always protesting something and the rest of us don't pay much attention to them.

Most of us are busy with our personal things, like making a living or keeping our family in one piece, so we leave the world problems to government officials in Washington and the college students. Sometimes, though, an important issue is brought to our attention so forcefully that we can't avoid thinking about it.

South Africa is a good example. I hope South African student protesters, both black and white, who were beaten recently with clubs and metal-tipped whips, know how much the beating they took did for their cause. Millions of Americans, who are normally disinterested, watched, and if they had been disinterested before, they no longer were after watching the storm-troop behavior of the South African police.

For several months, reporters have been barred from covering police activity in putting down the rebellions in the black townships in South Africa. We haven't heard anything but the statistics on how many protesters police killed, because the government won't allow reporters to go watch. Reporters and television cameras were there during this recent horror story because the action took place in the central part of Johannesburg. It made the rest of us more aware of why our college students are protesting the situation in South Africa, just as the nuclear disaster in Chernobyl made us sensitive to the cause of the nuclear protesters.

The students' protests at some of our best colleges put college businessmen in a difficult position. A lot of them don't like South African government policies any better than the protesting students do, but they're more practical about it. They invest the money to produce the most it can for their colleges without regard for how those companies conduct their business. Some college administrators have no sympathy for demonstrating students because those students often accept scholarship aid from the same college endowment funds whose investment policies they are protesting.

Milton Friedman, the economist who makes Ronald Reagan look like a pinko liberal, says that college students who demand that their colleges sell stocks in companies that do business with South Africa should first make some sacrifices themselves.

"Few temptations are so irresistible," the brilliant Mr. Friedman says, "as doing good at someone else's expense."

Friedman says that the students should first get rid of any personal possessions they have that were made by companies that do business in South Africa. He points out that this would mean "no more radios, electric clocks, hair dryers, etc. from General Electric. No more cars from General Motors or Ford or, for that matter, Honda or Nissan . . ."

It's a catchy idea. I imagine a lot of protesting students would be less ready to give up their record players made by a company that deals with South Africa than they are to have their college give up their stocks in those companies. Still, Friedman, in writing it, and I, in finding it catchy, are wrong.

There is something wonderfully pure and naïve about campus protests. The one thing they have in common is that they're always on solid moral ground. The students are usually right. Forget that what they demand may not be practical.

Americans are moral people. Our foreign policy should conform to our moral standards. When the President makes a decision on a weapons treaty, he should be thinking not of outsmarting the Soviet Union but of what's right, like protesting students do.

Doing what's right is where America's strength lies.

Questioning the Boss

Someone is always suggesting that doctors ought to be tested regularly to make sure they're still competent to practice medicine.

I suppose it's a good idea even though I'd trust my doctor if he never took another test. The trouble with testing doctors is, the doctors who are best at passing tests are not necessarily the best at diagnosing and treating their patients' problems. Taking tests is an expertise all its own.

Good doctors are embarrassed enough by the bad ones so that they'd probably go along with the idea even though they don't like it.

When they test the doctors, I hope they check out the people in their offices who do the billing. It would be interesting to see if any of them still remember how to subtract or divide. We know they can add and multiply.

Bosses get away with murder. Half the bosses in business don't know what they're talking about. There are a lot more incompetent bosses than there are incompetent doctors. Furthermore, we only see a doctor once every couple of years, if we're lucky. A lot of us see bosses every day.

If those lawyers who make a living off suing doctors for malpractice want to get really rich and do the rest of us a favor at the same time, they ought to start suing bosses for malpractice. Bosses are among the biggest malpracticers of all time. They can do the same kind of damage an inept brain surgeon can do.

If every boss in the country had to take an exam once every six years, I'll bet half the bosses would be barred from the practice of bossing. I've had as many as ten bosses in my lifetime who would have flunked bossing if they'd been tested. Some of them should never have been granted a license to boss in the first place.

The tests for doctors are usually administered by other doctors. This is probably wrong. Certainly a test for bosses should not be administered by other bosses. Bosses, like doctors, stick together. They tend to protect the incompetents in their ranks. They're protective and probably would never bar one of their numbers from bossing.

There are several questions I'd put to bosses on an examination:

1. Do you remember back to the days when you were not a boss?
2. Do you remember what your boss was like when you weren't one?
3. Which do you like better, working or bossing?
4. Do you think people have to be bossed full-time or can you let them alone sometimes?
5. Can you do what you're telling other people to do?
6. Do you enjoy firing someone once in a while?
7. If you didn't come in tomorrow, would it matter?
8. If you had to give up your reserved parking place in the company lot, would you cry?
9. What's more important about being a boss, power or money?
10. What would you like to be when you grow up?

There are a great many other people in our society in addition to doctors who should be tested for competence periodically. There are always some teachers who need to be checked. I think automobile mechanics and television repairmen need it.

The only people I'd exempt from these periodic checkups are writers. Not knowing what we're doing is part of the business.

God Is Not a Republican

Religion ought not be used by anyone as a sales tool. God doesn't do endorsements. If he did, Coke and Pepsi would have signed him up years ago.

If God listens to political speeches, He must be pretty surprised and probably a little annoyed at how often His name is used in a way that suggests He's a registered Democrat or Republican.

When a politician mentions God half a dozen times in a speech, it's to appropriate for his campaign the name "God." He's suggesting that God has endorsed the ticket and given permission to have His name used in promotional material in exchange for certain considerations, like school prayer. There are lots of cheap tricks used in political campaigns, and evoking God's name is one of them.

In his acceptance speech at the Republican convention George Bush, then a candidate, said:

"I am guided by certain traditions. One is that there is a God and He is good and His love, while free, has a self-imposed cost: We must be good to one another."

That's what I'd call a legitimate statement by a candidate. He's just telling us where he stands. He isn't pretending God wants him as President. Unfortunately, not many politicians running for office, including George Bush, stop at that. He used God's name constantly in relation to himself.

President Bush made an exception of Michael Dukakis in his pledge to "be good to one another" during that campaign by suggesting that, in addition to having God in his camp, he also loved America more than Dukakis because Dukakis opposed making the pledge of allegiance mandatory.

No number of compulsory pledges of allegiance has ever guaranteed the love of a person for his country, and endless repetition of prayer does not promise immortality.

Mr. Bush, like many politicians, often ends a speech with the phrase "God bless you." Do politicians think this will help? Do they think God may forget to bless us if they don't remind Him to do so? Or are the politicians saying, "*I hope* God blesses you."? If so, are they suggesting that they think you deserve it? What if God disagrees and doesn't think you have a blessing coming?

No matter what the case is, it doesn't seem as though a serious politician should use God's name so lightly and end each speech by saying "God bless you" with the same intonation and depth of feeling he'd use saying "Have a nice day."

It's difficult to understand why Americans accept the way people use God for their own purpose. Samuel Johnson said patriotism was the last refuge of the scoundrel, but maybe patriotism is only next to last. The least admirable people among us often hide behind a newly acquired religion when they're in trouble. On his way to the gas chamber, the murderer invariably announces he's found God. In the 1970s, several of the principals in the Watergate scandal "found God." They should have looked for God first instead of for those papers they stole.

The Middle Eastern terrorists don't call themselves terrorists. They call themselves names like "The Islamic Holy War." It is for God, as they see God, that they commit what the rest of the world sees as a crime. They are certain, as religious people, that what they are doing is right in the eyes of God. Religious people, no matter what religion, are always certain they're right.

We don't know whether the God that conservatives want in our public schools here is the same God to which Islamic Holy War members pray or not. Whose God, of all the gods of all the world's religions, should be the official one?

Religion doesn't belong in politics. The decision to protect the privacy of religious belief was not made lightly when the First Amendment to our Constitution was written.

"Believing with you," Thomas Jefferson said, "that religion is a matter which lies solely between man and his God, that he owes account to none other for this faith and his worship, that the legislative powers of government reach actions only and not opinions, I contemplate with reverence that act of the whole American people . . . building a wall of separation between Church and State."

Talk, Talk, Talk

Conversation may be disappearing along with good writing. In the average week, we hear hundreds of people talking but we don't hear much conversation.

Conversation involves an exchange of ideas, and hiya-how-you-doin'-

today-fine-thanks-how-about-you does not involve exchanging any ideas.

There's a place for pleasantries like "Good Morning. Nice day, isn't it?" but not if the small talk drives out serious conversation. When we talk, we use our mouths. In conversation, we ought to use our brains.

People are often reluctant to talk about anything serious. It's probably because they don't want anyone arguing them out of the things they believe for no good reason.

Two subjects that often are considered out of bounds are politics and religion. It's difficult to exclude those two important topics if we're going to have many genuine conversations. Why shouldn't we talk about politics and religion? Why shouldn't we argue about those subjects and expose ourselves to other opinions?

People are somewhat more willing to argue about politics because they can argue personalities, not issues. Personalities are easy. If a person dislikes the President, he or she can rant and rave about what an idiot Bush is without ever making any sense. This is not a political conversation, and most of us avoid serious political conversations for the same reason we avoid religious conversations. For the most part, we know what we believe but we don't know much more than that.

In the case of religion, most people have known since they were young what they are expected to believe by their parents and friends. They are Catholic, Protestant, Methodist, Christian Scientist, Muslim, Jew. They don't want to talk about it.

No subject is more interesting to discuss than religion but people are so uncertain about the details of their beliefs that they'd rather not have the subject brought up.

We like to talk to each other so we keep finding new substitutes for real conversation. These days sports have driven out the weather as the number-1 topic when we don't want to think much about what we're saying.

"Hey, how about those Dodgers!" has temporarily replaced "Is it cold enough for you?"

A real conversation takes too long for most of us. We greet each other on the street, in an elevator or pushing a shopping cart. This is no time to talk politics, the economy or whether we're spending too much on arms.

There are several other reasons why conversation may be a dying art. First, good talk takes time and we aren't willing to spend it on something that seems like doing nothing. Second, the best conversations are between two people, not among three, four or ten. The best conversations are those in which the participants can't wait to say what they have to say and, if there are more than two conversationalists, they don't get a turn often enough.

There's a third reason for the deterioration of good conversation. We're all more aware of how careful we have to be about what we say. We're nervous about being quoted in the newspaper or having our friends tell other friends, and enemies, what we've said. We can't be careful in a good conversation. We have to let the thought pop out of our mouths before we've finished having it. Good conversation is often a little irresponsible. We say things we don't really mean. We can't have the feeling it's being recorded because that makes a conversationalist careful and care kills conversation.

I'd like to have a serious talk with you about this sometime.

The Nuts

I like the nuts. We owe them a lot.

The nuts are the people who know everything about one thing and almost nothing about anything else. There are art nuts, wine nuts, stamp nuts, car nuts, baseball nuts and there are political nuts. You name it and there are people who are nuts about it.

Marty was a political nut. Marty lived in Albany, New York, and we were related but I don't want to talk about how. All during the forties, fifties and sixties, Marty got half a dozen newspapers from all over the country. He liked the *Chicago Tribune* best. It was indisputably the worst major newspaper printed in the United States during those years, but Marty loved it because no other newspaper was right wing enough to suit his political taste. We always hoped Marty was kidding but I don't think he was.

There wasn't any sense getting into an argument with Marty about politics anywhere in the country because he knew more about it than you did. His politics were never the same as mine but I had to admit he knew and I didn't. Marty was the kind of guy who could prove that Hitler was kind to dogs.

I'm not really a very political person. Most Americans aren't. Like people who watch baseball games only when the World Series is being played, most people pay attention to politics only during the last days before an election. That's me.

For better or for worse, average citizens leave the nitty-gritty of politics to those few people, like Marty, who are fascinated with the process. Fortunately for all of us, wherever there was a Marty reading the *Chicago Tribune* back in those days, there was some other nut reading *The Daily Worker,* and they canceled each other out.

While it may be the ambitious men or women who decide to run for office in the first place, it is the people who follow politics closely who pass on the candidates' potential for success, and they let the rest of us know who the promising people are.

Those political nuts among us who read everything and know everything have served us well. They're the people who walk door-to-door with the petitions and attend endless council meetings and neighborhood planning sessions. They know. The rest of us are guessing.

It's the people who are nuts about anything that bring the obscure things in their specialty to our attention. The art nuts recognize a good new artist whom the rest of us would live our whole lives without appreciating. If it weren't for the handful of people who know what they're talking about when they talk about art, Picasso would never have been discovered. He certainly never would have been discovered by me if he'd lived next door.

It doesn't matter what the subject is, it has to have some nuts of its own. Most of us don't know how to dress until the fashion nuts let us know.

Everyone would still be doing the minuet or the waltz if the dance nuts hadn't taken dance in a new direction that no ordinary dancer would ever have thought of or dared do.

We wouldn't know who to vote for in the Heisman Trophy competition if the sports nuts didn't give us some choices.

The wine nuts tell us '83 was a good year and we believe them and they're right.

I'll take a nut's advice on what he's nuts about every time.

The Devil Makes Them Do It

You have to feel sorry for the traditional little neighborhood churches across America.

The pope gallivants around the world attracting attention and money for the Vatican but very little of either for the local churches;

the preachers on television skim the cream off the top of the Protestant collection plate. In both cases, the Little Church Around the Corner has to take the leftovers.

The good, solid small-church Protestant ministers and Catholic parish priests must detest the neon evangelism of the TV hucksters. If these ministers and priests believe what they preach, they must worry about the perverse pleasure they take from the scandals in which so many of the big-money television pray-for-pay preachers have been involved.

It seems so unfair and yet inevitable that the most ignorant and the poorest people in America pay the most for nothing. It is, for the most part, the ignorant and uneducated who respond to the appeals from the television ministers. They are the same people who buy lottery tickets.

There is a correlation between buying a lottery ticket and sending $10 to Oral Roberts or Pat Robertson, because the results are the same. There are none. In each case the person putting up the money is looking for some disproportionately wonderful return on the money.

In the case of the lottery ticket, the person hopes to win $1 million a year for life. In the case of the money sent to the television ministry, the sender hopes to get back in return life everlasting or, at the very least, forgiveness for his sins. I'd give $10 to Oral Roberts myself for a little of that.

The television evangelists are good at what they do. Words flow from their throats like sugar from a bag. They never seem to be at a loss for words, and when they are, they say, "Praise Jesus."

Their talent is like that of the vaudeville performers who can juggle eight balls in the air or draw two rabbits out of a size 6 hat. Preaching is a trick they've mastered. It's sleight-of-mouth.

I was in the audience during the performance of a faith-healing minister in Philadelphia several years ago. Some kind of mass hypnosis took place. Many in the largely black audience actually fainted when he pressed his hand to their foreheads and shouted, "Heal this woman, God!"

He sent an assistant, who traveled with him, through the audience with a collection plate, which was actually a plastic bucket, while he told people to give. The assistant came back with the bucket brimming with bills—fives, tens and twenties. While his congregation waited, the preacher dumped the money in a suitcase. He made a hasty estimate of the amount in it, decided it wasn't enough and sent the assistant back into the audience for more.

Jesse Jackson, who is smart enough so he shouldn't have to resort to it, can do this vaudeville trick. Once on *Nightline* he appeared along with Jerry Falwell. Falwell has an appealing way about him if you don't listen to what he says but Jackson out-double-talked him that night.

When Jackson was backed into a corner by Falwell or host Ted Koppel, he turned on his invisible preacher-switch. His mouth started going while Falwell, Koppel and presumably the whole television audience tried to make out what he was saying. The words were all familiar. He sounded as though he were making sense but you realized that, like those double-talk nightclub comedians, it was an illusion of sense. He wasn't saying anything. It was his vaudeville act.

May I just say, in conclusion, that if I do not receive at least $1 million in the mail by two weeks from Tuesday, God told me He'd strike me dead!

Praise Jesus!

Please do what you can.

Beware the Company Memo

When the president or chief executive officer of a big company issues a statement saying how well the company is doing, you can bet the company is in big trouble or he wouldn't have bothered.

The first thing these memos try to do is establish the chief as Mr. Nice Guy. He'll say, "I'd like to take this occasion to share some thoughts with you." Or possibly he'll say, "I welcome this opportunity to speak to you."

The literature of the company memos is a genre all its own. Memos are often written for the president by a minor executive who also works on writing rosy prose for the stockholders' report at the end of the year and they reflect some of the style of those masterpieces of sleight-of-word.

To understand one, you have to be able to translate what's actually said into what's actually meant.

"In the past year, our company has undergone significant restructuring."

This usually means a lot of people got fired and one of the company's divisions lost so much money they got rid of it.

"We are confident that with your help we will be able to overcome the formidable obstacles . . ."

This translates as we'll be asking you to take a cut in pay.

"We have made great strides in recent months . . ." the memos always say. Then they go on to say, "While we have made great progress, there is still a long way to go."

What the head of the company is usually trying to tell employees is that they better brace themselves for a salary cut or some layoffs.

"Difficult times" always "lie ahead" in company memos.

"As you know," the company memo continues, obviously not believing that you know at all or it wouldn't be telling you, "the economy makes us particularly vulnerable to competition from outside interests."

"We can no longer count on" something. It doesn't matter what but they always say they can't count on something.

"In the future, as in the past, we will continue to" do something. It doesn't matter what, either. They always say they'll continue to do it.

The single most popular word in the memo from the company president is "challenge." The company faces "an unusual challenge this coming year," or it has already "faced a series of unusual challenges" in the year just past.

The president, nonetheless, looks forward "to a year of expanding growth and productivity."

The times are never just ordinary, everyday times in a company memo. "As we face the future," times can be "demanding times," "troubled times," or "the difficult times in which we live." Sometimes they are "turbulent times."

Even though it looks as though the company is going to fire people, cut salaries and reduce the quality of its product, "Our commitment is to excellence." Or "We are committed to a program of excellence."

If the rumor is already out that the company is going to lay people off, one of the first things the president says is "There is no truth to the rumor . . ."

There is never any truth to rumors in memos from company heads to employees. The company may go belly up three weeks later but at the time the president speaks, you can be sure "there's no truth to the rumor WHATSOEVER."

"Nothing could be further from the truth."

If the rumor of bad news has already proven to be true, the company head wants to "put the whole matter into perspective."

"Our greatest asset is you, our employees."

If you are one of the employees, BEWARE THE COMPANY MEMO.

The Cost Is More Than the Price

Why is it that everything always costs more than we think it's going to? How come we never get used to that fact and figure it in when we take money out of our pockets to pay for something?

We all know about the taxes on everything we buy. Why does it come as a surprise that taxes are added on to the price we see advertised? It may be unfair for us to expect people operating a retail business to absorb the tax and count it in when they write the price on a tag but that's what I wish they'd do. I hate surprises. I wish every price I see advertised in the papers, listed on the menu or written on the price tag attached to the item included everything I'm going to have to pay.

We call the plumber or the electrician or the television repairman, and we're invariably astounded at what he charges. We aren't surprised that we're making $50,000 a year but we're surprised that the oil furnace repairman expects to make a living too. We're shocked that, in order to make $35,000 working a forty-hour week with some hours he can't charge to customers, he has to ask $25 an hour for his time. It doesn't matter to a repairman that when he arrives to fix our television set he finds the only problem is that someone, while vacuuming the living room, pulled the plug to the TV set out of the wall and forgot to put the plug back in. It still used up his time.

Nowhere is the final amount we have to pay more surprising than in a good restaurant. The steak is listed on the menu at $16. You're probably with someone, so you double that and figure you can get out of the restaurant for twice that plus a few dollars. Maybe $40. You have a drink first, a salad, dessert and coffee. The waiter gets 15 percent. By the time you get out of the place, the dinner costs you not $40 but $63.

When I eat in a restaurant, I always guess what the check is going to be when I see the waiter coming with it. In all my years of eating out several times a week for either lunch or dinner, I have never . . . never . . . been surprised by a check that was less than I thought it was going to be.

We all know about cars. We all know that there are always additions to the list price. If you want your car with wheels and an engine, they are extra. No matter how many cars we buy, we're still surprised when the final amount we have to pay for a $15,000 car is $18,230.84.

The worst experience for a young married couple is finally realizing how much the $150,000 house is actually going to cost them. By the time the banks (there are usually several), the real estate agent, the surveyor and several lawyers take their piece of the action, the couple usually has bought a house they can't afford.

The trouble with having to pay more than you expect for everything is that when you get paid for anything yourself, it's always less, not more, than you thought you had coming. If you've ever stood in a line with people picking up their paychecks, you've watched while one person after another gets the check, rips open the envelope and looks at it shaking his or her head. Employees know about Social Security, they know about taxes and deductions for medical benefits, but they can never believe that they have so little left when the paycheck comes.

I yearn for a world where you get what you pay for and you pay what is asked for, nothing more. I want all the prices to be in even numbers and to include local, state and federal taxes. Nothing will cost $1.99 or $199. Any gas station advertising unleaded regular for $1.29.9 instead of the real price, $1.30, will be fined $999.99.9 and they'll have to pay in exact change.

For Fat People Only

I'm only talking to overweight people now. The rest of you can move on to another page.

Haven't you often felt it was unfair that, day after day, you see skinny people eating french fries and chocolate fudge sundaes and never gaining a pound? Haven't you noticed that a lot of people eat exactly the same things you eat and they stay the same weight while you blow up?

It is one of the unfairest things I've come across in my lifetime, but there's good news. Thin people of the world owe an apology to all of us average, normal, everyday overweight people.

If we'd all been falsely imprisoned, we wouldn't have been more falsely maligned than we have been by thin people all these years. They always suggest it's our own fault, and it is not.

Why? Because according to an article in *The New England Journal of Medicine,* which seems to have a monopoly on medical announcements, it isn't fat people's fault that they're fat. After all these years of being looked down on by people who act superior because their collarbones stick out, the truth finally has emerged. It isn't us, it's our metabolism that's to blame.

It was only a matter of time before the scientists, in their maddeningly slow, methodical way, discovered it, but they finally found out why a lot of people get fat through no fault of their own and why a lot of people stay thin through no virtue of their own.

I've suspected all along that it wasn't my fault. All overweight people know in their hearts it isn't their fault. We can be around thin people who are eating the same things we eat for weeks and while we get fat, they stay the same.

Make no mistake about this announcement; it's good news for overweights. It could mean the end of Weight Watchers and the feeling of inferiority we all feel because we're fat.

It's really good to know my weight is not a result of weakness or any flaw in my character. It is apparent that I have a very lethargic metabolism. A big piece of chocolate cake goes farther in my body than it does in the body of a skinny person. (I prefer "skinny" to "thin," just as I prefer the word "overweight" to "fat.") It isn't that fat people eat too much, it's that their furnaces are always banked.

"Obese people," says Dr. Jules Hirsch, a doctor at Rockefeller University in New York, "are born with a handicap."

"Just like people born with other handicaps," Dr. Hirsch says, "they'll have to learn to live with theirs."

Next thing you know, they'll be giving us handicapped, overweight people stickers for the windshields of our cars so we can park right up near the entrance to the store in the handicapped parking places.

The doctors who made this report say that when an overweight person makes a big effort to diet and loses weight, his or her metabolism declines even further. As the metabolism declines, the body uses less and less of the food taken in and turns the rest to fat. That's why it's so hard to keep off the weight you lose.

The researchers for this project kept track of their subjects for two years. They found that the people who were destined to gain weight burned eighty calories a day fewer than people of comparable weight. Dr. Eric Ravussin of the National Institutes of Health estimated that a person who burns a mere eighty calories a day less than usual would gain nine pounds a year.

According to these figures in the story, I must have a world-champion low rate of metabolism. I've been gaining nine pounds a year for years. It's wonderful to know that it isn't my fault. And if my body runs at idle all day long, I should think it would last longer than if I were racing my engine.

I can hardly wait to get home and celebrate with a big dinner and a bowl of ice cream for dessert.

Ms. Misses the Mark

The other day I was watching a little of the *Today* show with a cup of coffee and I heard Senator William Armstrong of Colorado call Jane Pauley "Miss Pauley."

I liked it and thought how unusual, how proper and how appropriate it was. The senator might have called Jane Pauley several things:

He could have said "Jane" as most guests do, even though they aren't on what is known as a "first-name basis."

He might have said "Mrs. Trudeau" because Jane Pauley is married to the cartoonist Garry Trudeau, but has not taken her husband's name for her professional career, so calling her "Mrs. Trudeau" would not have been appropriate.

Senator Armstrong might have endeared himself to some women by calling Jane Pauley "Ms. Pauley" instead of "Miss Pauley," but *Ms.* is awkward to use. It's awkward because, while the idea of not identifying a woman's married status may be a good one, people don't know what the letters stand for so they aren't sure how to pronounce it. Like Harry S. Truman's middle initial, the letters *Ms.* aren't an abbreviation for anything. They're just an invented word, and it's pronounced "Miz." (To further confuse the issue, that's the same way Southerners pronounce "Mrs.")

Senator Armstrong's "Miss" was perfectly friendly though slightly formal, and it sounded good for a change. He wasn't trying to kid us into thinking that he was one of Jane Pauley's close friends.

Guests on television shows who have never heard of each other before they go on the air often strike a false note by sounding too chummy. Everyone is Ed, Linda, Helen or George. You can listen to an hour discussion on television without ever hearing a person's last name. Politicians, in their effort to be everyone's best friend, are the worst offenders.

I often watch the *MacNeil/Lehrer Newshour* on public television. The guests usually call Robert MacNeil "Robin" because they've heard that's his nickname. A nickname should be reserved for good friends. If we don't stand back and preserve some of the little formalities, we're going to destroy the good things about genuine familiarity. When I call a close friend by his or her nickname, there's a touch of affection that goes with it. If everyone who meets that person for the first time also uses the nickname, the virtues of a nickname are lost.

Television hosts also do too much greeting and thanking. They thank everyone to death. When you thank someone, the implication is that the person has done you a favor. When the anchorman or -woman on a television news broadcast comes back on camera after a report from the field by a correspondent, he or she invariably says, "Thank you, Ed" or "Thank you for that report, Ed."

In so doing, the anchorman is assuming an importance for himself that he doesn't have. He's being condescending. The correspondent is not doing the report for the anchorman. The reporter is doing the report because that's what he does for his salary. They both work for the same company. It is no more appropriate for an anchorman to thank a correspondent than it is for the correspondent to thank the anchorman. Time is precious on network news broadcasts and even small amounts of it shouldn't be wasted on trivial and meaningless formalities.

There are several other meaningless phrases that ought to be eliminated from television interview shows. One is the obligatory "Come back and see us again."

The television host's idea of the best way to end an interview, no matter how dull it may have been, is to say, "Thank you for being here and please come back and see us again real soon."

He knows, the guest knows and everyone watching the show knows there isn't a prayer the person will ever be invited back.

Giving Business the Business

American businessmen spend half their time extolling the virtues of competition and free enterprise and the other half trying to eliminate them. They go to church on Sunday and start breaking the Golden Rule first thing Monday morning when they get to the office.

Making something these days is just a sideline for many big U.S. corporations. The product is nothing more than an inconvenience. It's a formality. Chief executive officers have people who do that sort of menial production work for them. They don't know anything about the product their company makes. They have little interest in the quality of their product and not much faith that quality makes much difference. They go with advertising and aggressive salesmanship. They worked their way up from salesman to sales manager to vice president of marketing to their present position. They don't know how to make anything. All they know how to do is sell, and they've reached the pinnacle of their profession when they sell the company . . . or buy another.

There are still thousands of good, small companies in the United States whose executives have a genuine concern for their product and the company's employees, but at the rate the small fish are being eaten alive by the sharks, not many of those will survive.

The first thing a big corporation does when it takes over a smaller one is to make an announcement: "We do not plan to make any immediate changes." Ha! That means it'll be three weeks before they start firing people.

Employees are often propagandized to believe that they belong to a family. This suits the business purpose of the company. When the business is sold, the family idea is dropped. No more bowling trophies paid for by management. Loyalty goes out the window and dismissal notices go out in the mail.

The sad fact is, employees usually feel more loyalty to a company than the company feels for them. Employees tend to endow the corporation with a heart it doesn't have.

It matters not to takeover corporations that they are firing employees who made the business worth acquiring in the first place. They do not concern themselves with such human aspects of employment as the production-line worker whose aging mother has cancer and whose wife has been in an auto accident and cannot take care of their three children.

For a long while unions had more power than was good for them. They demanded ridiculously inefficient work rules and companies had to accept them. Now unions don't have the strength they need. Paradoxically, it is union members who have helped to create the government that has reduced their power.

James Burke, the chairman of Johnson and Johnson, is an enlightened businessman and a wonderful guy to be with but he got in with the wrong crowd when he was young. Jim is upset because he says the American businessman is always shown as the bad guy on television and in the movies. He's trying to put pressure on the entertainment industry to show big businessmen as the good guys for once. He probably wants a lovable J.R. in the lead role in *Dallas.*

It's going to be a long while before Jim Burke sees the chief executive officer played by Robert Redford. Most writers feel the same way about company presidents as a producer I knew in Hollywood felt about lawyers.

An assistant came into Voldemar Vetluguin's office while I was sitting with him and showed him a report from a legal group in New York. The report said that lawyers had been portrayed as evil in 83 out of 100 parts they had played in Hollywood movies in the previous five years.

Vetluguin looked at the report for a minute, then handed it back to the assistant.

"Eighty-three out of a hundred?" he said. "Write back and say we gave lawyers a break."

Until businessmen stop buying and selling each other and get back to paying some attention to making something other than money, a lot of people are going to feel they get a break in the movies.

Rags to Riches

Last year, on the Tuesday after Labor Day, I was driving through one of the poorest sections of New York City, thinking how unpleasant it was. There was garbage everywhere. Unemployed young men who looked unemployable were hanging around the broken-down steps in front of the deteriorating brownstone houses, doing nothing.

A light changed to red in front of me and, as I pulled to a stop, I locked the car doors from inside. Across the street, two men approached a third standing in a doorway. There was an exchange among them, but the light turned, the man in the car behind me blew his horn and I moved on. I assumed I'd seen a drug purchase. I wondered whose car radio the buyers had stolen or whose house they'd broken into to get the money to buy the drugs. I wasn't in a court of law. I wasn't even speaking my thoughts to anyone. Sitting alone in the car, I could think all the prejudiced thoughts I wanted to in the privacy of my own brain.

"Scum," I thought to myself.

At the next light, a boy about seventeen approached me with a dirty, wet sponge on the end of a stick. He was going to make a gesture toward washing my windshield in the hope I'd give him some change. This is a common practice in New York City where traffic piles up coming on or off a bridge or highway. Young boys, always black, congregate there with their pails of soapy water. It's a sophisticated form of blackmail. When one of these kids comes toward your car, there's an implied threat. They seldom do any better than make a mess of your windshield, so almost no one really welcomes them. If you don't respond with at least a quarter, they often dab your windshield with one quick stroke, leaving a dirty smear for you to clean off yourself.

If you wave them off as they approach your car, the clever ones often say, "Hey man, it better than bein' out there stealin'."

Some drivers are angered, others shrug and pay up. A few feel the kids are at least showing a kind of ambitious enterprise that the ones buying drugs or sitting on the front steps doing nothing day after day are not.

Fortunately, on this day, the light changed before the boy with the dirty sponge could get to my windshield. I held my hand out the window with a quarter in it for him and drove off with mixed feelings. Does a quarter absolve me of any responsibility for his condition? Do I have any responsibility?

At the next light I was still contemplating poverty. If you have enough money yourself, it's easy to get to thinking it's their own fault. I was thinking a little of that when I had to stop a third time for a light. A simply dressed black woman stood on the curb holding a boy about seven and a girl eight by the hands. She glanced directly through my windshield to engage my eyes. The woman wanted to assure herself that I had seen her before she crossed in front of the car with her small children.

Each of the two kids had on a new pair of sneakers. They looked nervous but eager. Under their arms were little paper briefcases, which I decided contained new pencils, erasers and rulers the mother had bought for the children at the ten-cent store. The woman was obviously taking her two children to their first day of school for the new year.

Every negative thought I'd been having about the area disappeared from my mind. I was touched by the loving concern of this mother for her children. She could have been any mother anywhere in the world, rich or poor, black or white. She wanted her children to feel comfortable and protected going to school that first day. She was apprehensive for them, but determined that they be educated.

When the light turned, I pulled away, embarrassed at the prejudiced thought I'd had about the people living in this poor area.

DILEMMAS

A Time to Cast Away Stones

Our trash collector comes twice a week but this isn't enough for Margie. No, this recently born-again neat freak, who until yesterday was as messy as I am, gets religion and calls a guy in the Yellow Pages to cart stuff away for $25. Suddenly she's Mrs. Clean.

I am much perplexed by what has come over her until I learn that there will be a meeting of nine women on her speakers' committee in our living room Thursday morning. Presumably they won't be able to decide who to get to speak next fall if we don't have the trash in our driveway carted away before sundown Wednesday.

At the appointed time, a truck arrives with not one, but two trash men and they are trash men to behold. They are stripped to the waist and ready for heavy work. I'd strip to the waist more often myself if I was as muscular as they are. The truck is a compactor with capacity enough to crush all the junk in our town any given day. It is all ours today.

We have put some things in the driveway for them and Margie still is hunting for more. The pile consists of some old boards from a packing case the new refrigerator came in, a Coleman stove that never worked, some branches, fifty feet of hose that leaks and two plastic pails with holes in them. I could get the whole mess in the trunk of my car.

"Where's the stuff?" one of the men asks, standing three feet in front of the stuff. We point.

"Is that all?" He wouldn't have brought all his muscles if he'd known there was that little.

"What about those old skis," Margie says, and I'm not putting a question mark after that because she isn't asking me. She is planning to throw away the skis.

"They're beautiful," I say. "They're hickory."

"Yes," she says, "and you've had them since you were in high school. They're the kind they had before they wore ski boots and bindings. You just kicked the toes of your shoes into the leather strap."

"I like them," I say.

"What about that old tire in the back of the shed? Why don't they take that?"

"It's not an old tire," I say. "It's perfectly good. It doesn't have a thousand miles on it!"

"Yes, but you haven't owned a car it would fit for ten years."

"What if I get a car someday that it does fit?"

"Ridiculous," Margie snaps. "I suppose that's why you're keeping that broken shovel too, and that rusty lawn fertilizer. What about the half-bag of cement? Or is that a rock you put in that bag? What good is that board over there . . . the one you screwed the roller-skate wheels to when you wanted to move the refrigerator?"

"You can throw out the cement," I concede.

"What about the shovel?"

"I'm going to get a new handle for it."

"And that bicycle is no good. It doesn't even have gears. It's just taking up space."

"It's a good bike," I say. "I'm going to clean it up and oil it someday. That's what this place is for—to store things in."

"Not if you're never going to use them again, it isn't."

This idea is where the line is drawn between people who want to throw things out and people who want to keep them. When I keep something, it is not always with the idea that it ever will be useful to me again. There are useless things taking up space everywhere in my life that I keep because I like.

If I die with these possessions, someone else can throw them out. Someone it won't hurt to dispose of them. Why should I do it if it hurts?

"Oh say," Margie says to the two men, "come up the back stairs a minute, will you?"

A minute later they emerge with the crib we have kept in the house for Christmas and other visits from grandchildren. We have four children—three married, one unmarried. We have three grandchildren now, Justin, Ben and Alexis. Alexis is the youngest but she's five.

I hope Brian doesn't find out his mother has given up hope and thrown away the crib.

Everybody Does It Better

There are a lot of ordinary things I find hard to do. I either can't do them at all or I do them badly. For instance, I can't:

—Pack a suitcase neatly.

—Make a bed. I couldn't do it to the first sergeant's satisfaction in the army and I can't do it to Margie's satisfaction now. I don't try often.

—Attach a hose to an outside faucet without having it leak. New rubber washers don't help.

—Cut the fingernails on my right hand with the clipper in my left hand.

—Hold a telephone between my shoulder and my ear while I try to write something down.

—Open a waxed cardboard milk container. I usually forget to look to see which side I'm supposed to crimp open.

—Take ice-cube trays filled with water from the sink to the refrigerator without spilling water on the floor.

—Adjust to the approach of the year 2000. On the radio I heard them say they'd probably be sending a spaceship to Mars in 2003 because Mars will be close to Earth that year. They said it matter-of-factly as if the year 2003 were just around the corner. I don't think of it that way and frankly, I don't care what year Mars will be close to the Earth because I know what I'll be fourteen years closer to in the year 2003.

—Press a pair of pants. I end up with two creases up the front of each leg.

—Draw a sketch of something on a piece of paper to describe to someone what I'm talking about. This includes trying to draw a map for directions.

—Sign my name so a stranger can read it. Someone said an illegible signature is the sign of an egotist. I agree with that and I hope I'm not an egotist but, for the life of me, I can't write my name legibly.

—Sharpen a knife properly. I remember my grandfather shaved with a straight razor. Every morning he'd run the blade over a stone a few times and then slap it back and forth against a leather strop. It was called a strop, not a strap. The blade was always, proverbially, razor sharp. I can't get an edge on a kitchen knife, even my good pre–stainless steel knives.

—Read for more than an hour. I admire people who can settle in with a good book for three or four hours at a time but I get restless after forty-five minutes and usually put down the book and do something else. I blame it on my glasses but I think it's my mind that's inadequate, not my glasses.

—Put anything back in the package it came in. The Japanese genius is nowhere better exhibited than in the way their products come packed, but if you have to take it back, don't ask me to try to repack it.

I wouldn't want you to think I'm being unnecessarily modest by suggesting there's nothing I do well. There are things I do well. For instance, I can:

—Guess exactly what time it is when I wake up in the middle of the night.

—Eat a Chinese meal with chopsticks.

—Make salad dressing. Paul Newman bottles and sells his, but mine is better.

—Park a car in a space no more than eight inches longer than the car is.

If It Ain't Rev. Jackson

If the class will please come to order, today we'll take up the word *reverend*.

It appears now as though Jesse Jackson will be part of the American political scene for years to come and we might as well get his title right. According to every book on grammar that I can find, it is wrong, incorrect, ungrammatical and dumb to call Jesse Jackson "Reverend Jackson."

If you decide to use his ecclesiastical title just to stick it to him, as some people are doing, you may choose to continue using that somewhat comic "Reverend Jackson." If you mean it as a sign of respect, however, the proper form is "the Reverend Mr. Jackson" or "the Reverend Jesse Jackson." The word *reverend* is an adjective. It must be followed by either a title, like "Mr." or by a first name or initials. Catholics call Pope John Paul "His Holiness Pope John Paul." They do not call him "Holiness John Paul," which would be something like calling Jesse Jackson "Reverend Jackson."

Many of the people who were enthralled by Mr. Jackson's oratorical ruffles and flourishes in his first life as a fire-and-brimstone Baptist preacher responded to his bombastic style with high hosannas in church and popularized the tendency to call him "The Reverend" outside it. In some cases he was known simply as "The Rev." The term is popular with the people who call doctors "Doc."

The alarming thing about this now is that some network anchors and many of the reporters following Jesse Jackson's campaign have referred to him as "Reverend Jackson." This does not make it right. Most newspapers don't make the mistake.

For homework today, I'll ask you to memorize the following excerpts on the subject from a wide variety of textbooks:

"Reverend is used as we use Honorable. That is, the article the is required and the title cannot stand immediately before a last name. Either the given name or initials must be used or some title of respect must take their place as in "The Reverend Edward Pusey or The Reverend Mr. Pusey."
—*Dictionary of Contemporary American Usage*

"Reverend is strictly speaking an adjective meaning deserving reverence."
—*American Usage and Style*

"To describe a clergyman as Reverend Smith instead of The Reverend Mr. Smith is a common vulgarism, so common indeed that it may soon cease to deserve the description."
—Fowler's *Modern English Usage*

"Reverend is not used without the first name or initials of the person to whom it refers. The abbreviation is used in newspaper and informal writing as Rev. James Shaw or Rev. J. T. Shaw. NOT: Rev. Shaw."
—*Writer's Guide and Index to English*

"The Reverend Henry L. Brown; the Reverend Mr. Brown (*never* Reverend Brown *or* the Reverend Brown)."
—*The Chicago Manual of Style*

It's difficult to know where to draw the line when it comes to grammar. I'm not an expert, but I do use the language to make my living so it's always on my mind. The things that bother me most about misusing English are the things that confuse the meaning of something because they are illogical.

In most cases, clear writing or clear speaking comes not so much from knowing the rules of grammar but from clear thinking. Clear thinking and good grammar go together. If you know what you think, the chances are you can write it down or say it grammatically so that everyone understands it. If you're not clear what you think, you won't be able to speak or write grammatically.

I don't mean to make a federal case out of the word *reverend,* but we shouldn't let the language deteriorate along with our water, our air, our bridges and our cities. It doesn't cost anything to maintain the language. To call him "Reverend Jackson" isn't just a grammatical error. It ain't right.

Psychological Nonsense

Too many people are taking a little psychology in college these days. A little psychology is bad for the psyche. We have more people explaining the psychology of things than we need.

Amateur psychologists find truth in curious places. Nothing that's right there where we can see it is a good enough explanation for them. I know it isn't fair to a lot of good ones, but I'm suspicious of professional psychologists. I think of a psychologist as someone who wanted to be a psychiatrist but couldn't get into medical school.

You find amateur psychologists at work everywhere, but all sports announcers must have taken Psychology 101 as freshmen.

"Scoring that last basket before the half will give them a psychological lift going into the dressing room," the sports announcer tells us.

The team is behind 62–27 at halftime but the announcer thinks scoring those last two points is going to give them a psychological lift. The logical extension to the thought, which he means to suggest, is that the team will come out for the second half all revved up and go on to overcome the opponent's lead and win the game. This is the announcer's idea of how to make a dull game more dramatic. He's trying to hold on to his listeners until his sponsor gets a shot at selling them something.

"They've been here before," the football commentator will say about one of the two Super Bowl teams. "They know what the pressure is like out there. They won't be as uptight out there as the Bombers because they have the experience."

A rude expression often comes to my mind . . . for which the only polite substitute in writing is "Nonsense!"

If you did nothing but listen to the amateur psychologists reporting sports events, you'd think that it wasn't ever the team with the better players that won. You'd think the winners were always the ones who "had the psychological advantage."

It never seems to matter to the announcer/psychologist that one basketball team has three very good players seven feet tall and two others who are acrobatic artists at getting the ball in the basket.

"They have the home-court advantage," he says.

"State has the edge," the announcer tells us, "because in thirty-two of their last fifty-one games since they started this series way back in 1939, Central Western has been able to win on the road only nineteen times."

I don't know what he's saying. I just nod and figure State has the edge if he says so.

"Johnny Podolak's whole family is in the stands today cheering him on," we're told. "This could be a big factor in the game today because you can bet Johnny will be up, emotionally."

And, "Ed Werrgeles is playing against his old teammates this afternoon. This is going to give him a big psychological boost because you know he's got to be out there proving to them that they made a mistake when they traded him."

The psychology behind things was very big during the Olympics. It was either a psychological advantage or a psychological disadvantage to come down the hill first . . . or, possibly, last. She knew she had only one person to beat or he knew they'd all have to catch him now. The psychological pressure was on them.

Some of the Olympic performers who failed "weren't motivated," according to the announcers. "Motivation" is an important word with sports reporters and so is the athlete's "concentration."

Dan Jansen, the speed skater whose sister died the day before the 1988 Winter Olympics, competed twice and fell both times. The announcers attributed his falls not to the condition of the ice but to "a lack of concentration."

You can be sure that if Dan had won, the announcers would have been saying the tragedy "gave him added incentive."

Depending on what's going on in the world at the time, the diviners of the psychology behind things move from one event to the other. They explain politics, world events, sports, crime and marriage in psychological terms. Nothing is ever quite what it seems to the layman. It isn't the better team that wins. It's the team with "the psychological advantage."

A Nation of Exiles

Considering all the talk about illegal immigrants, not many of us know much about immigration. I got through high school without being certain of the difference between "immigration" and "emigration."

The process of giving a person from one country official status as a citizen of another is called "naturalization." It's sort of a funny thing to call it. You'd think it might be called "unnaturalization."

Those of us born here in the United States know how lucky we are. I'd hate to be outside trying to get in. The requirements for naturalization are so complex and vague that there isn't anyone who can tell you what all the rules are. I tried to find out and ended up with three fat volumes of double-talk law, very little of which I understood.

Do you, by any chance, know where most people came from to get here? There are some surprises. Here are some of the numbers on immigration to the United States from 1820 to 1981:

—The most immigrants came from Germany, 6,998,000. A relatively small part of that number can be accounted for by Jews who fled Nazi Germany.

—Italians were second, 5,310,000.

—There were 4,693,000 Irish immigrants and almost as many Canadians. I don't think of Canadians as immigrants.

—There were 4,319,000 immigrants from Austria.

—I was surprised to see that 3,395,000 people came from Russia.

—England accounted for 3,198,000 immigrants but that doesn't include two of my grandparents. They came from Scotland.

—The only other country exceeding a million was Sweden.

—The big surprise to me was France. During those years there were only 757,000 immigrants to the United States from France. I find that amazing when you think nearly 7 million came from Germany.

—There were 594,000 people who came from China but that statistic has to be qualified. While many Chinese came here before we had strict immigration rules, all Chinese were barred from entering from 1882 until 1943, when we opened that golden door again to them.

In another few years these statistics will change. The pattern of immigration has changed drastically already. Few people are coming to the United States from Europe today. Great numbers are coming from Mexico and Central America.

The mystique of the Statue of Liberty and Ellis Island is a thing of the past, of course. Anyone coming here now flies. No one comes in by boat unless they're running drugs, and more people are sneaking across the Mexican border every year than ever came in legally past the Statue of Liberty in a year.

The laws for entry into our country are not only complex, no one agrees on exactly what they should be. Congress has a new bill pending but it's brought up a major argument. Some people don't want to let anyone new in; others want to let everyone in.

Do you know the people who object most to the aliens who are sneaking in this year? It's the aliens who sneaked in last year. Last year's aliens are the ones who'll lose their jobs because the new ones will work cheaper in worse conditions.

It's an old American tradition to resent the people who come here after you do. I had a world-champion mother but she always felt a little superior to the Irish. She was probably a little embarrassed to have fallen in love with my father. In the small town in upstate New York where they both lived, the latecomers were the Irish. They mostly did the housework.

Prejudice has always been a fact of life in America. One group of immigrants has always found a reason to dislike the next.

Fortunately, I'm an enlightened person. I don't have the same prejudices my mother had. I think highly of the Irish.

It's all those Mexicans I worry about.

A Learning Experience

"No," I said.

"Why?" she asked.

"You just can't," I said.

It's Saturday morning and I've taken Alexis to the supermarket. Alexis is five.

The trick with a child in a supermarket is to snake your way up and down the aisles, without forgetting the things on your list, without losing track of the child, without buying one of everything she wants, while, at the same time, keeping her interested and happy enough so she doesn't make a scene.

"Can I get in there?" she asked, pointing to the shopping cart.

"You're a little big for that, aren't you?"

"Mom lets me."

"I'll bet she doesn't, but OK, get in."

I figured I'd have better control over her in the cart than out of it.

"Let's get some cookies?" she said.

"We'll get some cookies."

We passed the cookie shelves and I picked out two packages.

"Get chocolate," Alexis said firmly.

I got chocolate.

"Can I have a cookie now?"

"No. It's too early."

"Mom lets me have cookies," she said with a little tiny smile on her face, indicating she was kidding and that I knew she was kidding.

"You can't open them until we pay for them anyway."

"Why can't we?"

"They aren't ours yet. They still belong to the store until we get to the cashier and pay for them."

"Mom lets me," she smiled.

Being the father of Alexis' mother, I knew better.

A woman whose face was familiar but whose name I didn't know, passed by.

"Hello," I said, smiling more than I normally would have, trying to make up for not being able to recall her name.

"Why did you say 'Hello'?" Alexis asked.

"That woman is a friend of mine," I said.

"What's her name?" Alexis persisted.

"It doesn't matter," I said.

"Why doesn't it matter? Now can I have a cookie? Can I have some candy? Mom lets me have candy."

I don't know why I'd thought it was such a good idea to take Alexis to the store. Probably, in some general way, I thought it would be part of some educational process for a young girl to go to the store with her grandfather. As things turned out, it was more of an education for me than for her.

I had not realized, for example, how fiendishly clever all the companies had become at pushing their wares at us. After years of wandering through the aisles of supermarkets, I'd become inured to the attractive displays of food companies. We rolled the shopping cart to the car in the parking lot, unloaded it and I started to push the cart back to where they were stacked in front of the store.

"Can I push it?" Alexis asked.

"There are a lot of cars here," I said. "I better do it."

"Dad lets me," Alexis said.

It's about twelve miles home. I turned out of the parking lot and started down the road.

"Are we almost home yet?" Alexis asked.

By the time we arrived in our driveway, Alexis had eaten a small bag of popcorn and one big chocolate cookie. I had forgotten butter, lettuce and paper towels.

Don't Plan to Plan Ahead

Something's got to be done about slowing down the passage of time. If they can make cereal with ten times more iron than Shredded Wheat, they should be able to make a day last a week or a week a month.

In January I was relaxed and happy because it would be twelve months before I'd be a year older. Now, here it is only a short time later and I've only got seven months left till my next birthday. It's enough to put a person off birthdays for life. And while I'm on the subject, whoever decided that a birthday was an occasion for a party celebrating the day? I can understand kids having birthday parties, but no one past thirty thinks a birthday is any occasion for celebrating.

When a person gets to be eighty-five, then he or she has good reason to rejoice over still being alive. The grandmother who announces, "I'll be eighty-seven in August" shares pride in projecting the next step in age with the kid who answers the question "How old are you?" by saying, "I'm almost nine." You don't catch anyone approaching middle age, with a birthday six months past, saying, "I'm forty-two and a half" or "I'm almost forty-three." Right up until midnight of the day before the birthday, that person's going to be filling out forms and answering the question with forty-two." Never mind the details.

We keep moving things up—that's one reason birthdays come up so often. We're always hurrying time along by looking forward to things instead of enjoying what we have today. I keep hearing radio announcers saying that Memorial Day is the beginning of summer. Memorial Day is not the beginning of summer. Summer starts June 21. Let's not press it.

Planning isn't good for the passage of time, I'm convinced of that. I just know that planning things a month or two months in advance makes time pass more quickly. You get to those days quicker than you would if you had nothing coming up. In March, I was looking forward to May because I had some interesting things to do on my calendar. Now it's June, I've done those things I planned in May, but I've completely forgotten anything that happened in April. Did we really have April or did we skip it this year? I was so busy looking forward that I forgot to look around.

The days that drag are the days when you have nothing coming up in the future, so that's what we need more of to make time last longer—days that drag.

It seems unfair, but the longest days are the days we're sick in bed, in trouble at work or otherwise unhappy. These are the days we'd like to get rid of in a hurry but they won't go away. The good days, the busy days, are gone before you can taste them.

One of the most puzzling things about the passage of time is what happens in the middle of the night. I generally sleep well, but several times a year I have a bad night. I'll look at the clock at 2:00 A.M. and then look at it again at 3:30 and swear I haven't been asleep at all. Something strange has happened. I don't remember anything I thought during the hour and a half. The time passed and I was awake but unaware.

When I make my drive of three and a half hours every Friday to our summer home, I dread the thought of staring at the road for that long. I'll note by my watch that I still have two hours to drive, but an hour later I can't remember having driven the last hour.

There must be some condition of the brain in between asleep and awake. You can wake up even though you haven't been asleep. You can suddenly realize you haven't been noticing anything around you and start noticing things again. You've been awake but nothing registered. Your mind has been a blackboard but nothing got written on it. We have so little time, we should savor every minute.

HABITS AND
OCCUPATIONS

The Inadvertent Reveille

Early risers are good people. They do the work of the world while late risers are still in bed. All the things like cars, television sets, bars and all-night McDonald's never would have been invented if the world had waited for late risers to get out of bed and invent them. The late risers have the ability—they just don't get up in time to start.

Early risers have one serious problem. It has plagued me all summer. The problem is how to keep from waking the whole house when we get up. Being a typical early riser, I'm thoughtful of those who stay in bed and have to have a cup of coffee as soon as they get up. Once they're up, I'm not too nice to them but while they're in bed, I respect their disease. Staying in bed longer than it takes to get the rest you need is a disease.

When I rise at about six on my vacation, there are often other family members or guests in the house. I try to be quiet, but it's not possible.

I slip silently out of bed, trying not to move the springs under the mattress, and I head for the bathroom. I'm careful to open and close the bathroom door gently. I hold the doorknob and ease it back to its normal position, rather than letting the spring snap it back, which would shoot the catch noisily into the hole in the doorjamb designed to catch it.

Up until this point, I've done well every morning, but then come the problems. Being quiet is so difficult in a silent house. The silence is broken the instant I flush the toilet. That's like a public-address announcement. ATTENTION! ATTENTION! ANDREW ROONEY IS NOW UP!

It is not simply that I'm thoughtful. I want to be alone for two hours.

I don't want to interact with my dearest friends or family for a while.

I tiptoe back to the bedroom and silently pull on my socks while the sleepers doze off again after their rude awakening. The minute I start down the stairs leading to the living room, their sleep is interrupted again. At 6 A.M. the stairs make a racket that Rip Van Winkle couldn't sleep through.

The house is just sixty years old, and I'm sure that for all of those sixty years every time anyone came down those stairs, they have issued forth the same noises. Gingerly I extend the ball of my sneakered foot downward to the next stair tread. Each time I put my full weight down, there are a series of explosive little cracking sounds as the wood changes position in relation to the piece it is up against. I've tried coming down barefoot, I've made my way down placing most of my weight on the bannister and I've tried putting my weight on different places on the steps, looking for a spot that doesn't announce my descendancy. The stairs still snap, crackle and pop.

In deference to their sleeping habits, I don't get my breakfast first thing. Coffee making is quiet enough but squeezing oranges or even opening and closing the refrigerator door can create an impression in sleepers that the kitchen is going full blast and that they ought to get up.

Now I take the car and go get the newspaper. If the running water and the creaking stairs haven't permanently awakened everyone in the house, raising the garage door usually does. When I reach down and give the handle a jerk, the garage door starts up, and the sound of the little metal wheels in their metal tracks is like a drum roll echoing through the house. I open the car door quietly enough, climb in and close the door. Closing a car door is another one of those loud and inevitable sounds. There is no way to close a car door quietly. Car doors are built to be slammed. Slamming is what activates the little catches that hold a car door tightly shut.

What I need is a sound engineer to come into the house and find a way to muffle my morning. Or maybe I'm just going to stop worrying about it. I know late risers wouldn't be thoughtful if I were still in bed.

What I hate most about late risers is, they lie.

"I hope I didn't wake you," I say.

"Oh, no," the late risers say. "We were awake. We were just about to get up anyway."

Inside Outside Rightside Wrongside

How come, if I admire neatly dressed people so much, I didn't do anything about it this morning when I noticed I'd put my left sock on inside out?

It's still inside out as, sitting at my typewriter, I look down at it now. The ribbing looks a little different but not any worse, as far as I can see. To tell you the truth, it's hard to describe exactly how you can tell when clothes are inside out. They have a different look but not necessarily a worse look. I don't think anyone will notice.

That must be the difference between someone who dresses neatly and someone who doesn't. I put something on that isn't quite right and I just shrug and say, "Who's going to notice?" My collar may be a little frayed, there may be a small spot on my necktie and my pants are baggy at the knees. I wear them.

Being a neat person isn't something a person should get credit for. Neat people can't help it. They're neat, that's all. It isn't a decision they make every day. They can't help themselves. They wouldn't dream of leaving the house with one sock on inside out.

One reason I'm not better dressed than I am is because I get attached to some of my clothing. If a pair of shoes, a shirt or a necktie has been with me to a lot of interesting places, I hate to throw it away after it's seen its best days. These shoes, these very shoes I wear today, are a little down at the heels but I happen to know they have walked the streets of Moscow, were on board the U.S.S. *Guam* off Beirut and stood in the little garden by our house when Emily and Kirby were married. Could I throw them in the trash can as if they were something I hardly knew? I could not. This kind of sentimentality adds to the image I have of not being a very neat or well-dressed person.

I see Dan Rather in the halls once in a while. He's faultlessly neat. His pants always have a razor-sharp press, his hair is nicely combed, his shoes are shined, his shirt fits and there are no spots on his necktie. It all seems to come so easily to him that I resent him for it. He'd look perfect leaving a picnic in a rainstorm.

It may be that anchormen have neat minds that lead them to being neat dressers, because Peter Jennings is always faultlessly attired, too. Like Dan, he looks just right in his clothes.

This may be more than you want to know about my dressing habits but I assume that you will draw some interest from them as they parallel or diverge from your own. Last week I looked in the drawer in which I keep my shorts and undershirts and there were only a few pairs.

I asked Margie if she knew what happened to the rest of them.

"I threw them out," she said. "They were rags. You can't wear those."

Has there been a ruling from the Supreme Court on this? Does a wife have the right to throw out her husband's underwear simply because it's tattered? Have I no rights? Are not my dresser drawers sanctuary? Does another person have any business invading the privacy of what I wear under my outerwear?

If I let her get away with this, first thing you know she'll be throwing out my old flannel pajamas that are a little gone in the elbow; she'll be tossing out the ties that are worn at the knot and sorting out the shoes that are down at the heels.

When you can't be what you'd like to be, there's no sense eating your heart out about it. The best and easiest thing to do is simply change what you want to be. I've always wanted to be a neat dresser but it is apparent to me, after all these years, that I am incapable of being one. I am therefore altering my desire. I am convincing myself that my manner of dress is casual, informal, low-key, relaxed and homespun. The word "slob" will never cross my mind again.

Rethinking Breakfast

We have to rethink breakfast in America. No one in years has put any thought into the first meal of our day. How many times have you read in a cookbook or in the Sunday supplement of your newspaper a good new recipe for something to have for breakfast?

Once the recipe writers have run through pancakes, waffles, eggs Benedict and blueberry muffins, they're finished with breakfast.

There are reasons why we haven't paid any attention to breakfast, I suppose. For one thing, we're busy in the morning. Eating is part entertainment, and at breakfast we don't want entertainment, we want nourishment. We want to put something warm into our digestive tracts to get things going down there. People aren't interested in reading breakfast recipes.

You'd never know it from looking at the cereal advertisements but there are even a lot of Americans who start off their day with nothing more than coffee and a cigarette.

Another reason why the cookbooks don't spend much time on breakfast is that it isn't as social a meal as the others. You never invite someone over for breakfast the way you might invite someone for dinner, and you don't often have breakfast with friends or co-workers the way you often have lunch. People aren't much interested in talking at breakfast. They have their minds on what they're going to do that day.

Being creative or looking into new things to eat doesn't interest people first thing in the morning. They don't want to think about food. They're satisfied with more of the same thing they had yesterday.

Some people eat the same thing for breakfast every day of their lives. I know a man in his eighties who says he has had the same thing for breakfast for sixty years. He says he has one soft-boiled egg, two pieces of toast and three cups of coffee, black. We got to talking about it and we figured he has eaten 1,825 dozen soft-boiled eggs.

I like orange juice, toast, marmalade and coffee, but when I'm not home I end up eating bad muffins, soggy croissants or bakery coffee cake that smells of fake vanilla.

I've never read what doctors have to say about orange juice but it seems unlikely that anything as acidic as orange juice is the best thing to pour down your throat into your stomach first thing in the morning. I know the vitamins in orange juice are good for you but they certainly must be just as good at some other time of day. When you think of it, orange juice probably would be better consumed as a sort of breakfast dessert, after toast or cereal.

Weekend breakfasts are another matter, of course. I love breakfast Saturday and Sunday. Sitting there, in no hurry, reading the newspaper and drinking more coffee than is good for you is one of the great luxuries of life. Sunday morning is when I feel most sorry for the homeless.

On special occasions when the kids are home, I make waffles, pancakes or popovers. When we're alone on a cold winter morning, I make real, not instant, oatmeal. Directions on the box say it takes half an hour but it doesn't take more than about twelve minutes. You cook it like rice so it ends up dry. (The only Sunday-morning problem I've never been able to solve is getting them to deliver two newspapers on just that one day.)

I can't figure why Campbell's never pushed soup as a breakfast food. I've never tried it myself, I've just thought about it, but why wouldn't chicken or beef broth, with rice or barley in it, be a great breakfast?

I don't have it in for Wheaties or Shredded Wheat but why wouldn't hot chicken soup be the ideal breakfast? It's nourishing and it could replace the drink you want when you have juice, the hot jolt you want when you have coffee and the nourishment you need when you have eggs, toast, pancakes or cereal. Maybe we could have chicken soup with caffeine.

We have to reinvent breakfast. Bacon and eggs don't do it.

How to Read a Newspaper

Considering how much time I've spent reading newspapers in my life, it's amazing how little thought I've given to how a newspaper should be read. There's nothing I do so much of that I do so badly.

If I ate dinner the way I read the newspaper, I'd be starting with dessert; if I drove the way I read the newspaper, I'd be arrested for drunken driving because I was wandering all over the road; if I read a book the way I read a newspaper, I'd be starting near the end, working forward and then jumping to the beginning. My method of reading the newspaper makes no sense at all and yet there's no small pleasure I enjoy more. Anyone can read a newspaper any way he or she wants to. This is the great advantage of reading a newspaper over viewing television news. With television news, you take it the way they want to give it to you or not at all.

I wish I were more disciplined about the way I read the newspaper. It may be OK to start with the social notes, the gossip columns, sports pages, recipes, comic strips or the columnists, but my trouble is when I do that I often run out of reading time before I get to what I ought to read to know what's going on in the world. There is hardly a day that I don't put the newspaper down, fully intending to pick it up and finish it later. Unfortunately, there is hardly a day when I pick it up and finish it later. First thing I know, tomorrow's paper has come and the one I didn't finish reading is no longer news, it's history. I often wonder if newspaper editors read all of the things in their paper.

The reason I don't finish the paper is that there's a limit to how much time I can spend reading it before I have to get at life. I often feel guilty about that and so I save the paper. As a result, there are piles of newspapers everywhere in the house and office. They're on the floor next to my chair in the living room, on the radiator in the kitchen and on the table next to the bed. Every stack of papers reminds me that I don't get things done. Sometimes I wish that newspapers were printed on stock that evaporated into thin air when it was a day old.

We're bombarded by information from every side, and it's a good thing. The hardware for the distribution of intelligence is vastly better than it was even twenty years ago. Reporters, generally speaking, are not being given enough time to dig out the information they need for a complete story, but the means of spreading information around is so much better that we're getting more of it than we used to despite that sad fact. A little of that information is bound to sink in and make us better informed.

The trouble with reading novelty, gossip or sports items or reading half a news story is that we end up paying too much attention to things that have no bearing on our lives. They're dream-world stuff. They're interesting as entertainment but they have no practical value for our lives. Everything doesn't have to be important, but most of it ought to lead us somewhere, even if it's only to making a better cup of coffee or adding a tidbit of information about foreign policy that will help us vote intelligently in the next election. For all the information we have available, most of us are stupid and uninformed, and it isn't our newspaper's fault, it's our own.

It might be a good idea if schools had courses in "How to Read a Newspaper," although I don't know who is qualified to teach it. Not me.

The Worst Job in the World

People like their jobs. It isn't for the money alone that they work. Most men and women go to work with some anticipation of enjoying the companionship and the satisfaction that comes with accomplishing something.

Years ago, I talked to a group of women who were doing a repetitive, assembly-line job for the Parker Pen Company in Janesville, Wisconsin, and I remember being surprised to find that almost all of them liked the work. It took them away from the problems of their own homes.

It brought them together with people they liked to talk with, and the job didn't involve making any decisions. It had never occurred to me before that someone might actually like doing an assembly-line job.

While most of us like our own jobs, we'd hate to have someone else's. There are a lot of jobs I wouldn't take:

No one has asked me but I wouldn't take the job as president or vice president of the United States. I don't think I'm being too modest when I say I'm not smart enough. Not being smart enough has not kept a great many men from wanting to be president and some from actually being president, but I am not one of them. To tell you the truth, there is no city in the United States so small that I think I'm even smart enough to be mayor of it. And I'd rather be mayor than police chief of Los Angeles, Chicago, Miami or Philadelphia.

I don't think I'd want to be a dermatologist with people coming in to see me all day with skin diseases. I know darn well I wouldn't want to be a podiatrist, examining people's feet.

I'd even hate to be a shoe clerk in a store that sells expensive shoes to rich women. Whenever I pass by one of these stores, some poor guy is sitting there on that little stool at the foot of some woman with ten boxes of shoes on the floor around them. She can't find anything she likes and he's working on commission.

I'm thankful that there are compassionate people who will work in mental hospitals but I don't think I could do it.

There's an animal hospital I pass on the way to work every day and I hope the people who work there love dogs but it would break my heart to be around so many unhappy animals all day long. I certainly would refuse to be the one who picked out the dogs to be done in.

Being a plumber doesn't interest me. Trying to fix a leak under the sink is not my game . . . although I'd lots rather be a plumber than a school-bus driver.

I'd hate to be an airlines ticket clerk, a gynecologist, a prison warden or a Supreme Court justice. I'd never be able to decide what was right.

And can anyone who isn't one imagine being an undertaker? How badly would you need money before you'd work at a profession where you were daily exposed to the grief that goes with every bit of business you conduct?

In many states an undertaker cannot legally refuse to take in the body of someone who has died of AIDS. I'm sympathetic to AIDS victims but you wouldn't have to be a terrible person to be reluctant to do whatever it is morticians do with body fluids, to an AIDS victim.

Fortunately, most people like their jobs. They get up and go to work every morning with a lot of enthusiasm for what they're going to do that day. People who stay at their jobs because there's a pension coming at the end of the line are wasting their lives.

I don't know how a bright person stands being the president of a college. A college president consistently deals with people who are dumber than he or she is . . . people like students and alumni. If the president isn't dealing with them, he's dealing with faculty members, some of whom are brighter than he is, and this must be even worse.

No matter how objectionable a college president finds any of these groups to be, he has to be sweet and reasonable with them—especially the rich ones.

I feel selfish about my job. It may be the best job in the world and I'm the only one who has it.

Fall Falls Short

Whatever the season is, I'm not ready for it when it comes. You'd think this was the first time I'd ever seen fall arrive and faced an imminent winter.

Fall isn't a real season. It's merely an interlude between the end of summer and the beginning of winter. Spring is the same kind of intermediary season. It's that brief period between when it's too cold and when it's too hot. Summer and winter are the major seasons.

I needed a topcoat Tuesday morning for the first time. When I got out of the shower, the weatherman on the little radio in the bathroom said the temperature was in the thirties and I made the coat decision right there, standing wet and naked on the bath mat. That's where winter strikes first.

Before I left the house, I got my topcoat out of the closet, where I'd put it the last time I wore it sometime in April. I remembered instantly that I'd meant to have it cleaned and waterproofed last spring, so I'd be ready for this day. I never got at taking it to the cleaners, though. There seemed like plenty of time then, so it was just as I'd left it, spots, missing buttons and all.

I didn't really need gloves but there has been just one glove lurking around the shelf in the closet where I keep gloves and I've been meaning to look for the mate to it before I needed them. Last year I

went most of the winter with one glove on my right hand and my left
hand in my coat pocket.

When I came home from work late Tuesday afternoon, Margie was
in the kitchen, which is always warm. I changed into my sitting-around
clothes and came back downstairs and settled into my chair in the living
room to sit around. The room was uncomfortably chilly. I got up to
push the thermostat up to 70 from its minimal summer position.

I sat down again and the draft in the room reminded me that I'd
meant to cover the air conditioner and push some insulating strips into
the cracks around it.

The oil burner stayed on for longer than it should have to bring the
living room up to a comfortable temperature and I remembered I'd
never got at climbing up into the attic to cover the big exhaust fan in
the gable. It has louvered aluminum flaps that come down when it isn't
running but it needs more than that to keep it from letting the heat
out of the house.

The car is probably OK because I keep antifreeze in it all year long
now, but I meant to check that and to change the oil before it got cold.
Adding antifreeze from a plastic container I buy at a supermarket for
a lot less than a gas station charges is very satisfying although I don't
know what I'll do with the 37 cents I saved.

Our driveway is difficult when it snows and, instead of paying someone to plow it several times a year, it probably would be worth it to buy
some kind of snowplow or snowblower that would do the job. I mean
to do that before it snows but, knowing myself better than all but three
or four other people know me, I doubt if I'll look into the snowblower
until the morning of the first heavy snow when everyone else is down
at the hardware store looking for the same thing.

I haven't skied for the past couple of years. I don't want to lose it
so I've been meaning to do some exercises to get my legs in shape. It's
tough to hold that crouching position, with your knees bent, all the way
down a long trail unless you're in condition for it. I have the nervous
feeling I won't ski again this year because I didn't get ready and this
could be the end of my skiing career, never illustrious at its best.

Maybe what I ought to do is face the fact that I'm not ready for
winter this year and never will be. That way, I could start getting ready
for next summer early. I could do things like lose some weight so I'll
look good in a bathing suit and tennis clothes.

Where Are All the Plumbers?

For the past few days I've spent most of the time in my woodworking shop making a complicated little oak stool for Emily.

I like the whole process of writing but when I get back there in my workshop, I notice that I'm quite contented. Yesterday I worked until 2:30 before I remembered I hadn't eaten lunch. It even has occurred to me that I could give up writing and spend the rest of my life making pieces of furniture that amuse me. Who knows? I might get good at it.

It's a mystery to me why more people don't derive their satisfactions from working with their hands. Somehow, a hundred or more years ago something strange happened in this country. Americans began to assume that all the people who did the good, hard work with their hands were not as smart as those who worked exclusively with their brains. The carpenters, the plumbers, the mechanics, the painters, the electricians and the farmers were put in a social category of their own below the one the bankers, the insurance salesmen, the doctors and the lawyers were in. The jobs that required people to work with their hands were generally lower-paying jobs and the people who took them had less education.

Another strange thing has happened in recent years. It's almost as though the working people who really know how to do something other than make money are striking back at the white-collar society. In all but the top executive jobs, the blue-collar workers are making as much as or more than the teachers, the accountants and the airline clerks.

The apprentice carpenters are making more than the young people starting out as bank clerks. Master craftsmen in any line are making $60,000 a year and many are making double that. In most large cities, automobile mechanics charge $45 an hour. A mechanic in Los Angeles or New York, working in the service department of an authorized car dealer, can make $60,000 a year. A sanitation worker in Chicago can make $35,000 a year. All this has happened, in part at least, because the fathers who were plumbers made enough money to send their children to college so they wouldn't have to be plumbers.

In England, a child's future is determined at an early age when he or she is assigned either to a school that features a classical education or one that emphasizes learning a trade. Even though we never have had the same kind of class system in America that they have in England, our lines are drawn, too. The people who work with their hands as well as their brains still aren't apt to belong to the local country club. The mechanic at the car dealer's may make more than the car salesman, but the salesman belongs to the club and the mechanic doesn't.

It's hard to account for why we're so short of people who do things well with their hands. You can only conclude that it's because of some mixed-up sense of values we have that makes us think it is more prestigious to sell houses as a real estate person than it is to build them as a carpenter.

To further confuse the matter, when anyone who works mostly with his brain, as I do, does something with his hands, as when I make a piece of furniture, friends are envious and effusive with praise. So, how come the people who do it professionally, and infinitely better than I, aren't in the country club?

If I've lost you in going the long way around to make my point, my point is that considering how satisfying it is to work with your hands and considering how remunerative those jobs have become, it is curious that more young people coming out of school aren't learning a trade instead of becoming salesmen.

Writing the Written Word

If you have good handwriting, you're lucky and unusual. Mine is so bad that I'm all but lost trying to write something down on paper without a typewriter. I come on notes I've written to myself with little ideas and frequently they are so illegible that I have to throw them away, undeciphered.

Miss Rose, who in my memory looks like Diane Sawyer, taught me to write in the third grade but I can't blame my handwriting on her. I blame it on something called "The Palmer Method," a system used by many public schools when I was growing up.

I don't know anything about The Palmer Method . . . even today I hate to write the name . . . except it was a style totally unsuited to my character and ability.

The rules and manner of writing were drummed into my head so often that I recall every detail of how it was supposed to be done. I'm not certain whether my failure was because of a physical inability or a temperamental unwillingness to conform to rules that seemed silly to me.

Miss Rose was quite clear how she wanted us to do it. We were to take the pencil and hold it between the thumb and index finger. The thumb had to be completely extended, not bent at all. The pencil stuck almost straight up because it was held against the finger above the knuckle, not down in the crotch of the hand. The little finger was curled underneath and rode on the paper.

Each day Miss Rose went up and down the aisles inspecting our hands as we did push-pulls and continuous circles between two lines on a pad of paper.

Even at that age I recall being impressed by Miss Rose's beauty and being excited when she bent over next to my small desk and gently took my hand in hers to reform it in the manner prescribed by Palmer. She would lean over to see if there was light coming under my wrist, too. You were supposed to have light coming under your wrist. The wrist was not to touch the desk. The whole motion came from the shoulder, and your arm was an arch between your hand and the underpart of the muscle of your forearm. The fingers of the hand were not supposed to move by themselves. It was very unnatural.

I could no more do what Miss Rose and Palmer were asking me to do in those penmanship classes than I could eat an ice cream cone slowly. It was not my nature.

At home my grandfather, John Reynolds, worked with me. He had learned to write in a little school in Redruth, Cornwall, England, and he had a fine, firm, legible hand. When he put a word on paper, it looked as perfect as the model alphabet written over the blackboard in Miss Rose's homeroom. I remember the sample words my grandfather had me write. He thought they displayed the grace of the written word and they were words he himself wrote often. They were THE BALLSTON SPA NATIONAL BANK.

I greatly admired my grandfather but I was totally unable to duplicate his handwriting, and it strikes me now that I must have been coming of age because I recall not being very worried about penmanship. I wished I could write as he wrote but I simply felt he could and I couldn't.

My grandfather, I noted later, after I grew up, didn't do any better with his own son William. My uncle became a very successful commercial artist drawing charcoal sketches for *Vogue* magazine. As an artist he must have had a great ability to control the direction of the movement of his pen on paper, but his handwriting was as hard to read and childish-looking as mine.

It's a mystery to me why some people have good handwriting and why others have writing that's so hard to read. It's probably for the same reason that some people are six feet tall and others are not.

Maybe I'll ask Diane Sawyer to come over and hold my hand. I'll see if she can teach me how to be six feet tall.

Speaking of English . . .

Following are some miscellaneous observations on the use of the English language:

—Every few weeks I use a colon but I almost never use semicolons because I'm not sure what they indicate. I like dashes and three dots for punctuation. Three dots aren't officially recognized, though.

—Several times a year I look up the difference between *further* and *farther*. My reference books always say the same thing. *Farther* refers to distance. Everything else is *further*. You wouldn't say "farthermore."

—There are some phrases that should be given a long rest. Some examples:

The name of the game
World-class
What can I tell you?
No problem.
Have a nice day.
Will that be all?
More heat than light

I'd give up the phrase "having a dialogue" when I mean two people are talking, too.

—I don't use "whom" much, even though I know when I should. I use it sometimes when it's the obvious object in a sentence but I never use it at the start of a sentence even when it's the object. I say, "Who were you talking to?"

A lot of people get hold of a few grammatical points and are proud of themselves for knowing them. They don't miss a chance to point out the error in someone else's speech or writing.

" 'To whom are you speaking,' said he, for he had been to night school."

—In parts of Africa the natives have learned some English from the British and they've adapted it for their own pidgin English. Pidgin English is wonderfully colorful and inventive. For instance, they call one of their own native Africans who is uppity because he's been to London a "beento."

—Newspapers always put a period after Harry Truman's middle initial *S* even though it doesn't stand for anything more than that.

—An educated person is supposed to be able to use a hundred thousand words. A great language expert named Otto Jesperson once counted the different words in Shakespeare and found Shakespeare only used twenty thousand. He says there are only six thousand words in the Bible.

—One of my good books on English grammar says that when you use a quotation inside a sentence of your own, you don't start the quotation with a capital even though it's a sentence itself. For example: The President said last week that "we're not going to be fooled by the Russians." It seems wrong to me. I'd have capitalized "we're."

—I'm suspicious of a writer who uses "launder" when he means "wash," "inexpensive" for "cheap," "perspiration" for "sweat" or "wealthy" when he means "rich."

—I had an interesting ride into the city from the airport with Gloria Steinem. I liked her a lot better than I thought I would. She was talking about someone she knows who teaches writing courses. Gloria says the teacher just makes the students write and write. The teacher doesn't care what it is. Her theory is that if a person writes a lot, the person's natural personality will begin to appear after a while. Not only that, the person will begin to recognize himself or herself.

—People often replace the simple word *now* with something that sounds fancier to them. I don't know why they aren't satisfied with just plain "now." They say "currently," "presently" or "at this point in time."

—It makes fussy grammarians angry but I've forgotten any difference I once knew between *will* and *shall.* The distinction is so fine and so difficult to discern that I don't try. To me "I shall remember this" is the same as "I will remember this." The same goes for *should* and *would.*

—One of the few British words that American soldiers brought home to use was "queue" for "line."

Reporters

The other night I was watching Sam Donaldson, one of the best reporters in the news business, sitting in for Peter Jennings as anchorman on ABC's *World News Tonight.* Sam looked kind of pleased all over with himself, as if he'd been promoted. Shame on you, Sam!

Everyone wants a promotion because the money's better, but there needs to be some restructuring done in most companies regarding which jobs are considered most important and which get the highest pay. The whole idea of being boss or manager or anchorman needs to be rethought.

Being boss, for example, is just another job, and while it may be important, it's not necessarily more important than the jobs of other employees who work for the same company. Give the boss three phone extensions, his name on the office door so he can show his kids when he brings them in, and let him have a reserved spot in the parking lot but don't pay him nine times what anyone else gets. I don't notice many companies closing down when the boss doesn't show up for work or when he takes his month's vacation in summer and his ten days in winter.

In television, good reporters like Sam Donaldson are often promoted and made something else. Everyone forgets that Dan Rather, Walter Cronkite, David Brinkley, Peter Jennings and Tom Brokaw made their reputations as reporters. They were among the very best and, while I don't want to make any of them mad, because they're my friends, I liked all of them better as reporters than as anchormen. Those of us who are not anchormen have a secret disdain for anchormen even though we smile effusively when we pass them in the halls.

Making a good reporter an editor or an anchorman is like making a great chef the maître d' because he can make more money out front. Can't the networks find people who aren't good reporters to read the news? Getting facts and arranging them in an orderly way that will attract and then inform listeners has nothing to do with being able to read aloud. It takes ability to be an anchorman but it's a talent totally unrelated to a reporter's and a lesser one.

Even a lot of the television correspondents you're semifamiliar with are being turned into minianchormen and -women. Because their faces and styles of speaking are recognizable since they've been on the air a lot, they're considered more valuable as on-camera personalities than as reporters.

Good reporting takes a lot of time, and if correspondents do it all themselves, they have less time to be on the air. More than ever, TV reporters work with so-called producers, who are the actual reporters. The producers go to the location of the story, check it out, get the facts, arrange interview schedules, get the camera crews and then call the correspondent to come in and do twelve seconds on camera and the narration for a two-minute report prepared from information supplied not by the original source, but by the producer. The chef is out of the kitchen again.

On a newspaper, it's considered a promotion when a reporter is made an editor. Who wrote that? The editor should work for the reporter, helping, guiding and keeping the reporter from making a fool of himself or herself in print. (Reporters may stand and cheer.)

Every writer and every news organization has an obligation to get people to read or watch what they're about to tell them. That's what headlines are for. To this extent, news is show business. There's no sense putting the information out if no one's reading or watching. The danger comes for news organizations when they put too much emphasis on attracting a crowd and too little emphasis on telling the crowd anything once it's assembled. Get back in the kitchen where you belong, Sam!

A Few Cutting Remarks

I've just come from the barber and:
—My hair looks good now but it won't after I've slept on it tonight.
—If your hair looks as good after you've been to the barber as it did before you went, you've had a good haircut. This goes for women who go to the hairdresser, too.
—It shouldn't cost three times as much for a woman to have her hair cut as it costs a man. Confidentially, I think women are being taken.
—Men have their hair "cut" and women have theirs "done." The difference in price may be right there. Having it done sounds harder and more expensive than having it merely cut.

—I like my barber, Manny. He always asks me how my kids are and I tell him. He has kids too, and I never ask him how his are.

—I give 50 cents to the man who sweeps up and keeps my coat now. That's 15 cents more than a haircut cost me when I first started getting one from Mr. Kelly on Ontario Street.

—If Manny isn't ready when I get there, I look at *Playboy*. I wouldn't call it pornographic but it's pretty dirty and the naked girls look cheaper, less attractive than they did when they wore more clothes. I can't imagine buying a copy for $3.50.

—A barber always wants to wash your hair, and if you let him, he washes it before he cuts it. The worst thing about having a haircut is all the loose hairs that go down your collar the rest of the day. The time I want my hair washed at the barber's is after I've had a haircut.

—There are fewer and fewer barber poles outside barbershops and almost none of those move anymore. Why was a candy-striped pole a sign for a barbershop anyway?

—Manny's very quick with a pair of scissors. He never once has stabbed me with the scissors even though I always fall asleep and jerk my head up when I catch myself.

—When there are more than two barbers in a shop, they don't seem to get along very well among themselves.

—What would it cost, do you think, to have a barber's chair installed in your living room in front of the television set? Before I had it done, I'd want to test a dentist's chair to see which is best.

—A haircut looks worst the second day after you get it.

—An experienced barber can talk to you in the mirror as if he were looking you right in the eye.

—From what I learn from looking in barbershop windows in New York, prices run from a low of $6 to a high of $20. For $20, a man gets his hair "styled." "Styled," for a man, is more like a woman having hers "done."

—You're always seeing women who have just been to the beauty parlor. Half the time I feel like telling them they ought to demand their money back.

—You don't really appreciate how hard it is to give someone a good haircut until you've had kids and tried to save money by cutting their hair yourself.

—Getting a haircut is an event of some importance for men and having their hair done is an event of paramount importance for some women. If the possibility of something else comes up, "I have a hair appointment" takes precedence over almost everything else.

—They always have a lot of bottles of stuff. I've never tried any of it. I have a feeling it smells quite a bit.

—The worst mistake a barber can make is to try to give you your money's worth by taking off too much.

—When I left, two men were waiting for other barbers. One of them was reading *Playboy* and I thought to myself, "He looks like the type who would."

Short Skirts, Half Off

Short skirts come and go every few years as the fashion for women. When the dress designers are pushing short skirts, it's usually apparent on the streets that the designers and the people who write about women's clothes like short skirts better than the women expected to wear them. Except for a handful of women under thirty with great-looking legs, women hate short skirts.

A woman never seems comfortable in a short skirt. Watch a woman wearing one and you can see how careful she's being. She can't sit down, bend over, get out of a car or climb a flight of stairs without wondering about the angles of someone else's vision and about how much of herself is visible.

French women who go topless at the beaches along the Mediterranean seem casual and easy with their bareness but American women in short skirts are ill at ease. Their knees are always on their minds.

I hate clothes that constantly remind me of what I'm wearing and if I were a woman I certainly wouldn't wear short, tight skirts. The clothes I like best are the clothes I put on in the morning and forget until I take them off at night. Obviously most women feel the same. When a woman gets herself together for a special event, it's right that she should put on her drop-dead outfit even if she's a little uncomfortable in it. Wearing a skirt up to here on the street, in the middle of the day, is ridiculous and rude because it intrudes on the thoughts of everyone she passes.

People have never agreed on what to wear and I suppose it's more interesting that way. If you sit in a car and watch people coming and going on a busy street, you'd never guess they all come from the same planet. The variety is incredible.

One morning last spring, it was 37 degrees when I left the house. I noticed that a lot of the men going to work in their offices were dressed differently than they would have been on a 37-degree day in the middle of winter. Some of them weren't wearing any topcoat at all over their suit jackets. On the same kind of day in the middle of winter, they'd have had on overcoats, scarves and gloves. The temperature was the same this morning as it had been on several days in January but the men's dress had been decided on not by conditions but by the calendar.

One man who catches the same train I do every morning doesn't wear a coat all winter, and he never waits inside the station, either. He takes his position on the platform, jams his hands into his pockets with his newspaper under his arm and stands and waits, eyes straight ahead. It doesn't matter if it's below zero; he stands there and takes it like twenty lashes. I've never talked to him and I can't figure out why he does it. He must have admired the Spartans. Or maybe he thinks it's good for him, like a cold shower. Maybe he's showing the weather who's boss and proving it can't intimidate him. If he were a woman, he'd probably be wearing a miniskirt.

I've never believed the "thin blood" theory. That's the idea that people who grow up in warm climates are more affected by the cold than people who grow up in the North. The same people are always cold and the same people are always hot. It doesn't matter where they come from or what the conditions are. Being hot or cold is often more a state of mind than a condition of the blood. I work with a woman in a nearby office who always has a little electric heater near her. In the summer, when the rest of us are taking all the air conditioning we can get, she turns on her heater to fight it.

The businesswomen catching the train I take to work are a small minority and it's very apparent how much more of a problem clothes are for a woman than for a man in business. It's acceptable for a man to wear the same suit to the office day after day but a woman won't wear the same dress. I suspect this is something women have imposed on themselves because men don't care whether women wear the same dress to work every day or not . . . . as long as it doesn't have a short skirt.

Resolutions Don't Work

At the start of the New Year, when resolutions are so popular, it's disappointing to consider how infrequently resolving to do something really works. Breaking New Year's resolutions is as much a tradition as making them.

In my lifetime I've resolved to do a thousand things I have not done. I have been determined, on countless occasions, to stop doing the things I do badly. I've promised myself to think things through more carefully, not to be so careless with money, not to eat so much, not to make so many cutting remarks either in writing or in conversation and to finish every project I start. These are my weaknesses, and I must add to those my inability to correct them by resolving to do so.

Resolve simply doesn't seem to help anyone be a better person. Alcoholics who are determined not to drink again are unable to maintain their pledge without outside help; cigarette smokers are unable to stop smoking even as they lie dying of emphysema or lung cancer. Gamblers can't stop buying lottery tickets or playing the horses even though they know that in the long run they'll lose.

I'm sympathetic to everyone with a shortcoming who tries to correct it by determination. "Me too," I say.

We are led to put faith in resolutions because on rare occasions they do actually help. More than two years ago I noticed my arms were getting flabby and I decided to lift weights to rebuild my biceps. For what reasons I cannot say but I've stuck at curling a ten-pound weight every day for about five minutes an arm. I'm now up to doing it one hundred times with each arm and my biceps are noticeably firmer. I don't know why I've been able to do this exercise every day when I can't stick to a resolution not to eat so much ice cream. Whatever leads me to lift those weights also gives me false hope that someday I'll be thin through resolve. It's a mirage but I see it every day.

The news, recently announced, that there is scientific evidence that heredity has a great deal more to do with what we're like than the circumstances under which we live while we're growing up is seriously bad news for all of us. I hate to believe it's true. It means I'm hopelessly trapped being exactly the way I am for the rest of my life, and that isn't good enough. It means that all the people who are poor because they've been born without much ability to succeed are having babies born with the same natural inclination to failure.

The idea that our destiny is largely determined by the genes we inherit is a discouraging thought for many reasons. For example, it diminishes the importance of education. As much as I dislike accepting the theory, my failure at self-improvement has made me so skeptical of the power of resolution to improve me that I've all but given up making resolutions.

The only hard thing I've ever decided to do and then consistently done in my adult life is to get out of bed early every morning. I've stuck at rising before the crowd through light and dark, warm and cold. Getting going early seems to be responsible for most of any success I've had. I was congratulating myself on this just now as I thought it over but I couldn't help wondering how it fit into my belief that resolutions are almost never kept.

It suddenly occurred to me that the chances are that determination and strength of character have nothing whatsoever to do with getting up in the morning. I can stop congratulating myself on having followed through on a resolution. It's simpler than that. I get up because I can't sleep.

So, Happy New Year, but for better or worse, you might as well resign yourself to being about the same this year as you were last. Chances are, those resolutions aren't going to improve your personality or lose you a pound.

Ticket to Nowhere

Things never went very well for Jim Oakland. He dropped out of high school because he was impatient to get rich, but after dropping out he lived at home with his parents for two years and didn't earn a dime. He finally got a summer job working for the highway department holding up a sign telling oncoming drivers to be careful of the workers ahead. Later that same year, he picked up some extra money putting flyers under the windshield wipers of parked cars.

Jim was twenty-three before he left home and went to Florida, hoping his ship would come in down there. He never lost his desire to get rich but first he needed money for the rent, so he took a job near

Fort Lauderdale for $4.50 an hour servicing the goldfish aquariums
kept by the cashier's counter in a lot of restaurants.

Jim was paid in cash once a week by the owner of the goldfish
business and the first thing he did was go to the little convenience store
near where he lived and buy $20 worth of lottery tickets. He was really
determined to get rich.

Recently, the lottery jackpot in Florida reached $54 million. Jim
woke up nights thinking what he could do with $54 million. During
the days, he daydreamed about it. One morning he was driving along
the main street in the boss's old pickup truck with six tanks of goldfish
in back. As he drove past a BMW dealer, he looked at the new models
in the window. He saw the car he wanted in the showroom window but
unfortunately he didn't see the light change. The car in front of him
stopped short and Jim slammed on his brakes. The fish tanks slid
forward. The tanks broke, the water gushed out and the goldfish slith-
ered and flopped all over the back of the truck. Some fell off into the
road.

It wasn't a good day for the goldfish or for Jim, of course. He knew
he'd have to pay for the tanks and 75 cents each for the fish and if it
weren't for the $54 million lottery, he wouldn't have known which way
to turn. He had that lucky feeling.

For the tanks and the dead goldfish, the boss deducted $114 of Jim's
$180 weekly pay. Even though he didn't have enough left for the rent
and food, Jim doubled the amount he was going to spend on lottery
tickets. He never needed the $54 million more.

Jim had this system. He took his age and added the last four digits
of the telephone number of the last girl he dated. He called it his lucky
number . . . even though the last four digits changed quite often and
he'd never won with his system. Everyone laughed at Jim and said he'd
never win the lottery.

Jim put down $40 on the counter that week and the man punched
out his tickets. Jim stowed them safely away in his wallet with last
week's tickets. He never threw away his lottery tickets until at least a
month after the drawing just in case there was a mistake. He'd heard
of mistakes.

Jim listened to the radio all afternoon the day of the drawing. The
people at the radio station he was listening to waited for news of the
winning numbers to come over the wires and, even then, the announcers didn't rush to get them on. The station manager thought the people
running the lottery ought to pay to have the winning numbers broadcast, just like any other commercial announcement.

Jim fidgeted while they gave the weather and the traffic and the news. Then they played more music. All he wanted to hear were those numbers.

"Well," the radio announcer said finally, "we have the lottery numbers some of you have been waiting for. You ready?

"The winning number," the announcer said, "is eight-six-zero-five-three-nine. I'll repeat that—eight-six-zero-five-three-nine." Jim was still a loser.

I thought that with all the human-interest stories about lottery winners, we ought to have a story about one of the several million losers.

The Silent Sound of Music

At some point in life, everyone wants to learn how to play a musical instrument. My mother bought me a brass bugle for $5 when I was nine. I treasured it, polished it and tried to learn to play it. I learned how to get some noise out of the bugle but never what you'd call music.

Jew's harps became the fad one year. Every kid had one. It was like whistling—either you could do it or you couldn't. I could play a recognizable version of "Turkey in the Straw" on that, but another year Uncle Bill gave me a good Hohner harmonica for Christmas and I never mastered the trick of sucking in and blowing out at the right time.

I took one piano lesson in college and Bill Chernokowsky stepped on the back of my hand in football practice the next day and that permanently concluded my efforts to become a world-renowned musician.

The world must be filled with unsuccessful musical careers like mine, and it's probably a good thing. We don't need a lot of bad musicians filling the air with unnecessary sounds. Some of the professionals are, bad enough.

Instruments come and go in popularity and some go and never come back. I hardly ever hear an accordion anymore. The lute, the mandolin, the ukulele and even the harp seem to be instruments of the past. The saxophone is still popular but the trombone seems to be disappearing. It's too hard to hold up, probably.

The most enduring musical instruments are the violin and the piano, although people don't have pianos in their homes the way they once did. Most pop-music groups don't use either pianos or violins but the instruments will outlive the kind of music that's popular with young people now.

The violin and piano take more work and ability than many modern musicians have the time or patience to master. They want something they can bang on. Their idea of music is a noise so loud that nuances of sound are lost in the cacophony of reverberations produced on the eardrum. The favorite instruments of the rock musicians aren't made to be played so much as beaten. Drums are favorites and, while jazz drummers like Gene Krupa and Buddy Rich were artists, most modern-music drummers might as well be swinging a baseball bat.

The change of the guitar's standing among musical instruments is one of the most interesting recent developments. From the choice of the romantic, blanket-robed, gay *caballero* on horseback, the guitar has gone in two opposite directions. It has become a favorite of a group of serious musicians who hear in it sounds its Spanish inventors never dreamed of. And then, of course, electrified and plugged in, it's the weapon of choice for the modern rock singer who needs something to hold on to.

If all you read about music were the billboards on the concert halls, you'd think every good musician was well known and making big money. Our neighbor Ed Wright is a superb guitarist who plays in what I think of as the Andrés Segovia style. If Ed ever makes it big, he'll have good stories to tell about how hard it was getting started.

Four years ago Ed gave us a cassette of Christmas music he'd recorded on his own equipment, and it's a gem. It has every Christmas carol you've ever heard, played with clarity and finesse. Just for fun, I played it for myself on the Fourth of July last year, and I play it often at Christmas. I don't get tired of his sophisticated, understated style, but Ed's never going to get rich giving cassettes to his friends, and no business is tougher to break into than the recorded-music business. It's not so much how you play as who you play. I have the feeling you could be Arthur Rubinstein your whole life and not be discovered if you didn't get some kind of lucky break.

If I'd stuck with the bugle or the harmonica, do you think I'd be playing in the New York Philharmonic today?

Finishing Refinishing

Is there anyone reading this who hates to start a job but loves to finish one?

If there is, I'd like to get in touch with you because I've got at least a dozen jobs I've started that I never got around to finishing. Maybe we could get together. As a matter of fact, I'd love to have you living next door. We could make beautiful music together, with you finishing all the jobs I start and then abandon.

See if any of these appeal to you:

The air conditioner in one of the upstairs bedrooms doesn't fit in the window very well, and in the winter a lot of cold air seeps in. I started to fix it by buying one of those rolls of felt you stuff in the cracks. I also got some insulating material and special tape to do the job after looking it over carefully. Unfortunately, that's as far as I got. If you'd like to drop by to get the satisfaction of finishing it, you're welcome.

I got a good start on my taxes too. I was determined not to be in such bad shape next spring at income-tax time so several months ago I marked a folder IMPORTANT—IRS and started putting receipts, bank statements and canceled checks in it. It was a good start but I didn't keep it up. I notice, for instance, that since April 30 I haven't made any new entries in the diary the IRS tells you to keep.

If you like accounting and would enjoy finishing this kind of book-keeping work, I'd love to have your help. In exchange, I'll come over to your house and start a lot of things and then not finish them for you. That's where I excel.

The Sunday papers are piling up in the back room. I started reading all of them but never finished. I know there's a lot of good stuff in them so I can't throw them away but I never seem to get at reading them.

There are two articles I want to read in the travel section of May 8 and at least four editorials I started reading but put down when the phone rang. I also meant to look up the story of the fellow I knew at work who got married.

If finishing reading newspapers is your kind of thing, let's work out a deal.

Are you, by any chance, handy around the house? You aren't a careful woodworker who isn't satisfied until everything's just right, are you? Because if you are, I have a lot of projects I've started but haven't finished.

I began making a little coffee table for the living room last August but then I got sidetracked because I had to make a lean-to for the two big garbage containers out by the garage. To tell you the truth, I haven't quite finished that either, because it was supposed to have doors on it but I haven't put the doors on because I don't have any hinges. Maybe I'll quit what I'm doing and go to the hardware store for hinges.

While I'm there, I could get some varnish for that little table. I took the little table down in the basement one day to sand it but I couldn't find the right sandpaper down there so I just left it and I can't varnish the table until I sand it. Before I sand it, I ought to glue that stretcher between the legs that's loose. It makes the table wobbly.

I'm not sure, though. The table may be wobbly because the floor's a little uneven. I rented a big sander from one of those rent-all places. I thought it might smooth out the bumps in the wood floor. I sanded some of the floor but something came up and I had to take the sander back and I never got at it again. Anyone want to finish fixing the table and sanding the floor?

A lot of people are better at starting a job than they are at finishing it but if I'm ever offered a teaching job at a good college, I'd like to give a course in how to start more than you can finish. You won't find anyone better at that than I am.

By the way, I wrote some letters this morning but never mailed them. Do you like mailing letters?

Living Longer but Less

It always seems wrong for the head doctor in our country to be called the "surgeon general." Dr. C. Everett Koop wasn't even a general in real life. He was an admiral. Surgeon admiral?

Dr. C. Everett Koop fooled many of his critics who didn't want him put in the job by being a surprisingly good and active surgeon general. It was Koop, more than any other person, who pushed the country to stop smoking.

Smokers are so uncomfortable smoking around other people now that you see more and more people smoking as they walk along the street. They take any opportunity to do it when they aren't in a room or office with other people they may offend. When I take the train home from work, there is an attractive young woman who gets off at my station who heads for the door ten minutes before the train arrives. She gets her cigarette and her match out so that she can light up the instant the door opens. I look at her and think to myself, "Boy, I'd like to have the life she's throwing away."

One of Dr. Koop's most persistent themes was that a lot of Americans are eating themselves into the grave with bad nutritional habits.

Like most Americans, I read these remarks, think I ought to take them seriously and then forget them the next time I sit down at the table. If that girl who smokes could see me eat, she'd probably want the life I'm eating myself out of.

The question is this, though: How much time and effort should any of us spend in our lives trying to prolong our lives? My good friend Harry Reasoner is a heavy cigarette smoker with serious lung problems. He still smokes. He can't stop smoking and he justifies it by saying it gives him so much pleasure that he's willing to die a few years early in exchange for it. Dumb.

I've never smoked and if someone has never been hooked on cigarettes, it's easy for that person to think anyone who smokes cigarettes is dumb and careless with his or her life. I'm hooked on food, and I suppose it's just as bad and my attitude is probably the same as Harry's. I enjoy eating so much that, at what seems to me to be considerable distance from death, I'm willing to take the risk.

Last night, I made strawberry ice cream for dessert, ate two dishes of it at the table and then cleaned out the ice cream freezer with a spoon later. Dumb.

Unfortunately, there's no label on homemade strawberry ice cream saying, WARNING: THE SURGEON GENERAL HAS DETERMINED THAT TWO DISHES OF HOMEMADE STRAWBERRY ICE CREAM CAN BE DANGEROUS TO YOUR HEALTH!

Doctors do the right thing trying to make us all aware of the everyday things we do that are bad for us, but what would life be like if we all took all the good advice we get on how to live longer?

Even the first moment, being born, is hazardous. Ten of every thousand infants die in their first year of life. Would we take the chance?

If we survived infancy, we wouldn't want to be put in a crib, because there were 5,945 crib deaths last year. Too dangerous.

As children, we'd never get to school. Going to school involves crossing streets. Last year 7,157 pedestrians were killed.

If we were setting out to live as long as possible without taking any chances, we'd avoid steak, butter, eggs and most other food with any taste. We wouldn't travel, have sex or drink coffee, bourbon or beer. We wouldn't even dare drink the water in some places. We wouldn't travel and we'd stay away from dark alleys. We'd sterilize every doorknob before we took hold of it to turn.

We certainly wouldn't go anywhere in a car or an airplane. In 1987, 1,428 people were killed in airplane accidents and 44,822 in automobile accidents in the United States alone. Who needs it?

The medical experts tell you to exercise but you're always reading of some jogger keeling over. Why chance it? You certainly wouldn't get me out on a golf course with the number of people hit by lightning. Eighty-five people struck dead last year.

If we want to last forever, we should stay home, eat whole grains and vegetables, breathe through a mask, boil the water, avoid making close friends. Have a complete medical checkup often. See your dentist twice a year, avoid eye strain and loud noises.

Now to check the refrigerator to see if there's any of that strawberry ice cream left from last night.

PEOPLE

Horowitz, the Heavyweight Champ

In one twelve-hour period, I watched three hours of television comprising the best and one of the worst broadcasts I ever saw.

I'd be curious to know how many people watched both the Michael Spinks–Larry Holmes heavyweight boxing match and the Vladimir Horowitz piano concert from Moscow.

If it were up to me, I'd outlaw boxing as a sport, and yet I confess it holds a certain fascination for my baser instincts. There's no question its brutality is part of the fascination it holds for people who watch it. Two men are put into a small, fenced-in area together for the purpose of trying to hurt each other. The great Sugar Ray Robinson once said that he urinated blood for a week after a fight from blows he'd taken to the kidneys. And he took fewer than most fighters. You can imagine the effect of those same blows to a man's head.

Boxing appeals to the worst in everyone who watches it. The crowd at a boxing match are distant relatives to the crowds of Romans who came to the Colosseum to watch the gladiators kill each other.

It was one o'clock Saturday night—Sunday morning, actually—before I got to bed. I was ashamed of myself for having stayed up to watch such a dismal spectacle. It was as if I'd sneaked in to see a dirty movie. The fight and its outcome made it clear that boxing wasn't much better than those phony wrestling matches. It seemed clear beyond a doubt that Larry Holmes won, but Michael Spinks was declared the winner.

In an interview after the fight and just before I turned off the television set, Larry Holmes ended it with a tasteless vulgarity that was a perfectly fitting conclusion to a terrible evening.

The following morning, Marge and I had a leisurely breakfast lasting more than an hour while we read the Sunday paper. The Sunday paper always makes me feel like part of civilization again.

Toward the end of breakfast, at nine o'clock, I turned on *Sunday Morning with Charles Kuralt.* Charles had gone to Moscow with Vladimir Horowitz to broadcast the triumphant return to his homeland of one of the great pianists of all time. The broadcast was extended from its usual ninety minutes to two hours and it was simply the best television broadcast of all time. It was everything civilized, thoughtful and peaceful that the fight the previous evening was not. It was a miracle to me that I was watching it on the same little screen.

If you didn't see it, it's hard to tell you about it. Horowitz was magnificent and Charles Kuralt was very little less than that in writing and speaking the words that gave more clarity, shape and drama to the event than a mere piano recital would have had.

"Next comes one of the most powerful piano pieces Mozart ever wrote," Kuralt said, "very hard to play. Most concert pianists frankly duck this sonata. Horowitz plays it as if Mozart wrote it for him."

Then we watched and listened and appreciated how difficult it was.

Seeing one man play a piano for two hours doesn't sound like good television but it was better than good by a whole lot. It was smashing.

During the latter part of the concert, watching this eighty-one-year-old genius play, I found mist forming in my eyes for some mysterious reason I could not explain. I was not sad. I was exultant. It had something to do with my pride, at that very moment, in being part of the same civilization that this great and endearing man playing the piano was part of.

Almost at the same instant I felt the suggestion of tears in my eyes, the television camera left Horowitz's fingers on the keyboard and dissolved to the face of a Soviet citizen in the audience. He did not look like the enemy. His eyes were closed, his head tilted slightly backward so that his face was up . . . and one lone teardrop ran down his cheek.

It was the same teardrop running down mine.

A Genius Lost

Most of us find mathematics, physics and all the exact sciences too hard. We pretend our talent is more like that of the poet, the playwright, or the painter of abstract art. That's what I pretend but I know I'm kidding myself.

After all these years, I'm ready to concede that most of the good things in life come from the progress made by the mathematicians, the physicists and the practitioners of all the other exact sciences. Books, television programs, plays, paintings and all things cultural are only possible because the sciences enable us to live with ease and comfort and considerable time off from the work of feeding ourselves.

The talent of the poet, on the other hand, is not of much help to the scientist. Einstein may have enjoyed Shakespeare but he could have worked out his theory of relativity without ever having read *Hamlet.*

It is unlikely that many of you ever heard of one of the greatest Americans of this century. He died in Los Angeles in 1988 at the age of sixty-nine and he may have been the smartest human alive. His name was Richard Feynman.

Richard Feynman was a physicist who worked, as a young man, as one of the leaders in the atom-bomb project that led to the end of World War II. He went on to do his most important work in fields of theoretical physics so impenetrable to a mind like mine that there's no way for me to mention what they were. Feynman was so smart he could have been anything he wanted to be. He was, in fact, an accomplished painter and writer, but he was a physicist first. His brilliance came from his ability to master and simplify complex mathematical formulas, and his greatness came from a personality that would not have anything to do with nonsense.

He became more widely known than he ever had been before as a member of the presidential commission studying the disastrous flight of the space shuttle *Challenger.*

Sitting at a table with other investigators in Washington, he surprised everyone, and probably saved several million dollars in the investigation, by calling for a glass of ice water. When it came, Richard Feynman took a piece of the infamous gasket called the O-ring and dunked it in the ice water. After a brief time, he took it out and pinched it with a small clamp. The material from the O-ring did not bounce back to its original shape. In less than a minute Feynman had shown that the material was not suited for cold weather. That was Feynman's genius: making complex things simple enough for anyone to understand.

Much of the language of science, medicine, government and law is nonsense designed to exclude outsiders so they won't discover that, basically, the specialists' work is not so complex as it seems. Richard Feynman would have no part of that language. He spoke simply and directly of the most complex things.

"There were a lot of fools at the conference," he once said after returning from a scientific symposium, "pompous fools—and pompous fools drive me up the wall. Ordinary fools are all right; you can talk to them and try to help them. But pompous fools—guys who are covering it all over and impressing people as to how wonderful they are with all this hocus-pocus—that I cannot stand."

In spite of his impatience with people in his field he was much loved and respected by them.

"He's the most creative theoretical physicist of his time and a true genius," said Sidney Drell, former president of the American Physical Society. "He has touched, with his unique creativity, just about every field of physics."

Hans Bethe of Cornell University said Feynman performed magic.

"A magician does things that nobody else could ever do and that seem completely unexpected," Dr. Bethe said, "and that's Feynman."

Richard Feynman spent most of his life as a researcher and teacher.

"I don't believe I can really do without teaching," he said. "The reason is, I have to have something so that when I don't have any ideas and I'm not getting anywhere I can say to myself, 'At least I'm living; at least I'm doing something; I'm making some contribution.' "

We should all make such a contribution as Richard Feynman made.

My Three Friends

Bessie Reynolds was ninety. Bill Kramer was thirty-seven. Merle Miller was sixty-seven. They didn't know each other. No one but me knew all three. They had nothing in common, except me as a friend, until recently when each of them died.

Bessie must have had fewer enemies than anyone who ever lived. I say "fewer" but I can't imagine that she had any.

Bessie didn't have too good a life. Her left shoulder was noticeably smaller than her right so that she was slightly deformed. Her mother died when Bessie was two and her father left Bessie to be brought up by friends or relatives. She spent several years in the home of my mother's parents and that's how she got to be sort of an aunt of mine.

Bessie worked as a milliner in the days when women always wore hats. She had a little house of her own and she kept it the way we'd all like our houses to be kept. You could drop in on her unexpectedly and nothing was out of place. She made the bed when she got up, did the dishes as soon as she'd eaten, picked up the papers after she'd read them and then vacuumed.

Most of her last twenty-five years were spent in the sunny little back room behind the parlor she seldom used, with her sewing, her puzzles and the television set. It always seemed as if Bessie had lots of visitors, but twenty-four hours is a long day and I'm afraid Bessie was alone most of her life.

Bill Kramer was almost never alone. He filled his life with all the good things there are. When he and his wife, Angela, became parents seven months ago, they didn't have a baby, they had twins.

I spent just one month with Bill but it was an intense thirty days and I got to know him well. He and his friend Dave Wright were the pilots of a big Sikorsky helicopter in which we flew across the United States and back in May 1983.

When I read that a Sikorsky helicopter, provided to King Hussein during his visit here, had crashed, killing all four on board, I was worried. They didn't give out names, except to say Hussein was not on board, but I knew they would have given President Reagan's visitor the very best, and that was Bill Kramer.

Bill was one of those who knew all about everything. He didn't fake it; he knew. You could talk to him about ballet, Plato or how ethyl added to gasoline affects combustion in an engine. He must have been one of the Air Force Academy's prize students in 1971.

I'm not a nervous flier but you're always aware of how tenuous your position is when you're several thousand feet above the ground in a machine that weighs five tons and has no wings. The reason for the crash has not been determined but I can tell the investigators one thing. It was not Bill Kramer's fault. It must have been sabotage or mechanical failure. Bill didn't make mistakes in the air and he didn't take any chances. None. I'd often plead with him to get in a position for a better camera angle but if he thought it was in any way unwise he just wouldn't do it. I came to realize my life was in the hands of one of the best helicopter pilots who ever lived. Now, one of the best who ever died.

You should have heard of my friend Merle Miller. He wrote books.

"I've written a classic," he said with amused delight the last time I saw him. "My Truman book has been in print for ten years now and that's the definition of a classic!"

I first met Merle in London in 1942 when he was with *Yank* magazine and I was a reporter for *The Stars and Stripes*.

It was thirty years before I realized Merle was a homosexual. He distanced himself from the world and even from his friends, but when I was with him I always wondered how another human being could reach me with so many perceptive thoughts and yet have this hidden side I could not understand.

I don't know what my three friends would have thought of each other but I thought the world of all three.

My Friend Cary Grant

For the past four years, I've been thinking of Cary Grant as my friend.

I was sitting at my desk one day, pushing pieces of paper around, pretending I was working, when the phone rang. No matter how good telephone connections get, you usually can tell a long-distance call. This was one.

"Mr. Rooney?" the voice inquired.

"Yes," I said in a not-very-friendly tone. I'm initially gruff with calls from strangers because they're usually a waste of time and I'm seldom pleased to get one.

The next words the woman spoke abruptly changed my attitude toward the call.

"Cary Grant would like to speak to you. Will you speak to him?"

Will I speak to Cary Grant? Would I be too busy if Katharine Hepburn called? Could I spare a few minutes for Jimmy Stewart?

"Gosh, sure," I said, because the woman spoke in a manner that suggested the call was the real thing. She sounded more like a wife than a secretary, too.

"Mr. Rooney," the familiar voice said, "this is Cary Grant."

I'm not easily impressed with celebrities, but Cary Grant was a special person and I was mildly flabbergasted to actually be talking to him. He sounded more like himself than his best imitator.

"Good to talk to you," I mumbled weakly, groping for something gracious or clever to say and failing to find it.

"Say," he continued, "why don't you do something on all this packaging? It's getting so difficult to get into these packages we all receive.

"They have all this new kind of tape . . . very difficult indeed," he said.

"It's a good idea," I said. "I appreciate your calling. Thanks very much." By now I was just extending the connection with empty words. I didn't have anything to say and wouldn't have been able to think of it if I had.

That's the extent of my personal friendship with Cary Grant. It was one of the best telephone calls I ever got and certainly the least expected. I've been nervous ever since about who's out there watching.

Now Cary Grant is gone and I feel sad. For what reason I don't know but I never got around to doing the packaging piece he suggested while he was alive.

It isn't the first time I've had the feeling I let someone down. There are a few haunting memories of times in my past when I've disappointed people closer to me than Cary Grant.

In 1949 I was out of work and broke. I'd spent much of the previous year, with no income, writing a book about postwar Germany that didn't sell. We had our first child and it was a terrible feeling not to be able to support my family. I've never forgotten what it was like.

My mother and father would have given me money if I'd asked them for it but I couldn't. It seemed as though it would have disappointed them too much. Instead I went to my Uncle Bill and asked if I could borrow $500.

He must have been disappointed that I had to ask, too, but if he was, he never let on. He gave me the $500 and I made too much of a point of saying and repeating that it was a loan I intended to pay back within a year.

Three years went by. I was in better shape by then and although $500 wasn't going to be easy, I decided it was time I restored Uncle Bill's faith in me by repaying the loan.

Uncle Bill died that week.

It still hurts me to write that. Uncle Bill must have died disappointed, even though it is unlikely he would have accepted the $500 if I'd offered it to him.

Even though it cannot really be compared, Cary Grant's death reminded me of Uncle Bill and my unpaid debt to him. I waited too long again.

I wish now that I'd done something with the idea Cary Grant gave me on the telephone four years ago. He must have been just a little disappointed every time he watched me.

Song of the Unsung Heroes

Some of the best writing in a newspaper is often on the obituary page. I read the obit page of my newspaper, not because of any morbid fascination with the predictability of the eventual demise of each of us, but because it's interesting and because I feel an obligation to spend at least a few minutes considering the life's work of some people who have contributed more than their share to our fragile civilization.

The obituaries that move me the most are those that relate the substantial accomplishments of persons I've never heard of. It makes me feel terrible that I didn't know of the good things these people did while they were alive. The very least I can do is read of that person's accomplishments with respectful attention.

This thought came to mind when I read that Sidney Cohen died in Los Angeles. As a doctor, Sidney Cohen had done extensive research on the effect of drugs on the mind. He didn't do television commercials telling kids to stay away from drugs; he did the hard work. He set out to prove exactly why drugs should be avoided. Commendable as preaching the evils of drugs may be, it doesn't compare in importance with the work of someone who sets out to define, specifically, why drugs are bad to take. When someone says "Why not?" we'll know because of Dr. Cohen's work.

"Man," Dr. Cohen said, "has the capacity to be more than a flower-picking primate. We need more thinking, not less, and a society that does not value trained intelligence is doomed."

They ought to engrave that great line on Dr. Cohen's headstone. How many of you ever heard of Gordon B. Sherman? Not me. Not until I read his obituary. Mr. Sherman created the chain of Midas muffler shops but he turned out to be more maverick than businessman. He originally worked for his father's automobile-parts company. His idea for a muffler chain caught on and he became president of the company with his father as chairman of the board.

When Midas profits began to drop off, Gordon started fighting with his father, Nate. It turns out that Gordon was contributing company money to all sorts of good causes. He gave money to Ralph Nader, for example, and he also sponsored a group of Chicago businessmen whose goals were to help the poor, end discrimination and improve the environment.

Gordon's father objected and Gordon was forced out of the company. Eventually he moved to California and became a photographer and music teacher.

It's not the kind of story that comes to mind when you think of Midas muffler.

A headline that read THE REV. J. JOSEPH LYNCH, 92 caught my eye. As an omnivorous newspaper reader, I suppose I've read Father Lynch's name a hundred times over the years. He was a Jesuit priest and one of the world's greatest experts on earthquakes.

Although religion and science are uncomfortable bedfellows, Father Lynch was a member of the American Association for the Advancement of Science and was once president of the New York Academy of Sciences. When there was an earthquake or the threat of an earthquake anywhere in the world, it was Father Lynch all the reporters called for information.

So many of us prattle on with more opinions than knowledge that we can't afford to lose as genuine an expert in any field as Father Lynch was in his . . . or as Dr. Herbert Friedmann, who died in Laguna Hills, California, was in his. Dr. Friedmann knew more about birds than just about anyone ever has.

He once wrote a book about the cowbird, describing how devious it is. The cowbirds, he wrote, know how to trick other birds into raising their young for them so they won't have to bother.

Hail to you all and farewell! Farewell, Sidney Cohen and Gordon Sherman. Farewell, Father Lynch and Herbert Friedmann. It would be a better world if all of us did as much with our lives as you've done with yours!

Dinner at Eight

We were invited to dinner at Miriam and Jack Paar's house the other night. One of the things I noticed about the handful of well-known people I've met is how interesting they are in person. You can usually see how they got there.

Jack Paar is as good at the dinner table as he ever was on the air and, as I sat there listening to him, I had this crass, commercial thought. I thought about how much good material he was throwing away on his guests. A director could have taped the dinner and made a show out of it. Which, come to think of it, wouldn't be a bad idea.

I suppose any performer throws away a lot that could be sold. There are people who'd pay to listen to Vladimir Horowitz when he was just amusing himself on the piano or pay to sit in the bedroom while Luciano Pavarotti sang in the shower. Not that Jack plays the piano or sings.

The Paars are great hosts. I don't look forward to having to pay them back by inviting them to our house, though, for several reasons. Not only are they better hosts than we are but I suspect that Jack is a better host than he is a guest. He's itchy. A host can be itchy and move around among his guests but a guest has to pretty much stay put.

There's no doubt some people are natural-born hosts and others are natural-born guests. Jack is a host.

There are several things a good host does. When we arrived most of the sixteen other guests were already there. Jack greeted us before we were three feet inside the door, making us feel as though he'd been waiting for us to come. I've gone places where I've thought I was in the wrong house.

"Hey," Jack said, grabbing our arms, "I want you to meet some folks. Some of them you already know." He introduced us around without missing a name, making everyone feel special in the process.

Paar has an infectious enthusiasm for life. You have a good time when you're with him because his attitude is catching. He genuinely wanted us to see his friends, his new house, his daughter Randi and his grandson Andy. Particularly, he wanted us to see his grandson Andy.

At dinner I sat next to Peggy Cass. She'd be on my all-star list of people to sit next to at dinner. She's still limping from a medical disaster I hate to retell because it makes me think about it again. She had cartilage trouble with one knee and entered a New York hospital to have a fairly routine operation to fix it.

The surgeon went into the good knee in error. Realizing his mistake, he took Peggy back into surgery and did the joint he should have done in the first place. It left her unable to walk for months.

Peggy sued the doctor and won more than $400,000. A judge reduced it to $200,000 but she's still so mad she won't accept that.

After dinner, we left the table and Jack took me down into his basement. He wanted to show me the little battery-driven tricycle he'd bought his grandson. The basement looked like a cement-floored gymnasium with almost no clutter at all. It was perfect for a grandson's indoor tricycling.

The Paars' home could have been a picture in a magazine. Everything was in its place. The Christmas tree wasn't even dropping its needles. We could never make our house look like that. Their house is bigger and grander in every way but I know the answer. It isn't the house, it's the occupants. The only way we'd ever get our house looking like the Paars' would be to have them move in for a year.

We'd swap. I'd bring over my old newspapers, the magazines I've been meaning to read, the ticket stubs I've saved as mementos of old Giant games, the one new pigskin glove I can't throw away and some of the papers the kids wrote when they were in the third grade. I'd spread stuff like that around their living room and have the Paars' house looking like our house in no time.

Meanwhile, they'd make ours look like a page from a magazine.

Not Even Skin Deep

Three of the women in the room I was in recently while the Miss America Pageant was being televised were better-looking than most of the contestants.

The winner, Kaye Lani Rae Rafko, was attractive but not nearly so good-looking as Fawn Hall. At least six of the young women parading around pretending to be modest while they exposed as much of themselves as the committee allows, were several hundred yards short of being beautiful. During the bathing-suit display, all but three of the girls looked better from the back than from the front.

The Miss America contest proves one thing: The best-looking

women no longer enter beauty contests. All the Miss America contest decides is the best-looking girl among the kind of girls who enter beauty contests.

We didn't turn on the television set until late and didn't watch all of the pageant even then, but we got a good look at all the girls. It was interesting that none of the women watching where I was objected to the men watching. None of them said, "Turn that thing off." I think that was because none of those women looked bad in comparison with the contestants. And the guests were certainly a lot brighter.

The Miss America Pageant officials may not know it, but it has become a comedy show. People in their living rooms sit around doing more laughing than ogling. Most of the laughter comes during the so-called talent contest. The performances range from pitiful to not bad. Few are what anyone would call good. The new Miss America did a pretty fair and athletic hula dance that gave viewers a lesson in anatomy. One of the pop singers was quite good, but there were a lot of performances that could only be described as laughable. One poor girl tried to do some kind of ballet but couldn't get her feet three inches off the floor in her most determined jump.

"I couldn't even do that good," some kind soul next to me said, but that was not the point. My friend hadn't volunteered to do it in front of a television audience of millions. The Miss America contestant had volunteered and, in so doing, showed a confidence in herself that she had no business having.

There's something terribly wrong about the whole idea of the Miss America contest the way it's run now. All they'd really have to do to pick a winner is parade the girls out on a stage in their bathing suits and let the audience or a panel of judges decide which girl had the prettiest face and shapeliest body.

They don't do it that way. To make it into a television show, they've had to find a way to stretch it out. They pretend the competition involves the girls' minds as well as their bodies. Spare us the talent competition and the little talks the girls give! Just let us look at them and we'll decide who Miss America ought to be in about five minutes.

Atlantic City has turned out to be a fitting place for the Miss America contest. The Jersey Shore, from Sandy Hook to Cape May, is 125 miles of some of the prettiest oceanfront in the world. Nowhere have people moved in and destroyed the beauty of nature in a more thorough way than in Atlantic City. The gauche gambling casinos form a solid facade that hides the magnificent ocean shoreline from all but a few people who have rooms with a view. The hotels are all got up like the Miss America contestants. You sense there's beauty hidden there somewhere, but you can't see it for all the gilt and falseness.

There are people who go to Atlantic City for a weekend and never get any closer to a look at the Atlantic Ocean than the slot machine in the lobby nearest the boardwalk. Watching a little of the Miss America contest, I had the feeling we didn't get to know anything more about those girls than the gamblers got to know about the ocean.

Happy Birthday, Miss Jordan!

Miss Edith Jordan
Market Square
South Paris, Maine

It's great to be able to write to wish you a happy one hundredth birthday on January 15. I've read about a lot of people one hundred years old but I've never known anyone who was before.

When you were a teacher in grade school at the Albany Academy in the 1930s you must have been five times as old as I was. You aren't even twice as old as I am now so I feel closer to you.

I say I know you and I do, even though it's been half your life since I've seen you . . . fifty years. Once you know a person, though, you don't forget. I've certainly never forgotten you.

I suppose I'd be surprised at how you look. I have a perfect picture in my mind of how you looked when I knew you and I'm happy with that. You were never Miss America, but you always looked the way a teacher ought to look.

When I see my old school friends, we often talk about you. Did you know that? Except for our parents, you were the first real authority in our lives. We were lucky. You were so direct, patient and fair.

Are you still stern? You were quite stern, you know. You didn't stand for a lot of horsing around. You were the sternest teacher I ever had but all the kids liked you anyway. A lot of teachers think they can get in good with students by being nice and easy in class but a teacher can't fool students. Kids know when they're being taught and when they aren't.

I wish I'd been a better student. You were a better teacher than

I was a student. My mother always had a lot of excuses for why I wasn't doing well in school.

"He's the youngest in his class," she'd say.

"He's a very shy boy. He works best when he's alone."

My mother was wrong, though. It was because I was dumb, although you never made me feel dumb.

Do you think teachers are as good as they used to be? There are so many jobs that pay more money than teaching does that a capable person has to be a martyr to stick at teaching. When you were teaching jobs were scarce and a good school had its choice of teachers. Teaching was one of the few jobs an educated woman could get, too.

A lot of people work their whole lives to make enough money to retire on. You did better than that. You worked your whole life to make enough memories to retire on. If you live to be 150, I'm sure you won't run out of memories.

A mother and a father who bring up children sensibly and well take great satisfaction from that. A good teacher has that same satisfaction multiplied a thousand times. Somewhere in the world, someone is doing something because you got them started doing it that way thirty, forty or fifty years ago.

To tell you the truth, I can't remember anything specific you taught me. You had one section of the sixth grade and Miss Potter had the other, but classes didn't move around. One teacher taught everything to one class all day. About every forty-five minutes, you'd switch from geography to arithmetic or spelling.

It's good to hear of someone who went north to retire. I notice the temperature in South Paris, Maine, was minus 8 degrees this morning. It proves Florida or Arizona isn't the only place older people live and thrive.

I was thinking maybe you could get a job doing public relations for the state of Maine. Florida is always pushing itself with pictures of sun and sand and saying what a great place it is for old people to live. You're living proof that Maine is good for the health.

Last summer I went back to the Academy for a reunion. The old school is doing very well and it's seventy-five years older than you are.

Lonnie

Lonnie is an institution in the building where I do a lot of my work. He shines shoes but that's only a small part of what he does. The best thing Lonnie does is keep everyone's spirits up.

The other day I had a good talk with Lonnie while he fussed over making my shoes look better. We settled some world problems and straightened out our own company. As I climbed down off the chair Lonnie has mounted on a platform so he doesn't have to bend over much, I said, as you'd say lightly to a friend, "Thanks, Lonnie, you're a good man."

"Well," Lonnie said philosophically, "we're all supposed to try and make things better, aren't we?"

That's what Lonnie does in the small piece of the world he has carved out for himself. He makes things better. He makes everyone he meets feel better and he makes their shoes look better. If all of us did as much, it would be a better world. He not only does his job but he throws in a little extra.

Lonnie is black, gray-haired and lame. I've been guessing that he's about seventy years old. His left foot is in a shoe with a four-inch lift on it and he doesn't use his left leg much. When he walks, he lifts it off the floor from the hip and swings it forward. It doesn't seem to be able to move by itself. He parks his car, a car with special controls for the handicapped, in front of the building and it's a tough job for him to make his way inside. Still, Lonnie is strong, with muscular arms and shoulders.

He has a good-looking face with prominent bones. He gets to work about 7:30 A.M. and leaves, to avoid the traffic, about 4:00 P.M. In between, he shines as many as thirty pairs of shoes. Lonnie gives every customer the feeling it's his privilege to be working for him.

A shine is apt to be interrupted half a dozen times by people passing the open door behind him who yell, "Hi, Lonnie."

"Hey, there, Mr. Edwards," Lonnie will yell back, often without looking up. He knows almost every voice in the building.

Yesterday Lonnie shined my shoes again.

"I'll be packing it in in April," he told me.

"Leaving here?" I asked, shocked at the thought of the place without him. "Why would you do that?" I asked.

"I'll be seventy-five in April," Lonnie said.

"But you're strong and healthy," I said. "Why would you quit work?"

"I want to do some things," Lonnie said. "Fix up my house. Do some things."

"Can't you fix up your house and still work here?" I asked.

There seemed to be something he wasn't telling me.

"Oh, I could," Lonnie said, "but I want to go back to school."

"That would be great," I said. "I've always wanted to do that too." I wondered what courses Lonnie was thinking of taking but decided not to ask.

"Yeah," Lonnie said, "I been working for sixty-two years now. Want to go back to school. Never did get enough school. Never really learned how to read. I was a little lame boy, you know. Embarrassed to go to school. All the big kids. What I want to do is learn to read, good enough to satisfy myself."

I've known Lonnie for thirty years and never knew how handicapped he was.

My Friend the Horse Thief

It's too bad life isn't like the movies.

When they make a movie in Hollywood, the women are beautiful, the men are handsome and all the characters are either good or bad. We aren't confused about what we think of anyone. That's the way life ought to be.

Life isn't that way, though. In real life, it's impossible to tell the good guys from the bad guys because people are too complicated. Good people are always doing bad things and bad people keep fooling you by doing good things. The ax murderer drops bread crumbs out of his cell window to feed the birds.

The other night we were sitting around with some friends and, as will happen, we started talking about another person we all knew well who wasn't there. The subject of our discussion was Fred Friendly, onetime president of CBS News, a Columbia University professor and director of Columbia University Seminars on Media and Society. One of the people in the group referred to Fred as a "genius." A second man in the room exploded in anger and said some things about Fred that I wouldn't repeat here in print.

I didn't say anything because I was thinking they were both right. To almost everyone who has ever met him, Fred Friendly is "My Most Unforgettable Character." He is one of my best friends and I have not only great respect for his brilliance as an accomplisher of things but great affection for the way he is. I can't explain why I like the way Fred is, I just do. I don't fight with anyone who can't stand him. I understand.

Fred can be an egomaniac and a jerk. When he is, I just smile because he's my friend. I stopped judging him years ago.

That's the real problem. A person can be so many different things. He or she can be a loving husband or wife, a considerate friend who'd do anything for you in an emergency, but also someone who'd steal a sweater from a department store. This mixed-up quality of the character of all of us is hard to get used to and the movies make it harder because they condition us to expect people to be predictably all good or all bad.

The reason for arguments about people, like the one my friends had about Fred the other night, is that one person's memory of another is taken from that person's good side. The one who hates the person can only remember the bad things he's done. I know someone Fred Friendly fired twice. Fred fired him from one company and the man got a job at another. Two years later Fred moved to that company and fired the man again. I do not expect to hear anything good about Fred from him. I like them both and try not to mention one when the other is around.

Whether you like or dislike people can also depend on your relationship with them. I've known several couples I consider good friends. They came to hate each other and were divorced. I still like and see all of them but no longer at the same time because they don't speak to each other.

I understand the complaint these people have with each other. I like them as individuals but wouldn't want to be married to them, either. One of the former wives complained that her husband made her spend half an hour every day clipping coupons from the newspaper so she could get a dime off on things like boxes of laundry soap. I, on the other hand, always found her husband to be quick to pick up a check in a restaurant.

It would be best if we didn't take such satisfaction in our firm decisions about whether people are good or bad. We're amused by our initial reaction to someone and keep repeating it until it becomes our own opinion. In a conversation, we know it's a lot more interesting if we say someone is a genius or a jerk than it is if we withhold any comment.

I don't think any of us are going to change but I wish the movies would.

Death of the Handyman

Last weekend, we returned to the house in the country one last time to close it for winter.

The house has stood for sixty years and I guess it'll still be there on that windy hilltop looking out onto the Catskill Mountains when we get back in the spring, but there were a lot of things left undone. One storm window was missing, I never got to clean the leaves out of the gutters and I couldn't find any insulation to stuff under the door of the little building I write in. I'm sure some snow will drift in.

Those things are minor, though, compared to the big problem. Lloyd Filkins has been shutting off the electricity and the water and draining the pipes and the radiators every fall for about forty years. In the spring, he's been turning on the water and reconnecting the electrical system.

Lloyd knew where all the pipes and valves were because he put them in.

Lloyd knew which switches to throw to cut off the furnace and the electricity to the house and in my shop. He knew because he wired the place, too. Lloyd knew where everything was and no one else but Lloyd knew.

Lloyd died three weeks ago and took a thousand secrets with him.

We often said we couldn't do without him and now we're having to do without him. Lloyd was a wonderfully dependable old grump. You had to be careful who you mentioned in his presence because there were a lot of people he wasn't speaking to and if he wasn't speaking to them, he didn't want you to speak to them either.

It wasn't that he held a grudge for long . . . maybe fifteen or twenty years at the most.

He was more like a country doctor than a handyman. He knew the medical history of just about every house in the village and made house calls when things weren't going well. He had the keys to fifty of them.

Lloyd thought of it as his town. The rest of us lived there by the grace of his beneficence.

Just about everyone in the village had some job that Lloyd had started and was waiting for him to come and finish. He had so many emergencies that he usually couldn't come . . . sometimes for years.

Lloyd loved an emergency best. You could call him any time of day or night with an emergency. He'd grumble at you over the phone and he'd tell you that whatever had happened was your own fault . . . but he'd be there in no time.

When Emily and Kirby were married in the little garden by the side of the house, someone parking hit the standing hose connection up by the garage. The pipe broke and water gushed out. The well pumps only three gallons a minute so it's quickly emptied if someone in the upstairs bathroom takes a long shower at the same time someone is taking a long shower in the downstairs bathroom . . . or if there's a broken pipe.

The pump cuts out automatically when there's no water in the well and that means no water for washing dishes, cooking, showers or flushing toilets. With sixty people at a wedding party, this is bad news.

When I called, Lloyd dropped whatever he was doing and came. His routine never varied. Without looking or speaking to anyone, he went around to the back of his truck and pick out his tools for the job. He spent a lot of time at the back of his truck.

He fixed the broken pipe that day, restarted the well pump and grumped off without saying a word. Lloyd took some perverse pleasure in not giving me the satisfaction of thanking him. His visit that day of the wedding showed up on some bill with other items later in the season. FIX PIPE it said. LABOR . . . $8.00 . . . PARTS . . . GASKET $.12 . . . TOTAL $8.12.

There were people in town who said Lloyd had a heart of gold and others who were not sure. He never spoke to them unless they called him in the middle of the night with an emergency.

Goodwill Toward Men

When you consider all the groups of people who don't get along with each other in this country, it's surprising that the country works at all. You'd think we might have a Beirut or a Belfast here.

Blacks and whites, for example, don't get along. Our growing Hispanic population is alienated from both blacks and whites. There's growing friction between the young and the old. In small towns the Baptists don't have much to do with the Methodists and neither of them speak often to the Catholics. Southerners resent Northerners, and in every major city in the country there are enclaves of Italians, Chinese, Germans and Vietnamese who don't mingle much with anyone who doesn't speak their language. The farmers are mad at everyone, and doctors and lawyers aren't looking each other in the eye on the street because of all the malpractice practice.

Just when I get most depressed about all this, something happens to revive my confidence in the goodness of people, the greatness of our country and our common interest in things that are right.

Last Tuesday after work, I stopped by the Whitney Museum in New York City because there was an exhibition of Shaker furniture that I'd been wanting to see. It had been there for several months and was closing soon. I thought I'd be wandering around the museum more or less alone. It wasn't as if the Shakers were a rock group.

The Shakers were a religious sect of no more than six thousand people who lived in a handful of eastern communities in the 1800s. Not many groups that small have made such a lasting impression on some area of our culture.

Shaker furniture is some of the simplest, most interesting and graceful ever designed. The Shakers didn't selfconsciously set out to design anything. Design grew out of necessity. They made pieces of furniture and tools that did what they needed to have done. It wasn't design, the way we talk about design in overblown terms today. It wasn't built to sell—it was built to use.

Their furniture is beautiful because it is so instantly recognizable as useful. A small sewing table of cherry provides a good work space and it has a curly maple front edge an inch wide that is a yardstick. A Shaker woman measuring a piece of cloth never had to move. The yardstick is its own decoration. They applied nothing to furniture that was merely decorative. If Shakers had built cars, they wouldn't have put chrome on them.

Shaker craftsmen didn't turn out furniture to be bought by strangers and fitted into a strange place in a strange home, either. No two pieces of Shaker furniture are alike because each was built for a specific purpose to be put in a specific place.

You wouldn't think a wheelbarrow could be a work of art, but the museum displayed a Shaker wheelbarrow that would compete for any crowd's attention if there were a Rembrandt hanging next to it.

Impressed as I was with the Shaker furniture, I was even more impressed with the people who had come to the museum to see it. It is a small, unpretentious exhibit and yet here, on a hot summer night, several hundred Americans . . . Presbyterian, Chinese, black, white, lawyer, doctor, young, old . . . crowded into the Whitney Museum to stare thoughtfully at and enjoy, with a common sense of appreciation, the work of people from another age who had done something good.

In the subways beneath the same street, there was filth. At the very moment people gazed on a Shaker chest made of maple, cherry and butternut, there might have been a mugging in a nearby street, but here, in this one civilized place, there was evidence enough of intelligence, humor, compassion and respect for other human beings to sustain anyone's belief in the fundamental goodness of people for a long time.

It was exhilarating. The world, I thought, is not going to hell after all.

PLACES

The Living City

It's kind of nice that most Americans who live in a city are proud of it. They like their city and they want the rest of the world to like it too. New York is the only exception to this.

If you visit any city for a few days, you're left with an impression of what it's like and whether to turn left or right in a few places, but your impression probably doesn't have much to do with what the city is really like.

I have pleasant impressions of dozens of cities and unpleasant impressions of others but my opinions come from events or sights that were probably not typical of the place. Maybe I had a terrible breakfast in the hotel I stayed at that turned me against the city; maybe I asked directions from a stranger who was so pleasant and helpful that I went home thinking everyone in that city was the same way.

This comes to mind today because I just spent two days in Boston. I was reminded what a good place Boston would be to live in. A good city has a core where there are lots of people doing different things, and Boston's core is centered around the rebuilt Quincy Market downtown. (I'd be more comfortable if I was certain how to pronounce their historic old "Faneuil Hall.")

I could live happily in Boston, San Diego, Seattle, Pittsburgh, San Antonio or Madison, Wisconsin. There are some cities you couldn't make me live in but I'm not going to mention them in case a newspaper in one of those cities runs my column. Why go out of my way to anger a space salesman?

Here are some things for anyone thinking of moving to a city to look for:

—Check to see if the downtown parts of the city close up and move to the suburbs at 5:30 P.M. You want a city where there are still people on the streets after dark.

—The presence of one or more colleges is a good sign. You can't beat having a good educational institution in town for livening up the city.

—If the biggest cultural event of the winter season is the basketball game with the traditional rival, you might want to have second thoughts about moving there.

—The number and importance of country clubs is something to watch for. If everyone seems to belong to one, don't move there.

—Be wary of a town that allows diagonal parking.

—Don't move to a city in which the best restaurant is in a hotel.

—Watch out if there are too many churches and not many bookstores.

—If the mayor has been in office more than eight years, consider another city.

—Don't move to a place whose principal shopping center is called "The Miracle Mile."

—Make certain the railroad station hasn't been turned into a boutique.

—There should be at least one good hotel that isn't part of a big chain.

—It's not a good sign if all the police are in cars and none are walking the streets.

—Look for a bridge that leads into the main part of town. Bridges are a good sign. A bridge often means the place was worth going to some trouble to get to.

—Check to see how many intersections have signs reading NO RIGHT TURN ON RED.

—Make sure there's at least one bakery that bakes good bread.

—Perfect symmetry in the layout of the streets is not good. A city should be a little irregular, suggesting that its growth was somewhat haphazard.

—There should be at least one good news store that's open twenty-four hours a day.

—Make sure the city has a good newspaper. It's even better if it has two newspapers, one of which you hate.

—Don't dismiss a city that has a dishonest local government. Some of them are interesting.

—It's not a major city if you can see the water tower with the city's name on it from the center of town.

Canada, Oh, Canada

It's about time the United States gave a party for Canada.

No country in the world has a better neighbor than the United States has in Canada and our friends up there are having sort of a tough time. The Canadian dollar is worth about 72 cents, unemployment is high and Canada isn't getting any favorable mentions for paying people millions of dollars to lobby for them in this country.

It would be a good time to do something nice for Canada to let them know how much we appreciate their good neighborliness. For too long now, we've taken Canada for granted. Just look at some of the facts of our friendship:

—We share the longest undefended border between two countries in the world, 5,500 miles long and not a military weapon pointed in either direction.

—There are 70 million border crossings a year. Every once in a while a border guard will look in the trunk of a car to see if someone is smuggling something or hiding a criminal but most of the 70 million people go without much checking.

—We are each other's best customers. Canada sells us two thirds of everything it exports and we sell more stuff to Canada than to any other country. Canada buys twice as much from us as Japan does.

—I hadn't realized, before I looked it up just now, that Canada is bigger than the United States. It's close, but Canada has 3,849,670 square miles and the United States has 3,623,420.

The trouble with that figure is that a lot of Canada's land isn't usable. Most of the 25 million Canadians live in the narrow strip just above our border because if they go much farther north it's simply too cold to live in the winter. They cuddle up to us for warmth. There are places in Maine where the border with Canada is all but invisible. You can enter Canada without knowing it on a lot of dirt roads.

As a result of the way its population is distributed, a lot of Canadians have more in common with their American neighbors to the immediate south than to other Canadians a couple of thousand miles away to the east or west. For instance, Windsor, Ontario, is all tied up with Detroit because it's so close. The people from Windsor probably don't know any more about Canadians from Saskatchewan than the people from Detroit do.

For an American to go to Canada or for a Canadian to come to the United States isn't like going to a foreign country. It simply isn't any big deal. Canada gets so cold that a million Canadians head for Florida for some part of every winter and at least that many American tourists go to some part of Canada in the summer.

It must be hard for Canadians not to resent us sometimes. You can tell they're a little nervous about the possibility of having their economy, their language, their traditions and their culture flooded out by ours. How would we feel if we lived in the shadow of this benevolent giant? How would we feel if we were swamped every day with books, movies and television from the country next door?

On the other hand, Canada is sitting pretty. It knows no bully can come along and fool with it while it has this big strong neighbor on its side. Canada also has the luxury of taking the best the United States has to offer in culture and products and rejecting the bad things it doesn't want from us. In that sense, Canadians live in the best of two worlds.

If you think you know Canada, try naming their states . . . which they call provinces. I'm cheating. I'm looking in the almanac: Alberta, British Columbia, Manitoba, New Brunswick, Newfoundland, Nova Scotia, Ontario, Prince Edward Island, Quebec and Saskatchewan.

Good names and I say, "Hurray for our friends, the Canadians."

Some other time I want to talk to you about Mexico.

Sugar City Goes Sour

Sugar City is a little east of Ordway and north of Rocky Ford, Colorado. Otherwise, it's out in the middle of miles and miles of not much of anything in the plains of southeastern Colorado.

If Sugar City were a patient in a hospital, doctors would list it as critical. The patient on the critical list is the American farmer and if the farmer goes, so will the hundreds of little farm towns like this one.

We might as well face the sad fact that the farmer, whom we always have known and admired, is a disappearing breed.

Every farmer has a theory about what's wrong. There's something true about every theory but the problem is bigger than any one of them, and none of the theories matter anyway. All that matters is that most of the farmers are going broke. They're going to have to abandon their farms. There's no sense saying they'll have to sell their farms because there are no buyers.

The big cities like Colorado Springs are gobbling up the farmers' water in this area, and once a desperate farmer sells his water rights to pay his debts, he can forget farming.

If Norman Rockwell had been looking for a model American farmer for the cover of the old *Saturday Evening Post*, he could have used Albert Siegfried of Sugar City. Albert and Hilda Siegfried are in good shape compared to most. He's a good and careful farmer, and Hilda brings in money working as an accountant while he's in the field.

Albert works his 180 acres alone because he can't get anyone to help him, so he worries a lot about getting old. He still can do the work because he has a lot of heavy farm equipment but he's given up growing anything that has to be picked by hand. He has gone into the cattle business, and what he grows most of now is corn and alfalfa for the animals.

Albert buys four hundred head of young cattle at an auction every spring. Each steer or heifer weighs about four hundred pounds when he gets it, and he pays perhaps 72 cents a pound, or $115,000 for all 400. He takes care of the cattle and feeds them for six months until they weigh six hundred or seven hundred pounds. Then he sells them to a feed lot. The heavier an animal is, the less it brings per pound, so he only gets 62 cents, but they each weigh two hundred or three hundred pounds more, so Albert might collect $174,000 when he sells . . . if all goes right. That's the catch. In 1976 all went wrong with the price of beef and he lost $28,000 in cold cash. He still hasn't recovered.

Even if all goes right and he collects $60,000 more than he pays for the cattle, he has to run his farm before he has anything for himself. A growing steer eats thirty pounds of food a day. Fields need fertilizer, tractors take fuel and maintenance. Everything costs money. I didn't ask but I'll bet it's a satisfactory year when Albert has $10,000 left after expenses. I would hate to think what his hourly wages are with the hours he puts in.

"We go to bed at night pretty depressed sometimes," he says. "You wonder why you're doing all this work for nothing but then you get up in the morning and go right back at it because that's what you've always done."

The Siegfrieds were able to put their two boys through college, and their sons come home to help some on the farm but they're both teaching now.

"Imagine me having two sons teaching," Albert says, laughing.

The farmers like Albert Siegfried, who have sons who leave the farm, are sad to see them go but they understand.

Sugar City is a microcosm. It's difficult to believe our civilization can't organize its way out of this mess and save two cultures in the process. In one corner of the earth people are starving to death for lack of food. In this corner, death comes to the farm from too much.

Travel Tips for the Travel Industry

If you'd like to hear some terrible ideas for promoting travel in the United States, the Travel Industry Association of America has some.

It's starting a program to promote travel that will include, its members say, a sweepstakes, a photo contest, an essay contest, discounts and a Stay-Another-Day promotion.

Is there anything in all of that that would induce you to travel more? It sounds like the worst promotion campaign I ever heard of. It's all fake stuff.

Everyone, it seems, is trying to con us into buying something or doing something with a sales pitch or promotion scheme. The last way anyone thinks of trying to attract more customers is by improving the product. If this travel organization wants people to do more traveling, it ought to try to make some improvements in the things that would make travel easier and more enjoyable. I have some suggestions:

—Build more hotels and motels with rooms that are half the size and also half the price of current hotel rooms. Save money by eliminating the swimming pools. No one ever seems to swim in them anyway. There isn't going to be a big travel boom in the United States while a good hotel room costs from $50 to $150 a night.

—Make good road maps available for free again.

—Build thousands of rest stops along major highways and keep them clean. It shouldn't be necessary for a traveling family to buy gas to go to the bathroom.

—Discourage fly-by-night gift shops. Find a way for good local artists and craftsmen to sell their things to people passing through. Many travelers like a little memento of their visit to an area but too many of the items in tourist-trap gift shops were made in Taiwan.

—Upgrade postcards and sell them with stamps affixed.

—For air travelers, get the airlines to draw up an unambiguous schedule of air fares that anyone can understand and that don't change with the wind.

—Encourage tourists to go to places that are not tourist attractions. "Tourist attractions" are the worst places for tourists to go. For one thing, they're always crowded with tourists. A husband and wife with two children could have a more interesting and educational time if they spent a week in Chicago than they would at Disneyland. Everyone ought to see Disneyland, or Disney World, once but not twice . . . and not for long then, either.

—Encourage hotels and motels to have breakfast available at 6 A.M. instead of 7 A.M.

—Bring back long-distance rail travel with Pullman and dining cars. Most Americans never have traveled on a train. Steel wheels rolling on steel rails is the most pleasant, most efficient and cheapest way to get long distances. Anyone who never has been carried from New York to Chicago while sleeping in an upper berth of the *20th Century Limited* or ridden on *The Super Chief* has missed one of the great travel experiences. In Europe they still have real trains. Why can't they have them here?

—Teach people how to be in the big cities. People are afraid to come to New York, for example, because they don't know how to use the city. It uses them. Help them.

—Stop encouraging everyone to go to the beaches, the lakes or the mountains. When too many people go to the beaches, the lakes or the mountains, it ruins them for everyone. In a city, the more the merrier.

—Make it acceptable for people to travel alone. The world is filled with people who'd like to go someplace but feel ill at ease doing it by themselves. Hotels and restaurants often make single guests seem less than welcome. Educate the members of the travel association.

These are just a few suggestions I have for encouraging travel.

Philadelphia or Bust!

Road signs and direction markers in America are largely designed for the people who already know how to get there. Signs are seldom helpful to the stranger who is lost. We desperately need a set of rules for direction signs. Often you can't ever be sure which way an arrow is pointing.

Last week I drove from New York to Philadelphia, a distance of about one hundred miles, and almost all of it dull, sleep-inducing turnpike miles. I was due at the Warwick Hotel in downtown Philadelphia at six P.M. At about quarter to five I knew I was getting close to downtown. Ahead of me and over to the right I could see the clump of high-rise buildings that marks every city's business district.

PHILA CENTER CITY 1½ MILES, the big, official green highway sign with white lettering said.

I wasn't watching my odometer and it's hard to guess how far one and a half miles is. The next exit sign read something like HISTORIC BUILDINGS. I had two seconds to decide whether to take the exit ramp or continue on the highway. "Historic buildings" didn't interest me at the moment and I decided "Phila Center City" must be a few hundred yards along.

That decision cost me forty-five minutes. The next exit was in a dock area six miles from nowhere.

That incident is typical of how a lot of Americans will spend much of their summer vacations—looking for someplace. Direction signs are infuriatingly bad or nonexistent in many places. A large, well-placed sign will send you along a street toward something you're trying to find. Five blocks along there will be a major fork in the road with no indication whatsoever about which road you should take.

The world is divided between people who ask directions and people who push on whether they're going in the right direction or not. I tend to push on because experience has taught me that the average man-on-the-sidewalk either doesn't know where anyplace is or doesn't know how to get to it if he does.

"Three—wait a minute—four traffic lights and take a left," they'll say. Forget it. The turn you want is always at least six traffic lights away and half the time the turn you need is a right, not a left. I don't ask directions unless I'm desperate.

By 5:45 the other night, driving along Market Street in Philadelphia, I was desperate. I stopped for a light and asked an intelligent-looking businessman who came within a few feet of my open car window, "Do you know the Warwick Hotel?"

"Sure," he said. "Just stay on Market Street to Seventeenth. You'll have to go around City Hall and pick it up on the other side."

That seemed easy but when I looped around City Hall, it was not clear to me which of the streets feeding into the circle was the continuation of Market. When I found it, I saw that Market was one-way coming toward me at that point. So much for intelligent-looking businessmen. He must have thought I was walking.

Within what turned out to be four blocks from the Warwick, I asked a cop where the hotel was. "Take a right there on Sixteenth," he said. "It's way out on the parkway."

Finding any address is hard work in a strange city. You may have the street number carefully written down but it doesn't help. Only about one of every ten buildings in this country has a street address on it and half the time when they do, the numbers are placed where you can't see them from the street.

Road signs always are getting you started toward your destination and then leaving you for dead. If you see a sign that indicates you're headed in the right direction, you assume there will be another sign when you should make a left or a right to get there. Not necessarily.

My advice to Americans who are driving somewhere on vacation this summer is this: Try to enjoy where you are because you probably won't be able to find where you're going until after it's closed.

Florida: Love It or Hate It

Everyone who lives in Florida wants you to like it and you can't hate them for that. They want to convince you that Florida is the place to live.

I suppose it might be a good idea if everyone went to both Florida and California once every few years to see how they compare with where they live, because the question of moving to one of the two comes up in almost every American's life at one time or another.

I spent four days in Florida in February and talked to a lot of people. "This is the place to be, this time of year," the young woman serving

me a hamburger in Fort Lauderdale said. She paused a minute, looking
at me quizzically after I failed to agree with her. "Isn't it?" she insisted.
"Don't you think so?"

"Were you born here?" I asked.

"Yes," she said, "but I've been to Pennsylvania. It was snowing."

I had been in Florida for two days when the young lady asked me
the question and I wasn't prepared to answer because in forty-eight
hours I'd only been outside for about half an hour getting from the
airport to the hotel and even that trip was in an air-conditioned bus.
Floridians spend a great deal of time inside, considering they talk about
the weather outside so much.

I knew, though, that at the moment she asked me, it was cloudy,
windy, about 68 degrees and very, very humid. It did not strike me as
a beautiful day and Florida didn't seem nearly as good to me as the
brisk, cold morning I'd faced in Connecticut the day I left home.

The difference between the people in Florida and the people in Iowa
who boost their state by asking how you like it is that, unlike the girl
who asks you how you like her state, most of the people in Florida are
not natives. They've moved to Florida after having lived somewhere
else and the question often is motivated by the desire to be reassured
that they did the right thing.

A great many things annoy me about Florida but most of them are
petty complaints. It always has annoyed me that it's almost impossible
to get fresh orange juice or any other kind of fresh food in a state that
grows some of the best—but this is quibbling.

If the young woman wanted a real answer to her question, I could
have given her one. If you're talking about weather, "no," I do not
think Florida is the place to be at this or any other time of year. I do
not like Florida's weather. It is almost always a disappointment, not
because it isn't often good but because we've all been propagandized
to expect more from it than it consistently provides.

If, on the other hand, you're talking about the people of Florida, I'd
say "yes," it's a great place to be. Florida, at this point in history, may
be the most interesting of all our fifty states. No other has such a
growing and diverse population. If the United States is both great and
interesting because of the ethnic mix of its population, as we are always
saying it is, then the same thing can be said about Florida. There are
more secondhand Rolls-Royces for sale in Florida than anywhere else,
which isn't much to recommend it, but there are also more good large
and small newspapers than in most states.

The ethnic indigestion that paralyzed Miami for so long is going away. The process of assimilation that distinguishes New York City as the major melting pot in the nation is now at work in Florida.

It's easy to start thinking of Florida as a dumping ground for the elderly, and there are depressing areas where everyone in them seems to be the same age, but the biggest influx of newcomers to the state this year will be young people.

Florida, as much as any state in the union and more than most, has an incredible variety in both its population and its geography. If I could only get a glass of orange juice that was still in the orange when I asked for it.

Big-City Blues

I just spent two days in Toulon. You go there much?

Toulon, Illinois, is 125 miles southwest of Chicago, 40 miles northwest of Peoria and 7 miles from the town of Wyoming. Toulon's population, 1,390. How you feel about where you've been depends partly on luck. If you hit it just right and everything goes smoothly, you leave a place with fond memories. It only takes a flat tire or a bad meal to turn you against a town forever.

I hit Toulon just right. It was a lovely spring day when I got there, with temperatures bordering on summer. Everyone in town was brimming with friendliness, the flowers were blooming, the farmers just outside town were harrowing their fields. All was right with Toulon that day and I found myself wondering why the whole world wasn't headed there to live.

"You have to go back to New York tomorrow?" a native asked, incredulous at the thought of such a dreadful fate. "I was to New York," he said. "Or to New Jersey, anyway, right near New York. I had to meet these people at a motel all right but I was on the wrong side. Road was divided, you know. Took me nearly forty-five minutes to get back over there to meet them. Just maybe fifty feet away and it took me forty-five minutes. Traffic? Man! I sure wouldn't want to live in New York. You like it there?" he asked, challenging me to make a fool of myself by saying I did.

I hedged.

There's a continuing argument about the best places to live in the United States.

There are people who love Florida, people who hate Florida. There are those who wouldn't live anywhere but California. Southerners can't imagine living anywhere but in the South and Midwesterners think anywhere else is something less than 100 percent American.

There are those who love New York and those you couldn't pay enough to live in New York. The biggest argument of all is the argument over whether it's best to live in the big city or the small town. The strange thing is that the fewest people live where most people say they'd like to live; the most people live where most people say they wouldn't want to live.

Everyone talks as though they'd like to live in the country. Everyone loves the small town and the little village, but in spite of all the sentimental talk, the movement is out of the small towns and the country and into the big cities. Those who live in the city yearn for the country but they don't move there.

When you fly over the wide open spaces of America or drive to a small town, it's hard to keep from wondering why the crowded, unhappy, homeless people of the dirty cities don't go to the small towns.

I know there are good reasons. The homeless would still be homeless when they got there and the people already living in town wouldn't welcome them or have the same facilities for helping them that the cities have.

The argument between big-city and small-town life comes down to this: Is it better to fill your life with a wide variety of friends and events in a big city and expose yourself and your family to all the evils that exist there or is it wiser to settle down to the comfortable, the familiar and possibly dull, in a small town? Can you live a fuller life and thus make life seem longer by going places, doing things and mingling with more interesting people in a big city? Or is the quiet continuity of life in a small town more fulfilling?

I loved Toulon, but I'm back in New York by choice.

ANIMALS
AND PETS

Cats Are for the Birds

I have never met a cat I liked.

As an animal lover, I'm constantly disappointed with myself when there's a cat around.

Don't think I haven't tried to love cats, because I have. I always try to win their affection or, at the very least, try to establish some kind of relationship. Nothing. A cat will walk on my lap, jump on a table next to me where my host has put a dish of corn chips, or rub against my pants, but there is never any warmth in the cat's gesture.

"He likes you," the host will say.

Well, if those cats I've met like me, they have a plenty strange way of showing it. If I got the kind of affection from the people I like that I get from cats whose owners think they like me, I'd leave home.

Cat owners are amused by things their cats do that don't amuse me at all. I am not at all inclined to laugh when a cat walks in my potato chips or plants its claws in my clothes, the better to climb into my hostile lap.

"He can jump from the top of the refrigerator to the shelf in the pantry," the cat lover says as if it were one of the most desirable things in the world to have a house pet do.

"Cassandra!" the owner will say sharply to the cat with the cute name. "Get down, Cassandra!"

Has any cat in all history ever got down out of a stranger's lap when requested to do so? Cat lovers point out with pride that cats are independent and beholden to nobody. So who needs a cat as a pet? Our whole lives are filled with people who are independent and don't pay any attention to what we say. In addition we should have a cat who treats us like dogs?

I've known divorced couples who are friendlier toward each other than the average cat is to its owner.

Cats have come to my mind today because I just read a newspaper article that said cats are now more numerous as pets in American households than dogs. There are 56 million cats and 51 million dogs, according to the article, although I don't know how they got the cats to stand still long enough to be counted.

The story used the word "popular." It said "Cats are more popular as pets than dogs." That is ridiculous. Cats may be more numerous than dogs but it doesn't mean they're more popular. Easier to take care of, maybe. Inclined to reproduce quickly and in large litters, certainly, but if cats are more popular than the greatest animals that inhabit the earth, dogs, then I am more disappointed than usual in the human race.

I want to be honest with you—I hate everything about cats. I hate the smell of a house or a store that keeps one. I can't stand the way they gum their food, and having a pile of kitty litter in the corner of my kitchen is about as attractive a thought as inviting a horse into the living room before the parade.

Cat lovers find charm in the untamability of the animal. I concede that they are absolutely unsusceptible to taking direction of any kind from any human being but it is not an attribute I cherish in a pet. I was never amused by dogs that would roll over on request but there is something lovable about the dog's willingness to do the trick just to please its owner. I see nothing wrong with having a pet that gives the uncritical kind of love that most dogs give.

Cat owners go a long way looking for ways to praise them.

"We never have any mice, not with Cassandra around," the owner says with pride.

"No," I say, "and you never have any birds around, either."

It's true. Cassandra would just as soon torture a hummingbird to death as kill a mouse.

Killing things is Cassandra's idea of having a good time. For my part, I prefer mice to cats. At least mice don't climb in my lap. What worries me most is not cats but people. If people prefer cats to dogs, how can we trust them to choose a president?

Bless the Beasts

It's a mystery to me where wild animals go in the daytime.

This morning, like every morning of my vacation, I got up before six o'clock because I don't want to waste my vacation sleeping. As I pulled myself into my underwear, I looked out the window and saw a deer peek cautiously from the bushy edge of a wooded area that lines a path leading back from behind our house.

The deer looked both ways up and down the path and, seeing nothing and having no way of knowing I was watching it from my bedroom window, it walked out into the open and sauntered down the path. I judged the deer was just getting up too.

"How nice," I thought to myself, "to have a house far enough away from the crowd to have a deer living nearby."

But why doesn't it live here during the day? Where does the deer go? There aren't that many good places to hide. I don't know whether it's the same deer or not but I've seen a deer ten times this month and always at dawn or dusk.

The deer had come from a place about twenty feet behind this pentagonal-shaped little building I put up a few years ago to write in. I know the deer sleep there because the tall grass between the trees is matted down and there are well-worn paths leading through the woods.

Even though I've looked out back at all times of day and night, I've never caught one deer asleep. Last night I came out here at eleven o'clock and there was no deer there. Where were they?

There are lots of deer around and it's always a happy event when we see one. It's always "Hey, look! A deer."

Last year we had a mother with triplets. I wish I knew whether this deer I saw today was one of them. I wish I knew where the other two are. I have a terrible feeling about that, of course. We aren't here in the fall.

Deer have a remarkable ability not only to hide but to thrive side by side with people. They often live in residential areas. You wouldn't think there was much of any place for them to hide but they seem to find them.

It's a good thing people haven't scared away all the deer. They're so nice. I've never heard of a mean deer and they seem so vulnerable, so unwarlike. I guess there'd be too many of them if a lot weren't killed but I can't imagine shooting one. Bang, bang. You're dead.

Deer aren't the only animals good at hiding. I know they're here but we seldom see a raccoon, a fox, a skunk or a wildcat. I don't know why woodchucks are so fearless and why the raccoons are so afraid of being seen. Maybe the raccoons have decided to come out just after dark because they know the garbage is best after dinner.

Yesterday afternoon we had a torrential downpour. Where did the chipmunks go? I've never seen a chipmunk out in the rain. I'm kind of surprised animals don't like getting wet. Even the robins disappear when it rains. Where do all the robins go that are usually picking worms out of our front lawn? I can't believe the robins all go to nests. I see an awful lot more robins than robins' nests around here.

There has been a mouse around our kitchen at night for the past few weeks. I came out for a drink from the refrigerator the other evening and saw it. I can't figure where the mouse goes in the daytime. I can't find a hole anywhere that it could get in or out through.

When I find a box of cookies chewed open, I hate mice. I have some of the deer hunter in me. I get vicious. I decide to buy traps and kill all the mice. Then I remember the only time I did it and the sight of the mouse, eyes bulging, with blood in its mouth, caught by the neck with the spring-driven bar, was more than I want to face again. I shouldn't eat so many cookies on vacation anyway.

There are times when I wish I was as good at hiding during the daytime as the animals around here are.

Caught in a Trap

The organizations trying to eliminate cruelty to animals are right but they're a little shrill. They give people the impression they're on the lunatic fringe. Readers tend to associate them with the rich woman who dies and leaves a million dollars to her cat.

With the probable exception of Greenpeace, which has been effective against the baby-seal slaughter, and a few notable local groups, organizations trying to protect animals from abuse and torture have been largely ineffective. They certainly haven't discouraged women from wearing fur coats.

The steel-jawed spring trap with jagged teeth that snap shut on an animal's leg has been the object of humanitarian organizations' attacks for a hundred years. Their work has made animal lovers feel better but it hasn't done much for the animals. There are more leg traps and more animals being caught by the leg than ever before. Thoughtful, compassionate women who would open the screen door to let a fly out before they'd kill one do not associate the fur coats they wear with the cruel and bloody death of the animals whose skin they are made of.

I don't want to join these organizations or get their voluminous literature depicting the horrors of the leg-hold trap. I'm on the side of the people fighting cruelty to animals. I wish they were more effective. Maybe they ought to direct their campaigns against women who wear furs instead of against the trappers.

The men who make their living catching and killing animals are a tough lot. They think of their trade as a manly one and they've become inured to hard death. They're used to seeing animals that have been tortured or starved to death in their traps.

The way to make sure fewer animals are caught in traps is to discourage people from buying and wearing fur coats. The anticruelty organizations might try having some of their members follow fur-wearing women and men with signs reading, THIS ANIMAL DIED A HORRIBLE DEATH.

The fear of being the object of public scorn would discourage most people from going out in their fox, raccoon or mink coats.

Anyone who eats animals, as I regularly do, is on shaky ground talking about cruelty to animals. But, like most people, I don't associate the food on my plate with the animal on the hoof or the bird on the wing. My attitude toward steak is the same as a woman's attitude toward a fur coat—the animal and the coat do not seem related. The steel trap or the slaughterhouse do not occur to either of us.

We all look for ways not to worry. We don't worry about mink coats because the thirty or so minks that go into making a coat are raised on what they euphemistically call "ranches." The mink live for that one purpose. If they weren't valuable for their fur, they would never have been bred to life in the first place. We meat-eaters say that about cattle. It's weak. The ranches the mink live on are not to be confused with the kind of ranch President Reagan owns either.

These wild little animals are kept in tiny, filthy cages for all their brief lives because their skins are most valuable if they are unblemished. The mink are often drowned or suffocated when their time comes to become a coat. Even this is a little better than being caught in a leg trap.

Civilization's effort to become more civilized sometimes seems like a losing battle. How any society treats its animals is an indication of the degree of its civility. During our stewardship of earth's civilization, we ought not pamper our pets with vitamin-enriched dog food on one hand and close our eyes to the fur stripped from the animals caught in steel traps on the other.

A Feeling of Helplessness

Yesterday morning I had orange juice, toast, marmalade, two scrambled eggs and coffee.

After breakfast I headed for the shop in back of the house. It was pouring rain and, like always, I'd left my umbrella in the back of the car and my raincoat in the shop. There are a lot of trees between the house and the shop and I had old clothes on, so I made a run for it.

There's a cement pad in front of the door of the shop and a wooden sill on top of the six-inch step. The sill overhangs the cement by three inches. As I ran toward the door, there was a little flutter on the ground. It startled me briefly until I saw what it was. It was a small black bird and it half hopped and half flew into the bushes in back. I don't want to lie to you and give you the name of the bird because I don't know what it was. Lots of birds look like sparrows to me.

I didn't think much about it. It seemed as though it was probably a baby bird that hadn't learned to fly yet. There are a lot of nesting birds around. One purple martin chose the hanging plant on the side porch as a place to lay three eggs. Unfortunately, the hinges are gone on the screen door in front and we've been using the side door for going in and out. The bird obviously laid the eggs during the week we were away, when there was no traffic, and must regret it now. We all know how difficult it is to choose the right home.

About an hour after I first saw the little bird outside the shop, I went out and looked for her again. Under the wooden sill I saw what I hadn't seen before. It was one lone, baby blue egg. Suddenly I got the whole picture and felt terrible about having scared the bird away. It must have been the mother who had laid the egg there in desperation during the night. I suspect her nest must have been flooded out and the overhang of the doorstep was an emergency haven.

I got an old piece of towel and moved the egg onto it. After gently wrapping it, I took the bundle to the house and put the towel with the egg in a strainer over a lamp in the living room. With my hand, I tried to test for a spot that would have come closest to the warmth of a real mother bird's body. This is something about which I have no real knowledge, never having spent any time under a bird's body.

Later in the morning I did see the mother bird again. She was hopping around in the woods nearby. The temperature was way down around 60 and it was still raining heavily. Obviously, I needed a veterinarian specializing in ornithology. Should I go get the egg from its warm place over the lamp and put it back down on the cold cement in the hope that the mother would find the egg again? Though even if she did, there was no way she could hatch it and nourish it there until it could fly. For one thing, I'd be going in and out of my shop ten times a day, right over her. On the other hand, what if, by some wild chance, I did exactly the right thing with the egg and it hatches? What do I do then? Do I fly away and come back with flies or worms or whatever it is little birds eat?

It made me feel ill at ease all day. I knew the mother bird was out there and I knew that little chick was in there but I had no idea how to get the two together. There's an old nest under the eaves of the garage but birds don't go to old nests and she'd never have found the egg there anyway.

It kind of ruined my day. Every time I looked out, I thought about it. I'm no great bird lover but there was something poignant about the situation. It was such a tiny problem in my life and yet I was absolutely helpless.

When I went to bed last night, I left the light on for the blue egg in the towel. How long does it take for a bird's egg to get to be a bird, anyway?

For breakfast today, I had toast, marmalade and coffee. No egg.

Nature Seems So Unnatural

It's strange that Nature isn't nicer. It sure deals in a lot of death. The animals around our summer place don't have much of a life and what they do have doesn't last that long. The flowers don't have it much better, with either too much or too little rain, too much or too little sun and always a killer weed after them.

During July, I saw so much of the chipmunks that I got to know them apart. When I left the door of the shop open while I was working, the chippies would come and go past the door. I always spoke to them.

About a month ago I saw a cat around our place. I don't know whose cat it is—we're more than a quarter of a mile from the nearest neighbor—but the cat often was hanging around when I got up in the morning.

There has been a marked drop-off in the activity of mice in our kitchen since I first saw the cat. I imagine it has had something to do with the fact that I now can leave a bag of cookies on the shelf in the pantry at night and not have them nibbled during the night.

I noticed too, though, that I no longer saw my good friends the chipmunks passing my door or disappearing down their holes, and I was angered by the thought that the cat was killing the chippies.

This morning at about 6:15, there was a strange cat noise up by the shop as I was dressing. It wasn't the sound of a cat fight. It was a mournful wail. I didn't think much of it. I don't know cat sounds.

At 9:30 I was loading the car for the trip home. Margie went up to the shop looking for a checkbook I thought I'd left there. She came back with her hand to her mouth and a ghastly look in her face.

"Someone's killed a kitten up there," she said. "It looks as though its throat was slit."

I had seen the familiar cat in the area within the past ten minutes so I didn't think it was her.

"Kitten?" I asked.

"It's not real small but it looks young. It's terrible. We'll have to get a shovel and bury it."

I went down to the house for some things I wanted to load into the car, putting off the dreaded job. When I finally started up for the shop, I saw the old cat lurking by the far corner of it. The shop is surrounded by woods and brush.

The cat just looked at me and, as I got closer, I saw a furry object at its feet. She had dragged the dead kitten toward the woods and must have stopped when she saw me coming. You'd think the cat would know I wouldn't hurt her.

It seemed apparent that the cat who'd been killing birds, chipmunks and mice must have been the kitten's mother. She must have been the one who let out the sad, plaintive wail when she found her young one dead.

It was hard to know how to feel.

What killed the kitten? Its throat must have been slit with a sharp claw during the night. Could a raccoon catch and kill a cat? Why would it? Whatever killed the cat had no intention of eating it, as a fox might have.

Did the mother cat recognize the irony of her kitten's death right where she'd been killing chipmunks? If the cat was capable of grief over the death of her own, why was she not capable of understanding how sad it might be for the mother of a young chipmunk she'd mauled to death?

It was apparent we wouldn't have to bury the dead kitten, and I finally drove off. Going down the long dirt road, headed for the country road, I passed a row of maple trees. Several of the smaller trees had been overrun by wild grape, an eastern version of kudzu, the scourge of the South. Wild grape wraps itself around tree trunks, climbs the tree and pulls down its branches in a vicious stranglehold. Its mission killing trees in the big picture of nature is no clearer to me than the cat's mission killing birds, chipmunks and mice or the mysterious killer's mission in killing the cat's kitten.

On the Road to Recovery

The old station wagon is in intensive care. I'm not sure it's going to pull through this time.

Last Saturday I started out the driveway and heard an unfamiliar heavy, grinding noise. Over the years, during the time I've put 118,000 miles on it, my 1977 Ford Country Squire has made a lot of noises, each with its own meaning. This was different. It was no pebble in a hubcap.

I eased it into the Five Mile River Garage just a mile from the house and left it to be checked over.

Later in the day I dropped back and my worst fears were confirmed. It had a broken axle.

I talked with Malcolm in hushed tones about whether Old Faithful should be put out of the way or kept alive by heroic measures. If I gave him the thumbs up, the car would need surgery. Thumbs down, it would be gone from my life forever. Malcolm told me that first he'd have to operate to make sure there was no serious damage to the gears. If they were OK he could realign the axle itself and weld the axle casing.

I couldn't bear to see the car that had given me such good service for twelve years be put down so I gave him the go-ahead. The axle is being welded this week.

When a car has a problem, we're all inclined to think of a new one. We're looking for an excuse to buy a new car. It doesn't take much and car loans come easy. Even a dead battery can get you thinking the car isn't worth keeping. Buying a new car is the ultimate in recreational shopping and most of us do it a lot more often than necessary. The urge to buy a car is a disease for which they ought to develop a shot.

The idea of looking around for a new car appealed to me but as I stood there thinking about delivering the death blow to the station wagon, I knew I couldn't do it.

What would happen to my old car? It was only worth a few hundred dollars before the axle broke. It's not a wreck but there are the inevitable dents and scratches on it. You can't do anything about the people who open car doors and hit yours with the sharp edge of theirs in the supermarket parking lot. And there are other signs of use. After all, I did back into that high loading dock. I did catch the corner of the garage turning around in the driveway that day several years ago. That truck did skid into me on the cobblestone pavement down on Canal Street the day before Christmas in 1981. So the car has been through the wars. No prospective buyer could look at my station wagon and be fooled into thinking it had led a pampered life. It looks all of its 118,000 miles.

If I had decided to abandon the car, I know what would have happened. Malcolm would have towed it to the car scavengers, where they'd dump it out in the yard with all the others, occasionally stripping it of a door hinge here or a generator there. Malcolm probably couldn't get any more from the people at the car-parts dump than it would cost him to tow it there.

All that makes it even harder for me to abandon. I like it. I know it's silly to feel affection for any inanimate object but I'd hate to see that car get into the hands of someone who was going to abuse it or chop it up for spare parts.

My station wagon is being fixed now and I hope everything comes out OK. It's good to have a car you don't worry about denting. The wagon was always the one that got left out in the rain and snow. If there was a dirty job to be done, I did it in the wagon. I saved my good car because I wanted the good car to last. I've had three good cars since I bought the wagon. The wagon, mistreatment and all, has outlasted the cars I pampered.

When I get it back, the first thing I'm going to do is give it a nice full tank of high-octane gas, some clean, fresh oil and a warm bath. I want the wagon to know that it's loved.

Mr. Rooney Goes to the Dogs

There is no doubt in my mind that dogs have more good qualities and fewer bad qualities than people. They behave in an honorable way without the benefit of religion, too.

My high opinion of dogs in general was reinforced the other night by my annual visit to the Westminster Dog Show. There were 129 different breeds at the show, and backstage with the owners and trainers I must have talked to a hundred dogs of 50 different breeds. There were only three dogs I hesitated to reach out and pat without asking for the advice or permission of their owners first. They were (1) a mean-looking Doberman pinscher whose owner said he was a pussy cat, (2) a huge red Chow, known officially as a "Chow Chow" and (3) an alert German shepherd sitting at attention in his stall with a superior look on his face.

The owners assured me it was all right to touch their dog. The Doberman's master said, "You can pet him but just don't move your hand toward him too quickly."

I took his word for it that I could touch his dog but any time someone has to qualify how it is I can touch their dog, I don't touch it. I didn't pat the Chow either because I didn't want to encourage the owner into thinking people like Chows, but I did become acquainted with the German shepherd, whose owner I offended when I called him a "police dog." The German shepherd turned out to be cold to my advances but not aggressively unfriendly. He could take me or leave me.

There were some wonderful surprises among breeds I knew little about. The Rottweilers, big, strong, short-haired, brown-and-black dogs, were friendly in a big, rough way. I like rough, friendly dogs better than itsy-bitsy, fragile, nervous little dogs, although some small breeds that are relatively new to me like the Lhasa apso and the Shih Tzu seem nice.

One woman who weighed about eighty-five pounds was showing three mastiffs that weighed about one hundred pounds each. They were simply great.

Every time I go to this dog show, there are at least ten dogs I want to take home. Now, for instance, I want a mastiff. "We never bother to lock our house," the woman said and, looking at these huge, fierce-looking dogs, I could see why.

I don't like guard dogs, and the only reason these mastiffs would make good guard dogs is their appearance. I sat down with them, a total stranger, in their pen. I put my hand on the head of the big brown one lying on my right and immediately the gray one behind me put his huge head over my shoulder and licked my face. Some guard dog!

At that point the one at my side turned over on his side and plopped his twenty-pound head in my lap. They are magnificent animals and all I could think was that the American Kennel Club is doing a good job encouraging the breeding of all these relatively rare dogs that might otherwise become extinct. Like sailors, golfers or horse-lovers, dog people have one-track minds, but it's a good track to be on.

The winner of Best of Show that night was a German shepherd named Manhattan. It's the first time a German Shepherd has ever won and one woman who breeds German shepherds expressed delight, with some reservations. She said the trouble with a breed becoming too popular is a lot of people who don't know or care much about dogs start breeding and selling them for money without much regard to whether they are good examples of the breed or not and, as a result, the breed deteriorates.

You couldn't make that comment about humans. In the dog world it's acceptable to be racist. Breeders admit some breeds have both good and bad traits other breeds don't have. All dogs are not born equal.

I talked with a woman who had a pit bull, that tough, pink-eyed dog originally bred for that disgusting and most uncivilized "sport" of all, dog fighting. The pit bull, called an "American Staffordshire terrier" at dog shows, has a reputation of being good around people but death to other dogs. They are, therefore, difficult to have as pets.

The woman said her dog did not fight and breeders of pit bulls everywhere were trying to eliminate the fighting trait, along with the name "pit bull," from the breed. I wish they could breed a little of the mastiff's disposition into the Chow and the Doberman pinscher.

People tend to like any breed of dog they've known. That says something nice about dogs as a species. I grew up with an English bulldog named Spike and our children grew up with another named Gifford and, like most dog lovers, I argue with anyone who says English bulldogs aren't the best dogs in the whole world.

HOUSES

Adding on to a House

We're having an addition put on our house. It isn't much. It's a small bedroom being tacked onto the side behind the kitchen. It's only nine by twelve but we might as well be trying to build the cathedral of Chartres.

Work was started in June. The room would be finished now, as I write in August, except:

—The carpenter, who is also the contractor and very capable, couldn't start until the foundation had been dug, and the man with the bulldozer said we'd had so much rain that the ground was too soft where he had to bring the dozer in over the lawn, so he had to wait.

—The foundation took a lot of concrete but would only have been half a load from one of those big concrete-mixer trucks. They wouldn't deliver half a load so it had to be mixed by hand, which takes time and makes a mess.

—If they could have started right away it would have been finished July 15 but once the concrete was poured they had to wait for that to dry, so the carpenter started another job.

—Part of the project involved moving the washer and dryer in an adjacent room. Water pipes and electrical lines had to be moved. The house is in a small town. The electrician doesn't speak to the plumber and the plumber won't speak to either the electrician or the man with the bulldozer. The contractor is Mr. Nice Guy who'd rather leave than get into an argument with the plumber, the electrician or the man with the bulldozer, so he's been gone a lot.

—Everyone had to go back somewhere quite often for something they'd forgotten.

—The electrician said he couldn't put the outlets in until the carpenter had the wallboard up but the carpenter said he couldn't put the wallboard up until the windows were in, in case it rained, and he couldn't put the windows in until the plumber took the old washing machine and dryer out through the opening because he was afraid they wouldn't fit through the door or the window when everything was in place.

—Someone asked how we'd ever get the washing machine and dryer out if we wanted to replace them. I ignored the question.

—The windows hadn't been delivered yet, anyway. The carpenter said there'd been some mixup in the order. He'd dealt with Ed instead of Bill over at the building-supply place and Ed wasn't as reliable as Bill. He said he hoped they'd be in next Tuesday. "Next Tuesday" comes up a lot.

—There was some indecision about where the windows should go. Before you can decide where windows go, you have to know where you want the bed to be.

—You don't know where you want the electrical outlets, either, until you know where the bed's going, but it was hard to decide where the bed should go until the windows were in.

—We lost another day because it was the eightieth birthday of the ailing mother of the wife of the plumber who doesn't speak to the electrician, and the plumber had to drive his wife to Massachusetts to see her mother. The electrician said that if he'd known the plumber wasn't going to be here that day, he could have finished up but he didn't know it until he'd already promised someone else he'd come that day.

—The contractor got a nice young man to rake and seed the area that had been torn up by the bulldozer but we had a thunderstorm that night and everything was washed away, so he's going to have to do that again.

—The plumber was mad at the man who did the landscaping because he said the landscape man drove his truck over the pipe leading to the septic tank. If it was broken, the plumber said, it wasn't his fault. I was as nice to the plumber as possible. I agreed that if the pipe was broken it wasn't his fault because, if it is broken, I hope I can get him to fix it.

Some friends came over for dinner the other night and wanted to know why we hadn't put the new addition on the other side.

Maybe I'll have them move it when it's finished.

Thy Neighbor's House

Phil Donahue, the television talk-show host, bought a piece of property next to his house in Westport, Connecticut, for $6.8 million and tore down the house on it. Even if we get along with our neighbors, we'd all like to be rich enough to buy the piece of property next to ours and tear down the house on it. Most of us don't have the $6.8 million to do it . . . or even the $68,000, if that's what it would take.

The problem is that the house on the seven acres Donahue bought was the work of a distinguished architect named John Johansen. It was all concrete, no wood, and was considered highly unusual, so a lot of the townspeople of Westport are plenty angry at Phil for having it bulldozed.

Donahue bought the house and property from a man named Stephen Rapaport, who had it on the market for six months before the sale.

"It was a difficult house to live in and Mr. Donahue had every right to do what he did," Mr. Rapaport said.

The twenty-six-year-old house had been empty and untended for years. Grass grew high around it. Donahue complained that it attracted "vagrants, lovers and other strangers."

Westport's architectural historian, Mary McCahon, on the other hand, said, "I still get knots in my stomach when I think about it. It was a wonderful building."

Phil's answer to that was "If it's an architectural gem, why didn't someone take care of it?"

I don't know Phil Donahue but I've always liked him on the air. He seems bright, fair and sensible and a great popularizer of complex issues. Anyone who appears on television is considered a philistine by the I-never-watch-television crowd and it's anyone's natural inclination to be on the side of the preservationists, so Phil is taking a lot of heat.

The preservationists are usually the cultured, intelligent people in any community, but there are knee-jerk preservationists who'd save every building ever constructed for no other reason than that it's old. Age is no guarantee of excellence in people or buildings.

I don't know whether this building should have been saved or not but if three quarters of the buildings in most American cities were torn down, we wouldn't lose much of our cultural heritage. In many European countries, towns are constipated by their own history. In so magnificent a city as Florence, Italy, there are more great old buildings of historic significance than the living Italians can maintain. How much of the income of the living should be spent to preserve the history of the dead? It's always sad to see a building in which so much has happened fall into ruins but it's also sad to pass a cemetery and think of all the lives represented by the stones there. The fact is, there's a limit to the amount of time we can spend remembering anything.

Westport isn't Florence and the Johansen house was not an ancient artifact. I'm not much attracted to architectural *tours de force* anyway. The Frank Lloyd Wright houses called "great" are fascinating but they are not houses I'd trade my own house to live in.

Many of our best architects haven't served us well because they've devoted their talent to showpiece structures and not to the buildings that are most important to our lives. The average house in the average city is an artistic monstrosity.

The architects' defense to that charge is that too often houses are built without an architect's plan. This is true but architects have to find a way to make their skill more readily available. We have enough office buildings, banks, museums and churches. What we need from Mr. Johansen are fewer unusable unusual concrete gems and more help building or remodeling our homes.

If Phil Donahue puts up nine houses on the property where the concrete house was and makes a profit of $5 million on the deal, I take back every nice thing I've said about him.

A Car Wash in Every Garage

There are a dozen or so conveniences for the home that I'd like to have, except some of them haven't been invented yet as far as I know. I've been making a list:

—When I turn off the shower, I'd like to be able to switch on blowers that shoot hot air at me until I'm dry. I like a good, big towel but it's hard to leave it someplace outside the shower where I can reach it without getting water all over the bathroom floor.

—Is anyone so rich that they have a garage equipped with a car wash?

Why not? Every night when you put the car away, the washer would go on automatically as you turned out the lights. Every morning you'd go out to a sparkling clean car.

—It would be wonderful to have a dining-room table that would lift straight up and be conveyed to the kitchen on some kind of overhead rollers. In the kitchen, the dishes and leftovers could be cleared from the table. It then could be reset for dessert and returned, with another push of a button, to the dining room.

—Why don't we have dry-cleaning machines in our homes just the way we have washing machines? As far as I know, about the only difference is washing machines work with soap and water and dry-cleaning equipment uses some other fluid.

—I've always wanted a table that comes down out of the ceiling next to my side of the bed. A table big enough to hold all the things I like to keep next to me is in the way when I want to get in or out of bed. Lifting the whole mess into the ceiling is the only solution.

—I fail to understand why it's so expensive or impractical to have a swimming pool in the basement of a house. I think it's because most swimming pools are added to houses after the people who live there make big money. A basement swimming pool should be built into the house when it goes up. In the summer it would be fun to have outdoor pools in front and in back of the house so you could take advantage of the sun no matter where it was. The two pools ought to be connected by a channel, making it possible to swim from one to the other. It might be practical to cover the channel so you can walk over it.

—It certainly would be convenient if the table by the side of my big chair in the living room was equipped with faucets from which I could draw hot coffee, club soda, Coke, beer, lemonade, tea or bourbon, depending on my mood. This setup would save me a lot of trips to the refrigerator in the kitchen.

—I want a strong light in the ceiling aimed down at every chair in the house so that anyone who sits down can read easily from the chair without fussing with a lamp. I'm tired of lamps on tables next to chairs that throw a circle of light that falls eighteen inches short of covering the newspaper I'm trying to read.

—For our next kitchen floor, I'd like small tiles that sloped to a drain in the middle of the room. The kitchen floor could be washed with a hose.

—Our old refrigerator had the freezer section on top and the regular section on the bottom, which was inconvenient. Our new refrigerator has the freezer on the bottom and the regular section on top. It's an improvement but what I want is a refrigerator/freezer that's lateral instead of up and down so that both the freezer and the normal-temperature compartments are at eye level.

—I want a little elevator or dumbwaiter in the house that goes from the basement to the kitchen and upstairs to the bedrooms. Once it gets upstairs, it would be able to traverse laterally with an opening for delivery in each room.

—Every bed should have a telephone on each side of it, not just on one side. And the television set should be installed in the ceiling.

Realistic Ratings for Real Estate

We need some kind of official house-rating agency that would provide potential homeowners or apartment renters with hard information on the value of the property they're thinking of buying or renting.

Real estate people are often interesting and charming people but you wouldn't suggest that their word on a house they're trying to sell is always absolutely accurate. I'm not saying real estate agents lie. I'm saying that they . . . well, their statements about a place are . . . that is, when they tell you the good things they sometimes . . . what I'm trying to say is, they lie.

The real estate section of a newspaper would shake anyone's confidence in brokers.

"Beautifully landscaped," for example, usually means there are two bushes in front of the house. "Wooded lot," on the other hand, means there are two trees.

A house would be rated on as many as twenty-five major and minor features.

If a house was free of drafts, with tight windows and doors, good insulation and with a furnace big enough and good enough to warm every room, it would get a ten in the heating category.

There would be points off for drafts, rooms with radiators that are too small and for gaps in the insulation. If a house had steam heat instead of hot-water heat, it would lose five points.

Each house also would be rated for summer temperatures. If it was shaded or well insulated and air-conditioned, it would get a high hot-weather rating.

A prospective buyer would be able to get a realistic assessment of the amount of usable floor space in a house. The floor space in hallways wouldn't be counted, and any room that had to be used as a passageway to another room would lose points.

There would be major deductions if the front door opened directly into the living room instead of into a hallway.

There would be minor deductions for the following items:

—Doors that open into a room when they'd be better opening out or vice versa.

—Rain gutters that collect leaves from adjacent trees and get clogged up easily.

—A bathroom hard to find in the dark in the middle of the night.

—Misplaced and inconvenient light switches.

—A front lawn, with crabgrass, on a hill.

—A living room arranged so that when one person is watching television, everyone has to watch it, whether they want to or not.

—Cracks in the sidewalk that make it difficult to shovel after a heavy snow. A shovel should slide easily along the length of a sidewalk and not keep bumping into obstacles.

—Wet basement, leaky roof.

—Leaky attics.

—Noisy street with heavy traffic.

On the plus side, there would be bonus points for these good features if a house had them:

—Enough bathrooms for everyone at rush hour.

—A working fireplace.

—Ample electrical outlets in convenient places.

—Closet space enough for everyone and everything.

—A kitchen equipped with a big refrigerator, a good stove, plenty of counter space and two sinks so that two people can work on the dishes at the same time.

It seems likely that if a proper test and rating could be devised, it would give prospective homeowners a chance to get a fair deal. Instead of inflated prose, each house would have a rating number.

There are intangibles that would be hard to assess. Some houses have a kind of charm to which it's difficult to assign a number. In that case, a meaningful figure might be the average number of years occupants had stayed in the house. If a house is fifteen years old and has had six owners or tenants, it's probably a dog.

This Old House

You want to know why we could never sell our house? I'll tell you why:

Because there are a thousand things I know about this house that no one else would ever know, that's why. You think you know how to open a door? Try our back door. You think it's easy because you have a key? Forget it. The lock on that door takes a special little twist and jerk that comes with years of experience. A stranger couldn't get into our house through that door with a ring of keys and a crowbar.

And how would anyone else know how to turn the water for the outside faucet off in the fall and on in the spring? It's a routine I've performed twice a year for thirty-five years now. (I forgot to do it twice.) I go to the back of the basement where the washer and dryer are lined up against the wall. The faucet is up between two rafters right behind the washing machine. I turn my back to the washing machine, put my hands behind me and up on the front edge of the washing machine. I give a little jump and boost myself to a sitting position on top of it. My back is to the wall but by leaning back, looking up over my head and extending my right arm up behind me, I can reach the valve handle on the pipe and turn it on.

Who else would know you have to jump up and sit on the washing machine to turn on the outside faucet?

And how would you put your car in the garage if you bought our house? Would you have any way of knowing that if you pull the car forward just to where the divider between the front and rear door of the car is exactly opposite the leaf rake hanging from a hook that you won't bump into anything at the front of the garage but will still be in far enough so you can close the door? Would you know that?

And, by the way, don't open the garage door early in the morning if someone's sleeping in the little guest room over it because the door makes a loud rumbling sound right under the bed.

Would you know that the fan in the attic lets in too much cold air when it isn't working in the winter and has to be stuffed with insulation? And if you knew that would you know the best way to climb up into the attic through the small entry over the upstairs hallway? I'm sure you wouldn't. It's by using the little ladder I keep under Brian's bed. You wouldn't know that, would you? And anyway, if I sold the house, I'd take the ladder because I made it in 1957.

You certainly wouldn't know that when it rains steadily for a couple of days, the front part of the basement gets damp unless I put a sheet of plastic on the ground under the downspout where all the water pours out off the roof. While I'm basically an honest person, it is quite possible that if you were interested in buying my house, I wouldn't go out of my way to tell you about the damp basement.

If you don't jiggle the handle on the downstairs toilet just a little after you flush it, it keeps running. It takes a special touch to jiggle it just right.

When I come downstairs in the dark and want to turn the light on, I can put my finger on the light switch halfway down the hallway leading to the kitchen nine out of ten times without feeling for it. It's nothing I could teach anyone how to do. After thirty-seven years, I just know where every light switch is in the whole house. Every time I do it, I think what it must be like to be blind and still be able to find things.

I know our house too well to sell it. I know it's the seventh step from the top coming downstairs that creaks the most.

And if, by any chance, you did buy our house, you couldn't move in right away because it would take us at least a year to empty out the closets.

Going Out of the Buying Business

I hope it doesn't have an adverse effect on the economy of the United States, but very soon now I think I'll stop buying things. I was looking around the house last weekend and I think I have enough things to last me now.

I have my typewriters. I know for certain I don't need any more typewriters. In addition to the seventeen old Underwood No. 5's I've collected, there are two small portables in my work area in the base-ment and another I bought in an emergency at Sears in Indianapolis years ago. Sears had used it as a display model and sold it to me for only $59 because they couldn't find the cover to it. The typewriter works fine but, without a cover that has the handle attached to it, I can't take it anywhere.

Anyway, I've bought a computer that I write on when I take a trip because I can plug it into the telephone and send what I've written back to the office. I didn't think I'd ever use a word processor but I have, and it involves buying a lot of other things for it.

I've bought quite a bit of software that I don't know how to use. I'll start learning how to use that instead of buying anything more. I'm already at the very outer edge of my intellectual capacity for learning about computers.

It would be a good idea if I started writing more with pencils, too. Over the years I've bought a lot of pencils and I've brought a lot home from the office and, as a result, I suppose there are four hundred pencils in drawers, pockets, cabinets, car glove compartments and on the little tables next to the beds in the house.

The pencils will be good to write on all the small notepads I've got. I buy notepads and usually take the one in the hotel room next to the telephone, so I have a lot of notepads.

I'm not going to buy any more flashlights. I'll dig the ones I've bought out of the closets, fix some of them and get new batteries for the others. I have my flashlights.

While I'm not known as a clothes horse among my friends, I've bought quite a lot of clothing. I seem to be hooked on various kinds of casual jackets and sports shirts. There's what they call a factory store near us that deals in seconds and I often drop in there Saturday morning and buy a shirt of some kind. Beginning very soon now, I'm going to start wearing some of those shirts.

I have enough shoes, too. I must have six or eight pairs of those new running, walking or tennis shoes. I'm going to start wearing them regularly because, if I don't, there's still going to be a lot of good rubber left on them long after I have enough energy left to wear it off.

There are enough neckties hanging from the rack on the door of the closet to keep me properly dressed for many years to come. I must have fifty neckties, but I only wear the three I like. This is ridiculous and I'm going to start wearing the other forty-seven even though I don't like them.

Every time I go somewhere, I buy another little canvas or leather bag of some kind to bring home things that don't fit in my suitcase. I have enough little bags now, and if I go someplace I'll take one of them with me, empty, so I don't have to buy another.

I'm not going to buy any more tools. I have one of just about every tool known to man and I'll stop visiting hardware stores.

The only thing I buy more of than sports shirts and sports jackets is wood. I have more good wood in my shop in the country and in our basement at home than I'd have time to make anything out of if I started today and worked on it for the next twenty-five years.

I have boards in the spaces between the beams under the living-room floor, on supports I've put high up on the garage walls and under the stairway leading down into the basement.

Beginning any day now, I'm going to stop buying things and start enjoying what I have.

Homeless Sweet Homeless

Most mornings of my life, I arrive early in Grand Central Terminal. Grand Central is one of the most beautiful, complex and useful buildings ever built. It is a monument to our civilization. It serves hundreds of thousands of people every day, a sort of man-made beehive with people hurrying in all directions on a dozen different levels over its magnificent marble floors. A vaulted ceiling depicting what used to be called "the heavens" covers one of the greatest indoor spaces in the world, the main waiting room. It's called the main waiting room even though no one does much waiting in it.

When I arrive, there are as many as a hundred homeless people sleeping on the floor in various areas, covered with newspapers or tattered blankets. The public toilets in the station, originally built with the best plumbing fixtures available and made of the finest materials by the best craftsmen, are filthy sump holes now, abandoned to the homeless. Building management tries, perfunctorily, to clean the rest-rooms but it's a losing battle.

No traveler using Grand Central considers descending into the bowels of the building to use the toilet facilities. Not all the homeless bother to use them, either. They relieve themselves in the hundreds of recesses around the building. The little alcoves on the great ramp leading to the lower level of the station and to the superb Oyster Bar reek of urine.

Every day at midnight, the homeless are cleared out of the building and taken to what we once indelicately referred to as "flophouses." The homeless, like the rest of us, have their favorite places to be and every morning they're back in Grand Central.

Am I heartless if I resent the intrusion of these people, who cannot cope with life, on the beauty and efficiency of this public facility . . . and, to some extent, on my consciousness? Why did we bother to erect such a magnificent place? I have the clear impression that society feels sorrier for these people than they feel for themselves. If they are desperately unhappy, I don't detect it. Many of them are mentally unstable or alcoholic.

People in New York are divided about how they feel. One group yells, "Mea culpa! Take care of them!" Another group shouts, "Leave them alone! They have rights!"

As an observer, I have the clear feeling that the proud homeless who genuinely need and deserve our help because they are hungry, cold and jobless through no fault of their own are largely invisible. They are not on the floor in Grand Central.

Several years ago, New York State decided it was paying for the care of too many people who were mentally ill. It turned them out of institutions, and many of those people are on the streets of New York now. They are mostly harmless and, I suspect, happier than they were when they were institutionalized even though they don't eat regularly and are often cold on winter nights. Their presence in public places lessens the quality of life for the rest of us. Do we owe them that?

Recently Ed Koch, the mayor of New York, decreed that the mentally incompetent were to be removed, forcibly if necessary, from the streets. By "streets" he also meant such public havens for them as Grand Central. The edict did not include all the homeless, just those someone decided were "mentally disturbed."

Each of us thinks everyone else in the world is a little crazy. Exact definitions of what constitutes being "mentally disturbed" are hard to find. Many of these vagrants are, if not crazy, at least very eccentric. At what point does someone's eccentricity intrude on other people's freedom?

The argument rages in the courts of New York City. When it's over I hope the homeless have a home and we have Grand Central back, floors, men's rooms and all.

My House Runneth Over

Let me tell you a heartbreaking story of people with no place to sleep at Christmas.

Once upon a long, long time ago there was a house on a hill owned by a writer and his wife. They had four children and five bedrooms. Three of the children were girls and one was a boy. Two of the three girls were twins and sleeping accommodations in the house were ample.

Ah, but that was long ago. The house still has five bedrooms but since Margie took over one of them as her workroom, the bed that was there has been replaced by a convertible sofa that is only made into a double bed in an emergency and even then the foot of it hits her file cabinets.

Two of the remaining four rooms have single beds. The other bedroom sleeps two. Counting the convertible couch, this makes places for eight sleepers.

Our four children come from London, Los Angeles, Boston and Washington for Christmas. They are no longer little kids and they don't come alone. The twins, with one husband each and three children between them, come as seven. Nancy, my sister, is with us.

To save counting, that's twelve in all . . . twelve people in a house with real sleeping places for eight.

The couch in the living room and the old couch that was retired to the catch-all room in the basement are pressed into service. That's ten. I've never gotten into the details of where the others go. We close our bedroom door and hope for the best. We have two television reporters in the family but we've never seen overcrowding in the shelters they do stories about at Thanksgiving that can compare with the squalid conditions in our house at Christmas. It's enough to bring tears to a grown man's eyes.

There are clothes, open suitcases everywhere. The three bathrooms are strewn with stray toothbrushes, hair dryers and an assortment of beauty products . . . although I can't tell from looking at any of the six women in the house which one uses them. The refrigerator, the washing machine and the dryer get heavy use. The iron is never cool. Someone is always washing himself, herself, hair, clothes or the car. Because of nighttime sleeping conditions, there is random couch-napping during the day and some of the beds are working more than eight-hour shifts.

One year we rented two hotel rooms and another year we used the house of friends who graciously offered it while they were away for Christmas. Neither of these alternatives is popular with the family members who have to leave the chaotic, friendly warmth in our house Christmas Eve to go to sleep in a strange place.

All things come to an end and I dread the end of Christmas at our house. I'm not sure how or when it will come. Someone will probably decide it's too hard. The friends who loaned us their homes have made the Big Switch. They now go to the home of one of their children for Christmas. It could happen to us, I suppose. One more husband, one more wife or another grandchild might do it . . . but then where does everyone go? Do we break up the family and have separate Christmases in different parts of the country? Would this really be as merry? Am I suffering post-Christmas depression? I've thought a lot about it and I've decided what I want for Christmas next year.

I'd like Santa to bring me an addition to our house with two more bedrooms and another bathroom, even though they'd be empty 363 days a year.

Unreal Estate

Angela Nicolaysen
Weichert Realtors
Mendham, N.J.

Dear Angela,

Thank you for your letter, sent to my home in Connecticut, offering me a home in Mendham, New Jersey, for either $2.45 million or one for $2.55 million. If I take both of them, do I get anything off? From the drawings you sent along with your letter, I can't tell the difference between the two houses. Why is one so cheap?

I'd want to see the actual houses, too, because those dreamers' sketches of buildings never bear much resemblance to the way a place actually looks when it's finished.

You refer to the houses as "homes." "A house," as someone famous once said, "is not a home." When the builder finishes it and it's sitting there empty, as the places in your sketches are, it's not a home. It's a house. It isn't a home until someone moves in and leaves their belongings all over. I know "home" is a more attractive sales word.

I've been trying to figure out why you choose me to send your sales letter to. The only thing I can think of is you drove by my home and decided I could do better.

That's a pretty insulting thing for you to do, Angela. Yes, the place needs a little work but I'll be getting at that, probably, as soon as my vacation is over. I know, for instance, there are places that need paint.

Your letter reminded me that it wouldn't do any harm if I had a couple of loads of topsoil brought in so I could reseed the lawn and get some real grass growing.

The day you drove past, there may have been a beer can down front. Kids do that driving by once in a while, but listen, Angela, I can buy a lot of paint and topsoil for $2.45 million. The beer can I'll pick up myself. You say Mendham and the surrounding communities have "enticed a number of celebrities, among them Whitney Houston, Jacqueline Onassis, Mike Tyson and Malcolm Forbes."

I want to be honest with you, Angela. I've made good money the last ten years, but I don't have the kind of money Jackie, Mike and Malcolm have and, while I've never heard of Whitney Houston, I probably don't have the kind of money he or she has, either. If I showed up at their doors looking to borrow a cup of sugar from one of them, I doubt if I'd be dressed in the manner they've become accustomed to having their neighbors dressed. Mike Tyson is another matter altogether. If he was my neighbor I certainly wouldn't knock on the door and ask him for a cup of sugar.

Your letter is a persuasive sales pitch, but I do have some advice. You say that "This sophisticated, yet quaint rural environment is enhanced by its proximity to New York City . . . only fifty minutes away and easily accessible by car, train or bus." Take out "bus."

The idea of taking a bus into New York destroys the tony image you've tried so hard to create. If I moved out there, would I see Jacqueline Onassis, Mike Tyson or Malcolm Forbes on the bus coming into New York? I think your letter should read "easily accessible by limousine."

I know Malcolm Forbes rides a Harley-Davidson. I don't know

whether he rides his motorcycle to work every morning or not but if, by any chance, he lived next door to me, maybe he'd pick me up mornings. I could ride in sitting behind him on his bike.

You're knocking on the wrong door here, Angela. The biggest problem for me with a house in Mendham, New Jersey, is it would be two hours away from home.

HOLIDAYS AND VACATIONS

Free, Free at Last

Every one of us has imagined having something wonderful happen. We dream we suddenly discover a great athletic ability we have and win the big game or an Olympic gold medal; we think about having some distant relative die, leaving us an unexpected fortune; men dream of being in the company of Linda Evans, women in the company of Tom Selleck.

Recently I've been having a more practical dream. In this fantasy of mine, I'm arrested for some small offense. The judge sentences me to a year in prison. I am taken to a cell ten feet long and eight feet wide. In the cell, there is a bed, a chair, a desk, a lamp with a 100-watt bulb, a typewriter, a stack of paper three feet tall and, on a shelf above the desk, ten books.

Three times a day I am brought a simple, low-calorie meal that doesn't appeal to me. Each morning at seven, I am forced to take one hour of strenuous exercise and then returned to my cell. There is no telephone available to me, no television, no newspapers. I am trapped with only myself for company. There's no way to waste time, so I turn to the only things available to me, the typewriter and the books.

Then, in this prison fantasy of mine, I lay out my schedule. From 8:00 to 11:30 A.M., I work on a novel I've been meaning to write but never had time for. Then the guard comes with a glass of water and a tuna-fish sandwich on unbuttered bread for lunch. I hardly touch it.

After lunch, I take a little nap and then start writing a play. All afternoon I work on my play until the guard comes with a terrible supper at 5:30. Again, I eat very little.

Every once in a while, I stop writing my play or my novel and, for relief, I write half a dozen letters to people I never got around to answering when I was on the outside.

From 5:30 to 7:00 P.M., I just sit and think, and then I start reading. With two exceptions, the books are ones I never really read before. They are:

Webster's Third International Unabridged Dictionary. I've always wanted to read it from start to finish but never had time. I get caught reading a little of it when I'm looking up a word but I always feel I'm wasting time so I stop.

Crime and Punishment by Dostoyevsky. I don't really want to read this book but I'm tired of feeling guilty for not having read it every time it's mentioned by my intellectual friends.

War and Peace by Tolstoy. See reason above.

The Bible. I get into a lot of arguments, and having read the Bible thoroughly would help me win more often. I've heard there are a lot of good parts in it too. I've talked to people who claim to have read the Bible but I've never talked to anyone who convinced me they'd really read and understood it all.

On the Origin of Species by Charles Darwin. It seems as though everyone should have read a book as important as this one.

Don Juan by Lord Byron. I read this in college and was surprised to find out how good it was. I loved it. It was so interesting and complex that I'd like to read it again.

The Adventures of Huckleberry Finn. I'll pick this up toward the end of the evening when I'm winding down and want to relax and have a little fun.

The Sun Also Rises. I'm also ashamed of never having read Hemingway's classic.

Finnegans Wake by James Joyce. I couldn't make heads or tails out of this when I tried it twenty years ago and I'd like to try again.

Word for Word. This is the name of the book I wrote in 1986. I'd like to have a copy of it in my cell just to give me a little class with the guards.

By the end of my imaginary year in prison, I will have lost thirty-seven pounds because the food was so bad; I'll have read nine important books and I'll have written the novel and the play I've been meaning to get at.

Now, if I can only think of some nice, harmless crime to commit that will get me a year in the prison of my dreams.

Christmas Resolutions

While we're thinking about it, this might be a good time to make some Christmas resolutions for the coming years. Here are some proposals:

—Ban all recorded Christmas music in stores. Christmas music is too good to be used commercially. I sometimes have to flee a store and resume shopping at a later time because I can no longer take the repetitious sounds. It seems as though the people who work in those stores where the same recorded Christmas music is recycled time after time after time all day long could be driven crazy.

If a store had a band of school kids singing or live musicians playing, this would be perfectly acceptable. Some exceptions might be made for a store that didn't replay the same song more than twice a day.

—Appoint an inspector general of Santa Clauses. He would have the authority to ban all seedy Santa Clauses. Every Santa Claus would have to look right and sound right.

Department-store Santa Clauses have been pretty good over the years. The inspector would see to it that all Santas met this standard.

—Prohibit all Christmas advertising before Thanksgiving. Someone is always jumping the gun and filling a store window with Christmas presents in early November. They should be enjoined.

Most good stores voluntarily hold off until after Thanksgiving. It isn't fair to them when the schlock merchants start pushing too early.

—Stop fly-by-night Christmas-tree entrepreneurs who often steal the trees, bring them to town in a rented truck and set themselves up in an empty lot. They undercut the responsible places that sell Christmas trees from the same location year after year.

Every year tens of thousands of trees are cut and brought to town. When they don't sell, they're dragged to the local dump or burned on the spot. Any place that sells Christmas trees should have to pay a $5 fee for each tree they have left over by Christmas morning. There's no sadder sight than a lot full of unsold Christmas trees the day after Christmas . . . trees whose lives were shortened unnecessarily.

—Make it against the law to use Christmas music in any television commercial or newspaper advertisement. Santa Claus was never meant

to be a salesman; it lessens his believability when he's used as a symbol
for kids.

—Encourage recipients of gifts to give those gifts a chance before
rushing the day after Christmas to return them to the store from which
they were bought. Not liking a gift is not sufficient reason to return it.
That's between the giver and the receiver. If it doesn't fit or you already
have one, those are legitimate grounds for returning a gift.

—Make it mandatory that every Christmas card mailed out has both
the first and last name of the sender. It never seems to occur to people
that any one of us might know two or more people named Edith,
George or Linda. There's nothing more frustrating than getting a
Christmas card and not knowing who it's from.

—Ensure that every major religion in America finds a way to make
Christmas its own. There is no other time of year during which so many
people feel so good and so friendly toward so many other people. The
spirit of Christmas exceeds the narrow beliefs of any one religion.

Merry Christmas Cards

A few Christmas cards are still drifting in from friends who didn't
get at sending them out until it was too late. There's just so much you
can expect from the post office. I understand these cards because that's
when we send ours out.

I like sending and receiving Christmas cards but there are certain
things about the tradition that make me uncomfortable. For example,
I wish I had the names and addresses of all the good old friends I ever
had so I could send them cards. Someone ought to devise a system that
would make it easier for all of us to keep track of old friends when our
paths diverge.

There are eight or ten categories of Christmas cards.

1. There are simple cards with almost nothing on them but the
words MERRY CHRISTMAS AND A HAPPY NEW YEAR written in red and
green. Maybe there's a small wreath or border of holly. They're the
best. A Christmas card always should be basically red and green.

2. Lots of cards feature Christmas trees. Sometimes they look like
real trees. Other times they're stylized trees from an artist's imagination, usually attractive.

3. Many people send religious cards with pictures of the Virgin

Mary with Jesus Christ as a baby. These are often blue with silver, but I don't know why.

The religious people who send these cards don't like to hear it, but Christmas has become something more than Christ's birthday. Many people who are not interested in religion celebrate Christmas as a day to love their fellowman.

Another serious card is the one that says simply PEACE or PEACE ON EARTH. They're nice, although the cards don't seem to have any effect on world affairs.

4. We get two or three cards every year with family pictures on them. If you don't see the friends regularly, it's fun to identify family members you knew as children ten or twenty years ago.

5. One dear friend always sends us a Christmas card with a picture of a cat on it. It'll be a picture of a cat under a Christmas tree, out in the snow or with Santa Claus.

A cat, in my mind, has nothing whatsoever to do with Christmas.

6. Santa Claus cards are popular. Some of them are imaginative and clever, but a Christmas card can be too cute. Funny is not exactly the right mood for Christmas. I'm not enthusiastic about comic-strip characters on Christmas cards.

7. There were cards for sale this year that said MERRY CHRISTMAS TO MY WIFE or MERRY CHRISTMAS TO MY HUSBAND. Anyone who has to send a Christmas card to a spouse is in big trouble.

8. Everyone gets at least one card that says FROM JIM AND HELEN and has no idea who "Jim and Helen" are. In our house, Margie thinks they must be my friends and I'm sure they're hers.

9. Card manufacturers don't seem satisfied with the traditional Christmas cards. This year there were more cards in stores that did something. There were little windows in the front flap with Santa Claus looking out and when you opened the card you saw Santa sitting on his sled with all his reindeer. On others, Christmas trees popped out. They were made more like valentines than Christmas cards. Wrong.

10. Mimeographed Christmas letters have become a tradition with many families. They can be interesting but I'm not usually much impressed with the writing style or the reportorial skill of those who send them out. These Christmas letters are usually substantially rosier than real life.

Christmas cards are a wonderfully friendly tradition. I hope greeting-card manufacturers don't ruin the idea. Anytime there's money involved, someone usually carries the idea too far.

Some Don't Like It Hot

It's still only May but there are harbingers of heat in the air. (*Harbinger* isn't my kind of word. It sounds like it's a bird. A harbinger is a pretty vague thing and I wish I'd never used it but you know what I mean.)

Harbingers or no, I am one of the world's great haters of hot days. Some people hate cigarette smoke, some can't stand yogurt and others spend their time protesting against companies that do business with South Africa. I hate heat. When it's hot, all I want to do is lie down.

I am not alone. There is no question that the whole human race gets less done where the temperature is regularly above 80 degrees. Look at the world and see where most good things have been accomplished. In Pago Pago? In Tahiti? In Calcutta or the Philippines? They may be nice places to visit but for the men and women who have advanced our civilization, look toward countries with temperate climates. Heat saps ambition.

In the winter a lot of people go to Florida, Arizona, New Mexico and Southern California for the weather. I understand that. It can be very pleasant. What I don't understand is why those places don't empty out about now. I'm surprised some parts of the South don't have to hire guards to patrol their streets in the summer because all the residents have left to escape the heat. Why don't people head for Labrador, Iceland and Greenland in the summer the way they go to Florida in the winter?

There are so many reasons I hate the heat, I can hardly count the ways.

First, I don't like feeling sorry for people, but when it's hot I can't help it. I feel sorry for the policemen out there all day. I don't like seeing street-repair and utility crews digging in the broiling sun. I feel sorry for everyone who can't live in air-conditioned comfort on a hot day.

I'm even more uncomfortable watching how miserable dogs and horses are in the heat. Panting may be a dog's way of perspiring but it doesn't seem to work very well at cooling them down. It makes any caring human uneasy to be in the presence of a panting dog.

I even feel sorry for my car when I have to park it out in the open where I know it will be sitting in the hot sun all day.

There seems to be something basically wrong and counterproductive about having the air-conditioning unit of a car cooped up under the hood of a hot engine.

Air-conditioning itself, essential though it is, is not really lovable. In restaurants you sit where it hits you in the back of the neck and at home you bought a unit that's a little too small to do the job right. And then there's something pervasively unpleasant about the atmosphere in an air-conditioned room. You feel you're breathing old, canned air that has been previously breathed by someone else before it was chilled and pushed out into the room again. After a day in an air-conditioned office, you have a vaguely uneasy feeling somewhere in between a headache and a cold.

Clothes are a terrible problem in the summer heat. My clothes all seem smaller, tighter and less comfortable in hot weather. I wear lightweight clothes all winter and, as a result, don't have much to shift down to when summer comes. Hats shade your head from the sun but they increase the temperature of your head under them, so I usually discard a hat after a short time.

The most idiotic clothing custom in the whole civilized world is that of a man tying a piece of cloth around his neck and knotting it at the throat to make a necktie.

If daytime heat is ever tolerable, nighttime heat never is. I'd like it if I never had to sleep without a blanket again in my life. Beds should be made so that on hot nights we could sleep on firm nets allowing the air to circulate around our bodies. A mattress is like having a six-inch blanket under you.

The temperature reached 90 degrees in a lot of places last week. That's the harbinger I mentioned. I personally hope for a cold, wet summer.

A Vacation Postcard

It's wonderful having a summer house to retire to for vacation. If we didn't have a summer house, I wouldn't be having all this fun. For example, yesterday, when I made the mistake of turning on the toaster while someone was using the iron in the next room, it blew a fuse in the box in the cellar. It's a cellar; it isn't a basement. You have to go outside to get to it.

We all head for water on vacation so you can probably imagine what a joy it was for me when I opened the doors over the stone steps leading into the cellar and saw five inches of water down there. The fuse box is at the other side of the oil burner, fifteen feet from the steps. I don't know much about electricity, but I know enough not to wade into five inches of water to do any electrical work. I didn't change the fuse.

I don't want to go into the unpleasant details, but I don't want to leave you with the impression this was spring water in the cellar, either. It had backed up from a clogged pipe leading to the septic tank.

Unclogging the line leading to the septic tank isn't even half the fun I've had on my vacation. On my first day back on the tennis court, I made a clumsy move, tripped and came down with my full weight on my ankle in a turned position. It's as much fun as slamming your finger in a car door.

Then I've been having a high old time meeting people at the Albany Airport thirty miles away too. Martha and Leo were due from Washington at 2:30 on a USAir flight for the July Fourth weekend. It's an hour's drive from here to the airport, so I started at 1:30. It's also an hour's flight from Washington to Albany. When I got to the airport, USAir said the flight hadn't left National Airport in Washington yet. The flight was two hours and twelve minutes late.

Today Ellen was scheduled to arrive from Boston on Bar Harbor Airlines, a subsidiary of Eastern, at 10:05 A.M., on flight number 3753. I arrived at the airport at 10:00 and was told the flight had been canceled. "Mechanical problems," they said. I called home and Ellen had called Margie to say she was catching the next flight, number 3801, due in at 11:25.

The airline said there were air-traffic problems and that flight number 3801 would be arriving about noon. It arrived at 12:20.

Today I called the FAA in Washington. Eastern had not yet reported any mechanical problems to it on canceled flight number 3753. On-ground problems need only be reported once a month. I'll be checking. I hate being lied to even more than I hate waiting.

In meeting three flights, I've spent a total of six hours and fifteen minutes at the Albany Airport so I've had a lot of time to look around. One of the cops out front should lose some weight. Coffee is 70 cents a cup.

Joe gets $2 for a shine and Fred gets $10 for a haircut. I got a haircut, but I told Joe $2 seemed like a lot for a shine. Of course, Joe would have to shine a lot of shoes to make what I make writing so maybe it isn't too much. And anyway, during the whole time I was there, Joe didn't have a single customer. I felt kind of sorry for him, but I didn't get a shine because I was wearing old sneakers. By the time Ellen arrived and we drove back out to the house, it was after three. The dump closes at three so we're stuck with the garbage until Saturday.

Having a wonderful time. Wish you were here—Andy.

A Vacation Hangover

I'm back from vacation but everything feels strange.

My shoes feel strange because I've been wearing sneakers for a month.

My collar feels tight because I haven't been wearing a necktie, and my leather belt must have shrunk while I was away.

This typewriter feels strange because it hasn't been hit for a month. It's slow and sticky.

The city seems strange, loud and dirty.

There's no time of year that goes so quickly as those summer vacation weeks. I've been taking a month now for several years, and when I pack up to leave, the days seem to stretch endlessly before me, one vast amount of time to rest and catch my breath. And then the time flies. There's no good substitute for that cliché.

When I was eight and in between the second and third grade, we had a cottage on a lake for the summer, and I recall clearly the feeling of dread I had in the middle of the night even then. I'd awaken and start thinking about how close to its end my vacation was. Time was running out. It evoked in the pit of my stomach then the same feeling of dread I get in the middle of the night now, contemplating death.

It may be the clear delineation of a period of time that makes the time seem to go faster. Perhaps we ought to try to conserve time by dropping weeks and months as a means of dividing the years. We simply could number the days of the year. I am, for example, writing this on the 219th day. What would be wrong with calling it simply that? The date at the top right-hand corner of our letters today would say simply, "219th, 1988." Why do we complicate it by dividing the year into twelve months that have varying numbers of days? According to my calendar, it is, as I write, Sunday, August 7. I still would not be lamenting the passing of July if August 1 had been merely Number 213.

Variety makes a vacation seem short, too. It might be better if we all did the same thing every day of our vacation. We'd stay in the same place, see the same people and maintain a steady routine. Instead, we go places, take little trips, invite people to stay with us for the weekend and generally break up our days away from work into little patches of time. When you look forward to doing something the day after tomorrow, today and tomorrow pass quickly and so, of course, do the days on which you actually do something different. We nibble away at our vacation this way until there's nothing of it left for just doing nothing.

It's difficult to understand why we never get used to how fast the days of our lives go by. From the information that experience feeds our brains, we seem to learn everything else we need to know. We know when we're hungry, how much food to buy for ourselves. When we're tired, we know we'll have had enough sleep if we get six or seven hours, so we set the alarm for that. We know it takes half a glass of water to satisfy our thirst. We know all these things without even thinking about them, so how come we never learn how quickly our vacation goes by?

One of the most unfair things about vacations is that the people who do the least work and get paid the most money for it take the longest vacations. Everyone, though, is stealing more vacation time than they used to. It used to be they got two weeks and that was it. Now, more and more people are getting three weeks or a month and then taking extra days at other times during the year. I may steal a little myself during August. I'm not satisfied. I want a little more. I'll take a Friday here and there or use up all of Sunday and not come in until late Monday. I'll give the company its money's worth by coming in early and working late.

Plotting to steal a few long weekends for the next six weeks makes it easier to accept the fact that my real vacation is over.

After Many a Summer

Summer dies hard. We try to keep it alive for just a little longer.

Even though we're back at work and back at school, we try to hang on to a little of summer. We keep doing a few of the things we did on vacation, just as though it weren't really over. We do summer things on weekends. We continue swimming, playing outdoor games, wearing summer clothes. We wash the car and water the lawn but it isn't the same. The end is in sight. When *Monday Night Football* starts, can Fall be far behind?

It has been chilly in the house on several mornings recently. I can feel Fall coming. Driving through the hills Friday, I saw the first suggestion of some color other than green in the trees.

There's no sense pretending it's still summer when it isn't, but few of us can resist it for the first few weeks of Fall. The official end of summer comes about September 23 but we all know the Tuesday after Labor Day is really the day summer ends.

If the world were perfect, the seasons would be clearly defined. One season wouldn't blend gradually into another. We wouldn't have any warm summer days in October and cold winter days in April.

The problem is that the Earth got a bad deal when it was created billions of years ago. It wasn't put in orbit around the sun at the right angle. It's kind of cocked. The Earth's axis is tilted in relation to the sun, not facing it directly as it turns. The only times the sun hits the Earth straight on at the equator is in March and September, as I understand it . . . which isn't very well.

I'm not complaining about Fall. It's just that, like most people, I'm a little sad to have summer gone so soon. It isn't the weather I miss, it's the barefoot attitude everyone has in July and August. People aren't pressing so hard to get ahead. During the summer months, we're content to tread water and stay almost where we are.

People are divided about what they call this time of year. Autumn is more official, but I seldom use it. It seems too much like a poet's word for me. It's often used as a descriptive word to create a visual image of the season. You envision colored leaves when you hear the word autumn. I shouldn't think they'd use the word much in Florida or California.

Don't ask me why, but *Fall* is the only word for a season that I capitalize. I know it's inconsistent but it seems as though it needs a capital *F*. *Spring* could use a capital too, but I wouldn't think of capitalizing either *summer* or *winter*.

The best case that can be made for using *autumn* instead of *Fall* is that the word *Fall* has so many different and complex meanings in the English language. I'd hate to be starting out trying to learn English. Using *Fall* as the name of the season is way down on the list of definitions in both my dictionaries.

Fall means so many things. It isn't until definition number seven

that it says "the season between summer and winter." Among other
meanings for the word *Fall* are:

"To drop from a higher to a lower place."

"To take a proper place in formation; i.e., when a soldier 'falls in.' "

"When something comes or descends as 'the night falls.' "

"To happen; i.e., 'Election Day falls on Tuesday.' "

"To retreat or fall behind."

"A cascade of water coming down a bed of rocks."

"To quarrel or fall out with."

"One who receives the blame, slang; i.e., 'The fall guy.' "

"In wrestling, the throwing of an opponent on his back."

"In religion, the disobedience of Adam and Eve, The Fall."

No definition explains the use of the word *Fall* for the season.
Presumably it comes from what the leaves on the trees do.

It's all enough to make a person use the word *autumn*.

I don't care what anyone says about its beauty, though—Fall is a
little sad. A. E. Housman referred to it as "The beautiful and death-
struck year."

PLEASURES

The Art of Outdoor Cooking

This is the story of the fall of two of my heroes. Craig Claiborne and Pierre Franey write about food and I've always admired them greatly.

Now they've written a terrible article about outdoor grilling. I will never again accept their word for things about which I know nothing, because I've read their article on something about which I know a great deal and they're wrong. Imagine how crushed I was to realize that I know more than they do about cooking out.

Grilling anything outdoors is not an exact science. An outdoor fire isn't like an oven that can be set at a fixed temperature. Every fire is different and every piece of meat, fish or any other food to be cooked over it has to be treated differently.

Claiborne and Franey referred in their article to an "outdoor gas grill." Will someone please tell me why anyone thinks cooking over a gas grill outdoors is any different than cooking over a gas grill indoors? Outdoor cooking, Craig and Pierre, is done over wood or charcoal, not over gas.

These two experts quoted a third, a chef friend of theirs, as saying the use of wood wasn't important. I agree that mesquite chips or little bags of hickory chips bought in a gift shop are ridiculous but you can't beat cooking over hard wood.

The outdoor grill I cook over most often is built into the stone wall just outside the dining room. It is fortuitously situated within a hundred feet of six big shagbark hickory trees. Every time there's a strong wind, a few twigs and occasionally some major branches fall to the ground. I regularly pick up after the hickory trees and store their droppings in my wood box.

It's most convenient to start an outdoor fire with the store-bought "charcoal" that comes in those big bags. I put the word *charcoal* in quotation marks to indicate that it isn't really charcoal. It's coal dust that has been compressed with a large amount of clay that doesn't burn at all. I dislike it but it's convenient and it does hold its heat longer than wood.

Once I have a good fake charcoal fire going I add a few small pieces of wood. You can't use pine because the resins in it produce an unpleasant taste.

If I'm cooking meat, I put the meat on right away while it's smoking and before the wood catches fire. When the wood bursts into flame, this is where the experience counts. You have to judge how much flame to give the meat. You don't want it really charred, but cooking meat quickly at first seems to help it retain its moisture. If I'm trying to cook a thick steak or even chicken, I often put the meat in the oven first, at low temperature for fifteen minutes, to warm it through.

The big trouble with most grills you can buy in a hardware store is that they aren't adjustable. You simply must be able to move what you're cooking closer or farther away from the fire at different times. I keep four bricks handy and I'm always setting them up in different combinations to rest my grill on so that I can move the food away from the fire when it's flaming or closer to it if it dies. When I'm ahead of the cook in the kitchen doing the vegetables, I want to put the meat on hold for a few minutes.

Like most Americans, we're eating less meat. It isn't something we decided to do. It isn't diet or religion. Huge pieces of meat just don't appeal to us as much as they used to. Last night I cut two small zucchinis in half lengthwise and poured a combination of olive oil and safflower oil over them. I sliced big new potatoes half an inch thick and took the heavy stems off a big head of broccoli. I boiled the slices of potato for about five minutes and blanched the broccoli. I put some of the oil over the potatoes and the broccoli and put everything on the grill, the broccoli last and very briefly.

I thought to myself, "Craig and Pierre are probably grilling caviar on an electrically operated spit. I wish they were here to try this vegetarian dinner grilled over real wood."

Experience Is a Slow Teacher

I'd be a lot better going to school now than I was when I went to school. I wouldn't mind starting all over in about the seventh or eighth grade. That's when I began to lose it a little.

Miss Shute would stand in front of the class when she was teaching arithmetic and say something like this: "Seven. Multiply by three. Subtract nine. Divide by two. Multiply by eight. Add two. Andrew?" she'd say, looking quizzically at me for an answer.

Charles Gibson and several of the brighter boys had their hands up waving at Miss Shute to call on them because they had the answer.

"Fifty," they'd shout when she pointed at them.

The best I ever could do was guess. I don't think I ever got the right answer to one of Miss Shute's exercises.

Miss Boyd taught us English. "He cooked the steak a deep dark brown," she'd say. "What part of speech is the word 'deep'?" she'd ask, then pause. "Andrew?"

They were always calling on me, and I was always letting them down. I didn't know then what part of speech "deep" was in that sentence and, to tell you the truth, I'm not even sure now.

That's why I'd like to start over. I'd like to take advantage of an education. I'd work a lot harder.

I took Latin, algebra, biology and French in high school, and then in college I took good courses in American and English literature. I took lots of history and philosophy but, for the most part, I was more interested in passing than learning.

Kids going to school are lucky. When you see what a mess we make of our civilization, it's amazing we have local governments that govern us, water and sewer systems that work and pipes and wires that supply us with electricity and telephone communications.

As civilized as all these things are, nothing we have done with our world is any better than our determination to educate our young.

Phrases like "Experience is the best teacher" and "There are a lot of things you can't learn from books" are fine to pull out once in a while. These sayings are partly true but they're most popular with people who feel inferior because they didn't get a good education.

They're trying to convince themselves and their friends they didn't miss anything. They missed something and they know it.

Setting out to learn something in a program designed by professionals to teach the most about a subject in the shortest time is a wonderfully civilized thing to do and by far the most efficient way to learn. Putting aside a major portion of your life—often more than twenty years—to cram in facts that might otherwise never come to your attention is infinitely more efficient than experience. Learning from experience is slow and painful. Anyone can gain scientific knowledge about temperature by spilling boiling water on himself, but it's the hard way. Experience is a good teacher but it's no substitute for a real, live one.

The facts and background of subjects like literature, history, science and arts never come to the attention of people whose only teacher is experience because these people choose to quit school and go to work. Millions of people in the world less lucky than most of us never even have the opportunity to quit school. They go from their mothers' arms to work.

The institution of school in our society is almost too good to believe. In school you aren't expected to be doing anything else. You don't normally have a job or, ideally, even any major worries about money. You have special hours to learn in and a special place to go. Almost none of us recognize how good life is in school until we're out of it.

With all the kids going to school, we should all take some satisfaction in having done this one thing right.

Playgrounds for Grown-ups

One of the saddest days of my life was the day I realized I'd played my last football game. As a young boy I played in pickup games in vacant lots on Saturdays in the fall. I was already certain that I loved the game better than any other.

All through high school and into college I played my favorite game and then, one day, it was over. It was my last game and I knew it.

There are school administrators who emphasize to students the good sense of playing what they call "carryover" sports in high school and college. These are the games like golf and tennis that you continue to play as you age. I understand the argument in their favor but as bad as I felt the day of that last football game, I wouldn't trade my football days if I could have started playing golf in grade school and grown up to be Arnold Palmer.

It's a problem, though. The problem is that too many games we play in our youth turn us into fans instead of participants when we're older. There's no question that Americans are watching too much and doing too little when it comes to sports.

If I ever run for office—and you're safe because I never will—I'd run on a ticket that endorses spending federal, state and local-government money for an adult sports facility in every village, town and city in the country. They would be on equal footing with our schools, our museums and our libraries.

There ought to be a big field house in every community where adults could play the year round. There's no reason for gymnasiums to be limited to the use of school kids. I don't know many adults who wouldn't get a lot more exercise and enjoy themselves playing games that demanded some physical exertion if there were facilities for it in their communities.

Would it really be too expensive for this rich country to have buildings with racquetball and tennis courts, swimming pools, gymnasiums, weight and exercise rooms and good locker-room facilities? I always look toward our $300 billion defense budget. Just give us one of those billions and we can build a thousand adult sports complexes and spend $1 million each on every one of them.

I've never spent much time in a women's locker room but there's something very open, friendly and honest about a men's locker room. I like the smell, the steamy atmosphere, the camaraderie and the disheveled look of it. They're islands of civilization in a mean world. (I have heard . . . and this is only hearsay, mind you . . . that in a women's locker room the showers are usually divided into individual stalls so that women have privacy bathing. If this is true, it wouldn't have the same spirit as a men's locker room. If elected to office, I will vote to take down the walls in the women's shower rooms all across the country. Women, like men, have got to face the fact that we're all a little funny-looking naked.)

Athletic clubs in most big cities have good facilities but until recently they've been exclusively men's clubs and they're prohibitively expensive. Membership in the New York Athletic Club costs thousands of dollars and it doesn't let everyone in who has the money, either. Even at the famous West Side YMCA in New York, membership in the Business Men's Club is $810 the first year.

As a result of all the high-priced athletic clubs in town and the exclusive golf and tennis clubs in the country, not many people can afford to do much about sports, once they're adults, except sit and watch the games on television.

I hereby propose an adult sports facility for every community in the United States.

One Hot Ticket

The medium-size fellow wearing the blue baseball cap looked OK to me as I got off the bus in front of the stadium for the Giants-Dallas game. I was carrying a small canvas bag with my radio, binoculars, two tuna-fish sandwiches, four cookies, a thermos of coffee with cream and no sugar, and a raincoat. In my pocket was an extra ticket to the game.

My idea of a week's vacation is going to a Giants game alone on a Sunday afternoon. I couldn't have been happier. If I could whistle, I'd have been whistling.

There were a dozen young hustlers all around yelling for tickets.

"Who's got one? I need a ticket here."

Most of them were scalpers who would resell any ticket they got at a profit. The guy in the blue cap didn't look like a scalper, and I felt selfish going into the stadium with two tickets so I went up to him. "You looking for a ticket?" I asked.

"Yeah. Sure would like to see the game. I went to school with Lawrence Taylor."

It amused me to see the look on his face when I handed him the ticket and walked away. "Mr. Nice Guy," I thought to myself about myself.

Even though I go to the games alone, my friend Gene sits immediately in front of me, and I'm surrounded by dozens of other friends whose names I don't know because we have met only two hundred times, at eight Giants home games a year for the past twenty-five years. I don't know their politics, their religion or what they do for a living. They may steal for all I know but eight times a year for three hours they're my closest friends.

"What did you do with your other ticket?" Gene asked.

"I gave it to a guy out front," I said. "He was OK."

"He'll sell it," Gene said.

"No," I said. "He was OK. If the guy who comes isn't wearing a blue cap, you're right."

As I was bending over to dig my sandwiches out of the canvas bag, a voice said, "Pardon me. I have that seat."

The black guy standing next to me with the ticket stub was six feet four inches and must have weighed 240 pounds. He should have been down on the field.

Gene turned, gave me a look and said, "Where's the blue cap? You're some judge of character, Rooney."

"Where'd you get the ticket?" I asked the man.

"Outside," the big guy said. "Paid fifty dollars for it."

Mad is too mild a word for how I felt over having been taken.

I settled down to enjoy the game and the big guy turned out to be an OK fan, but I was still mad. At halftime, the big guy went out back. He returned with a Coke and said he'd just seen the fellow who sold him the ticket.

I jumped out of my seat and ran up the stairs and through the tunnel to the refreshment area.

The guy with the blue cap was just coming out of the men's room. I grabbed him by the arm.

"Give me the fifty dollars," I screamed.

"Let me explain," he said as his face went white.

"Look," I said, "I don't know who's gonna win this fight but we're gonna have one."

At that moment, my friend Gene appeared at my left shoulder.

"Is this the guy?" Gene asked menacingly.

Gene looks and talks like a retired New York City cop.

"I don't have the fifty dollars," the wimp said. "I'm with some other guys. We needed three tickets."

"I'm gonna get the fifty dollars," I said.

"Look," he said, showing me his empty wallet.

I reached quickly for his wallet and took out an American Express card.

"When you get the fifty dollars, I'll give it back," I said, and we left him.

Midway through the third quarter, the wimp in the blue cap appeared, holding a lump of bills.

"Here," he said, handing me the bills, "but I want to explain."

"Get lost," I said, taking the money and returning his American Express card. I passed the $50 on to the big guy and went back to the game.

On the bus home Gene said, "Did the big guy ever pay you seventeen dollars for the ticket?"

"Listen," I said, "when the Giants beat Dallas, it's worth thirty-four dollars to me."

The Best Hotel Room I Ever Had

Anyone who's never been broke cannot possibly appreciate having money as much as someone who has been broke. I never thought I'd live to think so but I know now that it was a good thing for me to have lived through a serious, jobless depression of my own years ago. I never get over appreciating being OK now.

I got thinking about being broke this morning because I just read that YMCAs across the country are closing their residential rooms. Twenty years ago Ys across the country had sixty-six thousand rooms they rented to young men looking for temporary places to stay. Last year they were down to thirty thousand rooms and more are closing.

During a period of almost a year when I was desperately broke, I often came to New York City looking for work or for someone who'd buy an article I'd written. My budget allowed little for a hotel room and I often stayed at the YMCA on Thirty-fourth Street for 50 cents a night.

Of all the things I've ever bought with money, nothing compares with what I got for that 50 cents. The rooms were tiny. I suppose their dimensions were something like twelve feet long and eight feet wide. The bed took up most of the room. Beyond the bed there was a small dresser on one side of a little window and one chair on the other. When you checked in, there was one clean towel, a washcloth and a small bar of soap waiting for you on the bed. The bathroom was down the hall.

One bitter-cold January day I arrived in New York during a raging snowstorm with nothing but a small suitcase, a portable typewriter and high hopes for a job from an interview I was to have with an advertising agency. The job interview left a bad taste in my mouth for job interviews that lingers after thirty years. Who do job interviewers think they are? They sit there, all smug and certain of their righteousness, ready to blackball the applicant for the look of his haircut, the sound of his voice or because of his "bad attitude."

I was curtly dismissed after a brief interview and walked out into the snow that was swirling through the canyons of the city. How would I tell Margie the interview came to nothing and that I was still without a job? It was 4:30 and darkening. I walked the fourteen blocks to the Y with my suitcase and typewriter. It was important to save the dime a bus ride would have cost me.

At the front desk at the Y they weren't sure they could give me a room. Please wait and come back in half an hour. I went to a nearby Automat cafeteria and spent 55 cents for dinner—a hard roll, rice and fricassee chicken.

The Automat was good and there were always people there worse off than I was. The desperate ones made soup by pouring ketchup in the bottom of a cup and adding the free hot water meant for tea.

I felt better after my dinner and made my way back to the Y. Glory be, a room was available. I took the key, bought a nickel candy bar at the newsstand and went to the room.

That may have been the best hotel room I ever had. It was warm and cozy. Through the window I could see the cold, cruel world outside and that made it seem even better. I turned over one of the drawers in the dresser and slid it back in upside down so that I could use the bottom of the drawer as a table for my typewriter.

Because the rooms were all occupied by men, you could walk down the hall wrapped in a towel then. I undressed, tied on my towel and walked to the bathroom, where I took a beautifully warm, steamy shower. How good, I thought, that the YMCA can provide such hot water on so cold a day.

Back in my room, I put on my pajamas, unwrapped the Milky Way and sat down in front of the upside-down drawer to write.

The job interviewer at the ad agency was rotten, I thought to myself, but the whole world is not rotten . . . not when the people at the YMCA provide something like this for an anonymous person like me.

Dear Sir, You Jerk

For every letter I actually write and mail, I compose a hundred in my head. Here are some samples of the kinds of letters I think of writing.

To the boss.

DEAR BOSS:

You can be a real jerk sometimes. If I didn't need the money, I'd have walked out of here about ten times in the last nineteen years.

You know how to make money, I'll admit that, but you don't know how to treat people. Once you hand out that little Christmas bonus, with the snappy memo saying what loyal employees we all are, you think you're Mr. Nice Guy. Big deal. Could you really afford the bonus after the profit the company made last year?

If things weren't so bad and if I was younger and if I didn't have three kids in college, I'd be out of here.

I'd come here early in the morning to clean out my desk. I'd park in your place by the front door marked RESERVED FOR THE PRESIDENT. When you dragged your butt in here around ten o'clock, there wouldn't be anyplace to park.

Maybe I'll see you in the company cafeteria at lunch and give you a piece of my mind. Ha! That'll be the day when you eat the garbage they serve us.

Sincerely,
Andrew R.

P.S.: By the way, what did your snooty secretary do with all those ideas I put in the suggestion box? I suggested your company car ought to be a Ford instead of a Cadillac, for instance.

To the owner of the gas-station garage.

DEAR ED,

I just got your bill for the job you did on my car. Isn't $237.50 a little stiff . . . considering parts and labor were extra?

What's this third item here? It says GRDLLCK MAC'ET INST FRD OPP. (BOTH SIDES) $81.65.

You have a sign posted over your cash register that says LABOR $45 AN HOUR. If your mechanic works ten hours a day five days a week and four hours on Saturday, he could be making $126,360 a year. Or don't you give him all of it? You're always complaining about how bad business is. If business is so bad, how come I have to book three weeks in advance to get the air changed in my tires?

Sincerely,
Andy

I've often written unmailed letters to the president of the bank:

Ralph Forsythe
President
First National American United Home Federal Bank
DEAR MR. FORSYTHE:

If there was a *second* National American United Home Federal Bank, I'd take my money out of your bank and go to it.

What's all this gobbledygook you send me every month? I can't read it. Just tell me how much money I have left and how much I spent. That's all I want to know. I don't need a lot of your numbers.

How come the number on my checking account is bigger than the total number of people in the United States? And how come you send me my statement on the sixteenth instead of on the first day of the month? It's real convenient . . . for you but not for me.

Those cash machines you've put in must be saving you a lot of money because you don't have to hire so many cashiers—whom you paid $3.50 an hour to handle $500,000 a day.

Customers no longer have to stand in line waiting for the cashier to cash their checks. Now we stand in line waiting for one of the machines.

Sincerely,
0072294783279

(You wouldn't know my name even though I've been banking there for twenty-three years.)

Look at it this way. I've just saved myself 75 cents for not mailing these.

Play It Again, Sam

It would be nice if all of us could use the instant-replay system in our lives to decide whether we made the right decision.

For those of you who don't follow professional football, it should be explained that when the officials on the field make a call and there's some doubt about whether they are right, other officials in a booth above the playing field review the play from all camera angles available to them on television. If there are eight cameras trained on the action, all shooting from a different position, the officials can look at the play from all eight angles and have a better chance of deciding what really happened.

That's what I'd like to do with my life. I'd like to have eight cameras trained on everything I do and then, when I make a mistake, I could replay it and see what I did wrong. Too often I can't remember exactly what I did or why I made the decision I did.

Last night I started to pull the car into the garage. I've done it thousands of times but this time I heard a terrible scraping, crunching noise and realized I'd caught the right side of the car on the side of the garage door. I'd like to review that.

By the time I was ready to go to bed, I realized I'd eaten too much for dinner. I'd like to review all eight camera angles of me at dinner last night to see if I can determine exactly where I went wrong. Next time we have it, I think I'd reverse my decision to have another helping of linguine with white clam sauce and I know darn well I'd overrule my call for more ice cream.

There are hundreds of decisions I've made that I'd like to see again:
—It would be interesting to replay the conversation Margie and I had when we decided to live in Connecticut instead of New York or California.
—The details of how we ended up with three cars for two people are vague to me. I'd like to see that again.
—If there had been cameras in the store where I bought the terrible-looking suit that doesn't fit me, I'd like to look carefully at those pictures to determine whether the salesman was out of bounds.

To be given a second chance, after reviewing the evidence and the facts, would change all our lives, I suspect three out of every ten important decisions I make would turn out to have been wrong if it were possible to go back over them and spend some time looking at every aspect of the problem.

The NFL owners are meeting in Phoenix, and the question of instant replay is on their agenda. They're talking about eliminating the rule that calls for it. I can't imagine why.

The instant replay has been a great satisfaction to both players and fans. They all get a better deal. I should think that even the officials would like it because they've come off looking good. The instant-replay feature was invoked 490 times in 210 football games and the officials were found to have been wrong only fifty-seven times. In other words, they were right almost 90 percent of the time. We should all have such a good right/wrong average in the decisions we make.

One objection NFL owners have is that it takes the officials in the booth too long to make their decision. That's true, but it takes advertisers too long to sell their stuff in the commercials too, yet the owners don't complain about that.

Instead of eliminating instant replay from one sport, it should be spread to all sports where television cameras are present. Anytime you watch a baseball game, you see two or three bad calls a game. Some are so obvious that even the home-team rooting announcers can spot a bad call that went in favor of their team. The World Series would be improved with instant replay.

Baseball and I should both have instant replay so we could review what has just happened and correct our mistakes.

Mr. Rooney Goes to Church

My old school classmate Howard Hageman has done very well in religion and he was the guest preacher at the beautiful little New England church in our tiny upstate New York town. I liked Howard in school and I was curious about how he did it, so I went to church.

When I knew Howard best, he was manager of our undefeated high school football team. He went to Harvard and subsequently became president of the New Brunswick Theological Seminary.

There were thirty-nine people in church Sunday morning, a pretty good crowd. The interior of the church is perfect. It is absolutely plain, about sixty feet across and eighty feet long, painted a kind of Williamsburg off-white. There are twelve rows of pews, divided by a center aisle. The minister stands at a simple mahogany lectern, framed by two white, fluted columns that go from the floor to the roof.

Howard greeted the congregation and then, before asking the members to pray, and realizing some of the people had come a distance to hear him, said that if anyone had to go to the bathroom after the service, they could do it at the Palmer House Café just up the street.

The Palmer House is one of the best things that ever happened to our town. It's a serious little restaurant that has even arranged to get the Sunday papers so we no longer have to drive twelve miles for them. Sunday morning I can pick up four fresh-baked cinnamon Danish and *The New York Times* by eight o'clock.

When the restaurant opened two years ago, it was having trouble getting a liquor license because it was less than the two hundred-foot state-mandated distance from the church.

The Palmer House has a wine license now and it sounds as though it has arrived at some quid pro quo with the church: The people who pray can go to the bathroom at the restaurant and the restaurant can have a wine license only 198 feet from the last pew.

Howard has gained a lot of weight but he has gained a lot of presence too. He's no Jimmy Swaggart, but he knows how to do it. He began by speaking to us about the Lord and was very professional with his change of pace and change of volume. He would speak softly for a minute and then, with a dramatic gesture, turn up the volume and shout at us. He was good and never at a loss for words.

The congregation was good too. Everyone in it but me knew when to stand and when to sit down. I was brought up a Presbyterian but had forgotten that they don't kneel. Howard said he was Dutch Reformed but later at lunch when I asked him to explain the difference, he was enjoying his chicken salad and deflected the question.

During prayers, Howard called on the Lord to end all wars, heal the sick, console the grieving and also asked Him to "give His blessing to this country and this land." I'll be interested to see what happens. The theme of Howard's sermon posed the question of whether people are happier now than they were two hundred years ago when our small town was founded. He said that just because we have all these "instruments of pleasure" doesn't mean we're happier.

"Pleasure," Howard said, "is doing what we like to do." There was a clear implication in his sermon that this could lead us to what he called "the hell of fire." Being a pleasure seeker myself, I was uneasy.

When Howard and I were in the academy together, we attended chapel every morning and sang four or five songs, including one hymn. I love those hymns I learned and I thought Howard was letting me down until the last one he chose.

It was one called "Love Divine." It starts: "Love's divine all love's excelling." My favorite line is: "Take away our bent to sinning alpha and omega be." I never knew what it meant but it was great to sing.

Howard was tough on us sinners, and I was pleased to note at lunch that Howard himself is mortal, when he smoked ten instruments of pleasure in a little more than an hour.

My Guest, Mr. Gorbachev

Next time Mikhail Gorbachev of the Soviet Union comes to the United States, I'd like to show him around. A visit here would be a college education for him and I'm not sure he'd want to go back.

It would be fun to show Gorbachev around. I think a visit here would change any Russian's attitude toward the United States. We'll never do it by arguing with them. Most Russians are better informed about communism than the average American is about democracy and capitalism, but if every Soviet citizen spent just one day in the United States, it would be more effective than all the talking that has ever been done.

I'd like to have Mr. Gorbachev as my guest if he comes here. He seems like a pretty good guy.

First thing I'd do is I'd bring him home. I'd put him in Ellen's old room next to the bathroom and tell him he's welcome to anything he wants in the refrigerator in case he feels like a beer or some cheese between meals. We're a little short on borscht but the average American refrigerator would look pretty good to a Russian from what I've seen of food in the Soviet Union.

After getting Gorbachev settled, I'd suggest we take a drive around our small town in Connecticut.

"You want to drive?" I'd say to Gorbachev. I figure he might enjoy that because, as an important official, he always gets taken in a chauffeur-driven limousine. He'd probably love to get his hands on an American car, anyway.

Gorbachev and I would drop in to visit with friends who live in houses with three rooms per person instead of three persons per room the way they do in the Soviet Union.

I'd take him over to the supermarket and show him the shelves full of loaves of bread, the refrigerated cabinets full of milk, cream, butter and eggs, and no lines anywhere but at the checkout counter.

After the supermarket, we'd head for the fancy new mall. I hate it myself but it would surely impress a Russian.

If there was time, I'd take him over to the Giants' training camp to watch practice.

That night we'd have dinner, watch television, argue until eleven and go to bed after the late news.

Next morning we'd give Gorbachev fresh-squeezed orange juice, bacon and eggs, and pancakes with maple syrup, just as if that's what we ate every morning for breakfast. The fact is, of course, I grab a piece of toast and a cup of coffee, but he doesn't have to know that.

The next morning we'd drive into New York City. We'd go at rush hour to make sure we got trapped in a traffic jam. The Soviet president isn't going to believe there are that many cars in the whole world.

Cars are hard to buy in the Soviet Union. One of President Reagan's favorite jokes was about a Russian trying to buy a new car.

He goes to the official government car dealer, puts his money down and the dealer says he can deliver the car in ten years.

"Morning or afternoon?" the man asks.

"In ten years," the dealer says, "what's the difference?"

"Because," the man says, "the plumber's coming in the morning."

In New York we'd park the car and go over to Crazy Eddie or 47 St. Photo to look at electronic gadgets, television sets, kitchen appliances and computers. We'll walk or take a cab. I wouldn't let Gorbachev on the subway because the subways are better, cleaner and safer in Moscow. I don't want him to get one up on me.

For lunch, we'll go to the Russian Tea Room, a fancy restaurant near Carnegie Hall that specializes in celebrities and pretends to be Russian. We'll see what Gorbachev thinks of an American restaurant that thinks it's Russian.

This is only twenty-four hours but I'll bet I'm beginning to get to Gorbachev already and I haven't even taken him to the Empire State Building, Texas, Maine, California or Disney World.

The Gentle Rain from Heaven

It's raining. It's a gentle, steady rain. I hear it on the roof, see it running down the windowpanes. The grass out there obviously loves it. The garden by the side of the house is gulping it down.

Call it perverse if you wish, but I love a rainy day.

This is no recent love affair for me. I remember liking a rainy day when I was a child. I think I know why, too. When it's raining, it cuts down on the number of options you have for action that day. There are things you know won't be possible to do so you don't worry about them.

A rainy day is special. On a normal day, we are all faced with so many things we ought to do that we go through it with the vague, gnawing feeling that we're leaving a lot of things undone. On a rainy day, we can't mow the lawn, go swimming, play golf or tennis, have a picnic or cook out. Everything, except staying dry, is simpler.

We needn't leave the house at all on a rainy day if it's a Saturday or Sunday. All inaction is excused by the unavoidable circumstance of weather. "It's raining." I even recall my mother saying she wasn't going to do wash because it was raining and she wouldn't be able to hang it out in the backyard to dry. Many of you may have thought that even though Adam and Eve had no clothes, they had a washing machine and a dryer, but that is not true.

A sunny, bright day doesn't call itself to your attention the same way a rainy one does. You appreciate life more on a rainy day. A day with the sun out is an average day. You don't inspect it much. Even the weather reports on radio and television are dull when the sun is shining.

People think better on rainy days. This is not a scientific observation but I'd be willing to bet it's true. The sound of the patter of water coming down in equally spaced drops on everything drowns out distracting noises and it's easier to concentrate. Sun, on the other hand, is bad for the brain. Left out in it long enough, the brain becomes frazzled and inoperative. I'll bet Albert Einstein never got a sunburn.

Even though I could stay inside all day today, I know I won't. Just as soon as I finish this, I'm going to lace up my old shoes with the waterproofing on them, put on my yellow slicker that really sheds water and find some excuse for going out in the rain.

One of the good things about rain is the fun to be had trying to stay dry. It's a game, and people like it even though they seldom win it. The best raingear usually leaves you wet somewhere. If everything else works, the drips run up your sleeve when you lift your arm, or your headgear is less than perfect and the rain finds its way down your neck. The space between the bottom of your raincoat and the tops of your shoes is vulnerable too.

While I like to go out in the rain properly dressed, there is still some work to be done on rainwear. An umbrella is great fun in a good rain. It doesn't really keep you dry but having the rain spatter overhead without actually hitting you gives the illusion that you're defeating the weather. Umbrellas are efficient from the top of the head to somewhere around the waistline, but from there down umbrellas don't help at all. Also, while umbrellas are good when rain is coming straight down, rain is so often accompanied by high winds that drive it in a slanting direction that umbrellas are of limited value in the average rain.

Cars have been made remarkably impervious to rain. I'm always surprised that you don't get wet at all driving a car in a rainstorm. I wish they'd make truck-size windshield wipers for cars that went straight back and forth across the windshield instead of wiping in that half-moon shape. I imagine they'll get to that because the half-moon shape leaves too much of the windshield unwiped.

There now. That's done—I can go out and play in the rain.

FOR THE BEST IN PAPERBACKS, LOOK FOR THE

In every corner of the world, on every subject under the sun, Penguin represents quality and variety—the very best in publishing today.

For complete information about books available from Penguin—including Pelicans, Puffins, Peregrines, and Penguin Classics—and how to order them, write to us at the appropriate address below. Please note that for copyright reasons the selection of books varies from country to country.

In the United Kingdom: For a complete list of books available from Penguin in the U.K., please write to *Dept E.P., Penguin Books Ltd, Harmondsworth, Middlesex, UB7 0DA*.

In the United States: For a complete list of books available from Penguin in the U.S., please write to *Dept BA, Penguin*, Box 120, Bergenfield, New Jersey 07621-0120.

In Canada: For a complete list of books available from Penguin in Canada, please write to *Penguin Books Ltd, 2801 John Street, Markham, Ontario L3R 1B4*.

In Australia: For a complete list of books available from Penguin in Australia, please write to the *Marketing Department, Penguin Books Ltd, P.O. Box 257, Ringwood, Victoria 3134*.

In New Zealand: For a complete list of books available from Penguin in New Zealand, please write to the *Marketing Department, Penguin Books (NZ) Ltd, Private Bag, Takapuna, Auckland 9*.

In India: For a complete list of books available from Penguin, please write to *Penguin Overseas Ltd, 706 Eros Apartments, 56 Nehru Place, New Delhi, 110019*.

In Holland: For a complete list of books available from Penguin in Holland, please write to *Penguin Books Nederland B.V., Postbus 195, NL-1380AD Weesp, Netherlands*.

In Germany: For a complete list of books available from Penguin, please write to *Penguin Books Ltd, Friedrichstrasse 10-12, D-6000 Frankfurt Main I, Federal Republic of Germany*.

In Spain: For a complete list of books available from Penguin in Spain, please write to *Longman, Penguin España, Calle San Nicolas 15, E-28013 Madrid, Spain*.

In Japan: For a complete list of books available from Penguin in Japan, please write to *Longman Penguin Japan Co Ltd, Yamaguchi Building, 2-12-9 Kanda Jimbocho, Chiyoda-Ku, Tokyo 101, Japan*.